MICHAEL COLLINS

Also available in the NEL series

THE BLACK AND TANS
by Richard Bennett

THE EASTER REBELLION
by Max Caulfield

FAIRY TALES OF IRELAND
by Sinead de Valera

THE ORANGE AND THE GREEN
by Clifford King

Michael Collins

REX TAYLOR

NEW ENGLISH LIBRARY
TIMES MIRROR

To
Anna and Frank

First published in Great Britain by Hutchinson & Co. Ltd. in 1958

*

*

FIRST FOUR SQUARE PAPERBACK EDITION 1961
Reprinted July 1961
Reprinted April 1963
Reprinted April 1965
Reprinted April 1966
New NEL edition May 1970

NEL Books are published by New English Library Limited from Barnard's Inn, Holborn, London, EC1. Made and printed in Great Britain by Love & Malcomson Ltd., Redhill, Surrey.

45000616 6

Acknowledgments

I should like to place on record the help, kindness and understanding of the following people.

Sean O Luing, who has given much time and labour on my behalf in helping to get this book into print; Sean McGarry; Lieut.-Gen. Sean MacEoin, T.D.; Judge Barra O Briain, S.C.; Gerard Costelloe; Miss Eithne O'Kane; Sean MacBride, S.C.; Dr. G. A. Hayes-McCoy, M.A., Ph.D.; P. Moylett; Mrs. Anna Kelly; Frank Kelly; Maurice Wilkins, M.A.; Kevin O'Brien; Michael Collins, B.Comm., Dip. Pub. Adm.; Sean Deasey; Patrick Hodges; Thomas O'Neill, M.A.; Martin Sheridan; Frank Gallagher; John O'Connell; M. B. Corry; Diarmuid O'Hegarty; Frank O'Connor; Eamonn Dore; Florence O'Donoghue; Capt. J. M. Maynard (rtd.); T. J. McCallum; J. M. Hone; Michael J. Hargrove, M.I.A.A., F.A.L.P.A.; Capt. W. P. Ahern; Capt. J. M. Feehan; P. MacBriain; Liam MacGabhann; R. H. Owen and the Guaranty Trust Company; Miss Eileen Murphy; Mrs. Murphy; Mrs. M. J. McHugh; Mrs. Agnellis; Mrs. Hyde; Mrs. B. Middleton; Mrs. M. Delaney; Eric E. A. Norris; and others who, for many and varied reasons, wish their names to be omitted.

The *Sunday Independent*, Dublin; *Irish Independent*, Dublin; *Irish Press*, Dublin; *Sunday Express*, Ltd.; the Manchester Editor, Assistant Editor and the Dublin Editor of the *Sunday Express*; *Daily Express*; *The Times*; *Nationalist and Leinster Times*; *Cork and West Examiner*; *Clare Champion*; and other Irish newspapers.

The staffs of the National Museum of Ireland, the National Library of Ireland, and the Lancashire Branch Library, Morecambe.

I am deeply in the debt of the following authors and publishers:

Sean O Luing for *Art O Griofa* (Sairseal Agus Dill); George G. Harrap and Co. Ltd., for permission to quote from *Michael Collins and the Making of a New Ireland*, by Major-General Piaras Beaslai; Frank O'Connor for *The Big Fellow* (Nelson); *The Path to Freedom*, by Michael Collins (Talbot Press—T. Fisher Unwin); Commandant-General Tom Barry for *Guerilla Days in Ireland* (Mercier Press); Padraig de Burca and John F. Boyle for *Free State or Republic?* (Talbot Press—T. Fisher Unwin); *Recollections of the Irish War*, by Darrell Figgis (Benn); *Lady Gregory's Journals 1916-1930*, edited by Lennox Robinson (Putnam); Sir John

Lavery for *The Life of a Painter* (Cassell); Miss Dorothy Macardle for *The Irish Republic* (Gollancz—Irish Press Ltd.); Michael MacDonagh for *William O'Brien* (Benn); *With Michael Collins in the Fight for Irish Independence*, by Batt O'Connor (Peter Davies); Mrs. E. O'Hegarty and the late P. S. O'Hegarty for *A History of Ireland under the Union, 1801-1922* (Methuen) and *The Victory of Sinn Fein* (Talbot Press); Frank (now Lord) Pakenham for *Peace by Ordeal* (Cape); 'Sceilg' (J. J. O'Kelly) for *A Trinity of Martyrs* and *Stepping Stones* (Irish Book Bureau); W. B. Wells and N. Marlowe for *A History of the Irish Rebellion of 1916* (Maunsel); Mrs. W. B. Yeats, Messrs. Macmillan and Co. Ltd., and A. P. Watt and Son for the quotation from W. B. Yeats' *Collected Poems*; Major-General C. E. Callwell, K.C.B., for *Field-Marshal Sir Henry Wilson, Bart., G.C.B., D.S.O., His Life and Diaries* (Cassell); *Sloinnte Gaedheal is Gall*, by the Rev. Patrick Woulfe; The Earl of Birkenhead for *Frederick Edwin Earl of Birkenhead: The Last Phase* (Thornton Butterworth—Eyre and Spottiswoode); Hayden Talbot for *Michael Collins' Own Story* (Hutchinson); Maurice Headlam, C.B., C.M.G., for *Irish Reminiscences* (Hale); Terence de Vere White for *Kevin O'Higgins* (Methuen); the many contributors to *Dublin's Fighting Story* (Kerryman); Denis Gwynn for *De Valera* (Jarrolds); the *Irish Times* for the *Sinn Fein Rebellion Handbook, Easter, 1916*; the publishers (Talbot Press) of *Dail Eireann Official Report, 16th August, 1921 to 8th June, 1922* and *Debate on the Treaty between Great Britain and Ireland*; the publishers of *Hansard*, Vol. 127; the publishers (Oxford) of *The Concise Oxford Dictionary*; the authors and publishers of the various pamphlets, and the publishers of the newspapers, listed in the Bibliography.

As I am unable to trace Lieut-Col. Andrew J. McCarthy (Brugha's death, p. 192), I can only acknowledge the printed source of his article (*see* footnote to p. 192).

If there are other books which I have inadvertently omitted from this list, I trust that the authors and publishers will pardon me.

To the following for kindly placing at my disposal various photographs: Mrs. Anna Kelly; Judge Barra O Briain, S.C.; Mrs. A. Hogan (Hogan, late Dublin, now 'London Wedding Photos', London); Keogh Bros.; Joseph Cashman; J. Horgan; Mrs. M. J. McHugh; Independent Newspapers, Ltd., Dublin.

I wish to express thanks to my wife and to my daughter for their help and understanding of the problems involved; to James McCarthy and James Crawford for the pleasure afforded me by their conversation; and to Iain Hamilton, Editor-in-Chief of the Hutchinson Group.

Foreword

Ten years ago I commenced the task of seeking material for this biography—a task which has proved at times to be pleasant, and at other times extremely unpleasant. There was, naturally, some suspicion of me, an Englishman, wishing to write on the subject of an Irish soldier and statesman.

Nevertheless, there are people who have assisted me with information simply because of the fact that I am an Englishman and an 'outsider'. In doing so, some have broken a silence of many years' standing. I feel bound to record my pleasure at being so honoured.

As an 'outsider', removed from the Irish scene and from Irish politics, the conclusions arrived at in this book are not motivated by any political adherence whatsoever; and, indeed, as will be seen, I have been at great pains to document, whenever possible, statements made by myself as the result of private information and from other sources.

Much of the material placed at my disposal throws new light on many controversial issues; and, in the belief that a forthright approach to these matters is best for the interests of all concerned, I have sought to be honest in my approach and frank in my statements.

The purpose of this biography is to present, in the light of previously unpublished material, a new assessment of Michael Collins. The aim of this book is not a detailed history of the years 1916-21. In concentrating on the character of Collins and the events of his career, I have, of necessity, had to omit some information relevant to the times.

Silverdale
Lancashire
June, 1958

REX TAYLOR.

Author's Notes

In the spelling of such words as 'organization', 'realize', etc., the more modern form (vide *Concise Oxford Dictionary*) is used, but where the words occur in letters, directives, etc., in the period covered by this book, the old form, e.g., 'organisation', is used when required to conform strictly to the quotation.

The form of W.T. (William T.) instead of L.T. (Liam T.) Cosgrave is used because of the familiarity attaching to the former christian names in this case.

For the sake of readability and simplicity in type, accent marks are omitted from Gaelic names.

Many of the notes made by Michael Collins during the London Treaty discussions—and quoted in this book—were later expanded and used as material for his book *The Path to Freedom* (Talbot Press—T. Fisher Unwin).

Many of the Collins directives quoted in Chapter 6 are addressed to Michael de Lacy of the Mid-Limerick Brigade. The author considered it best, in the interests of the reader, to use a batch of directives addressed to one particular brigade, in preference to using a random selection.

All sources are indicated in Appendix K (*see* pages 273 to 282), and are denoted by numerals placed at the appropriate place on the appropriate page. Explanatory matter which directly concerns the body of the text will be found as footnotes on the appropriate page. In this respect I have endeavoured to please both the general reader, who prefers a straight narrative, and the student, who will, no doubt, desire the addition of such useful information as sources.

Introductory Note

The genesis of the revolution which swept Ireland in the first two decades of the present century lies far back in history. Throughout the long centuries of British rule, the will to freedom remained a vital and activating force and submission to British rule, though often apparent, was never real. Time and again Ireland, seemingly pacified, blazed into revolt afresh.

In approaching the study of Ireland's history we will find that certain vital ideas which gave force to Ireland's early twentieth-century revolution are to be sought in the writings of Molyneux, Swift, and Berkeley. A glance at the Irish writings of Dean Swift is instructive. For example, a pamphlet of his, printed in Dublin in 1720, bears the following title: *A Proposal for the Universal Use of Irish Manufacture, in Cloaths and Furniture of Houses, etc., Utterly Rejecting and Renouncing everything wearable that comes from England*. It is but one of many similar writings, and their import is significant. Here is the key to the Sinn Fein doctrine of economic self-reliance, one of the basic notions of Arthur Griffith's national philosophy. A similar exposition of the idea of self-sufficiency in Berkeley's *Querist* is widely known.

Among the personalities who directly influenced later events the name of Theobald Wolfe Tone will be found. In turn, the ideas of Wolfe Tone were influenced by (*a*) the ideas of the French Revolution, and (*b*) the writings of Tom Paine (*The Rights of Man*). Paine it was who introduced the political concept of the Independent Republic, with equality of status and opportunity. He died, a prisoner in British hands, in 1798—the year of the rising which was led by Wolfe Tone. The ideas of Paine and his resolute efforts to put them into effect presaged the democratic movements of the nineteenth century. The nineteenth-century democratic movements in Ireland were based on three motivating forces:

(1) Religious and Civil Rights: Movement led by Daniel O'Connell; and which was successful in 1829 when the Catholic Emancipation Act was passed.

(2) Land: Agrarian reform, security of tenure, peasant proprietorship, the 'land for the people' are terms and phrases which occur during different phases of the land agitation. Apostles for the 'land for the people' idea were James Fintan Lalor (died 1849) and Michael Davitt (influenced by the writings of James Fintan Lalor and John Stuart Mill). The land agitation was successful: Land Acts of great importance which were passed towards the end of the nineteenth and at the beginning of the twentieth centuries gradually abolished landlordism and secured the land to the people.

(3) Political Freedom: Important figures in the political struggle are: Robert Emmet (the symbol of youthful idealism), hanged in Thomas Street, Dublin, in 1803; the personalities of the 1843-8 movement: Thomas Davis ('Educate that you may be free'); John Mitchel ('There is no solution save the edge of the sword'); the broad-based democratic movement of Fenianism, 1858-67 (known in Ireland as the Irish Republican Brotherhood, and in America as the Fenian Brotherhood), the leaders of which included James Stephens, John O'Leary, Jeremiah O'Donovan Rossa, Charles Kickham, and, in America, John O'Mahony. A popular movement this, few aristocrats or liberals in it. Militarily it failed, but the organization remained in being on both sides of the Atlantic and transmitted its political message to succeeding generations. It is worth noting, in connection with later events, that the I.R.B. (of which Michael Collins was a member)

'. . . was a separatist organization rather than a republican one. The object was an Irish Republic, and the oath was an oath to an Irish "Republic", but this was because nothing but a republican form of government could be envisaged for an independent Ireland, it was not from any conviction in favour of a republic, as such. And, down to the end, it preserved its aloofness from questions as to the form of government, or the "rights" or privileges of the various sections of the people. . . . Its business was to beat England out of Ireland and not to commit the Irish people beforehand to any particular form of government. . . .'[1]

The constitutional Home Rule movement led by Charles Stewart Parnell, 1879-90, operated side by side with the agrarian movement led by Davitt and Parnell. The Parnell movement owed a great deal of its success to the magnetic personality of the leader. When the split came, in 1890, the movement collapsed.

Between 1891 (the year of Parnell's death) and 1905 (the year of the founding of the Sinn Fein movement) the more youthful forces of Irish nationalism took stock. There emerged Douglas Hyde (cultural and intellectual nationalism), Arthur Griffith (economic nationalism, self-reliance, passive resistance), Padraic Pearse, and others; and there commenced the rise of Labour (an urban movement) under the direction of James Connolly and James Larkin; and the reorganization of the I.R.B. with the return to Ireland from America of Thomas J. Clarke (Tom Clarke).

Chapter 1

CHARACTER

THE country is Ireland, the city Dublin; and the time the early months of the year 1921.

It is a time of great event: for the Irish, struggling to throw off the shackles of seven hundred years of rule by the British, in this latest phase of their efforts there is the possibility of at last gaining their cherished independence. For the British, engaged in a war which smoulders and occasionally flares to intensity, there is the possibility that their hold on Ireland is about to be relinquished. Since the ending of the 1914-18 war, the British Government and its Authority in Ireland have recognized that Ireland has become, once again, a major issue in the affairs of the United Kingdom.

At this time, the city is the haunt of the spy and the informer: British khaki and the uniform of the Auxiliaries to be seen everywhere; the streets alive with the sound of the engines of Crossley tenders and Lancia cars; the patrol; the cordon; the lightning swoop; the people of the city alert to the sound of rifle and revolver shots—all the terror created by a force uncertain of the measure of its strength against an enemy expert in guerilla tactics.

Into the front snug of Kirwan's public house in Parnell Street—set in its labyrinth of little lanes, stalls, sheds, and old lofts—a man strides. Tall, burly, athletic, he stands upright, one hand in his trousers pocket; every now and then throwing back his head to toss a falling lock of dank hair. He speaks to his companion in a rich, chuckling voice.

On the counter is a small glass of sherry. The moment it was placed there, he did no more than look up, his glance meeting that of the barman, followed by a quick look around the room, populated by a mixture of civilians, British 'Tommies', and Auxiliaries. Nor does he protest when the barman takes away the barely tasted sherry, and replaces it with a pint of stout. He merely glances again at the barman, and around the room, noting the exit of a customer.[1]

To all appearances, and by the brusque, strongly accented pronunciation of his speech, the man is a visitor to Dublin: a commercial traveller, perhaps, up from the south of Ireland, intent only on spending a quiet evening in a city public house. The presence of the 'Tommies' and the Auxiliaries serves to further the illusion regarding the man. The soldiers drink their stout, oblivious to the fact that they are in the company of a man on whose head is placed a reward which could make them rich for life.

By means of contacts in the public houses of Dublin, Michael Collins waged a major campaign against the British. The threads of the intelligence system which he organized and headed took in most of the bars and taverns. What better place in which to create the illusion of innocence than a public house, populated by men from all walks of life, and of all shades of character, and with a ready 'cover' unwittingly provided by the British army?

From 1917 to the Truce of July, 1921, the most 'wanted' man in the whole of Ireland walked and cycled about the streets of the city; and remained free. Strangest of all facts in regard to the hunt for Collins is that once seen he was remembered for a long time afterwards, so striking was his physical appearance. Again, he had certain very noticeable mannerisms: that toss of the head, for instance. But chameleon-like, with his companions, though without any tricks, he merged with the company he was in; and when alone, walking or cycling, he wore the air of perfect innocence that almost always goes unnoticed. He never impersonated, never went in disguise; the secret of his continued freedom lay in a rigorous self-control which shunned recklessness. Collins was, if anything, the direct opposite to the man as portrayed by journalists and writers in search of a story. The 'dare-devil', the 'laughing, glamorous gunman', never existed in the person of Michael Collins. The real Collins was a man with work to do; a fastidious, methodical go-getter; and an exacting, sometimes tyrannical, task-master to those who worked under him. The most lethal weapon ever carried by Collins was a fountain pen.

At the other extreme, it has been stated in print that he was not a man of mystery. If we are to accept this statement as fact, it is to give the lie to many of Collins' actions; and to disprove what he himself wrote in letters, notes, and diaries; also, it will insinuate that many of those who knew him deliberately cultivated a legend. But there is nothing of the legend concealed in his writings; nor is there in this statement by a former close acquaintance of his:

> 'I can claim to have known Michael Collins as well as, if not better than, most people. Even so, I thought my personal knowledge of him to be no more than surface knowledge. He was a very difficult person to really know.'

Others, who worked with him on the closest possible terms, will say that they knew just so much of the work he had in hand; beyond that limit the knowledge was for Collins alone.

Examined from a time distance of thirty-odd years, the character of Collins is a complexity which almost defies analysis. The broad outline is there for all to see: dynamic, ruthless in pursuit of his objective, domineering, generous qualities allied to those of coolness, calculation, and, in lighter moments, a gay rumbustious bonhomie; as well as a trait which seems in odd contrast to these, a hatred of being beaten or usurped in any way. There are many examples, too numerous to detail, in proof that Collins hated being beaten. Yet even this last trait has two facets. It was not so much that Collins hated the thought of being beaten, but rather that he lived his life with such intensity and at such a power level that the pedestal which he himself had built with his own efforts must never be chipped or even tarnished in any way. These were the traits of character which Collins gave to the world, or at least to those interested enough in the personality of the man. It is the 'half' which may frequently be seen in the anecdote and sometimes in the documentary.

The other 'half' of the man is to be found only in his letters, notes, and diaries; and, on very rare occasions, in a sudden outburst during conversation. It is the part which Collins rigorously suppressed from the eyes and the ears of the general public and even from his closest acquaintances. Joe O'Reilly, Collins' general factotum, saw it once. With the storm of 'Bloody Sunday' raging around him, Collins said testily: 'When will it all end? When can a man get down to a book and peace?'[2]

It is a fleeting glimpse of the real Collins, the man who secretively withdrew into himself on certain emotional occasions. In this 'secret' half of his character may be found the serious-minded intellectual; the man of restless impatience, which sometimes concealed a state of near panic; the part which had a tendency, at times, to bask in the praise showered on him; the part which came near to a state of collapse under the stress of great emotion—in short, the part which contained all of his shortcomings and his weaknesses. It is only fair to add, however, that he was well aware of these shortcomings and weaknesses, and he fought strongly to repress them.

Three natural gifts, born with him, account for the rapidity of his rise to power. He had the instinct of the visionary, the calculating watchfulness of the strategist, and the ability to organize. Apart from these natural gifts, the Easter Rising moulded his character; and the sojourn in Stafford Jail and internment in

Frongoch Camp matured him from the raw idealist which he had formerly been. Only his intellect required further development; but death intervened. Collins shared with de Valera the distinction of great promise, which in the latter was to mature, but in the former was cut short after an all too brief period of brilliance. Collins belongs to that rare band of men who stand out in the history of any country and in any century. Recognized for their individuality, and by the blessing bestowed on them of gifts which, because they are at once complete, require no further training in order to reach exacting standards. They leave their mark on the history of the country which they serve, whether as soldiers, statesmen, scholars, or in other ways.

Former acquaintances of Collins' are reluctant to criticize him and for reasons which are at once apparent. The character of Collins was such that he was never a follower, but always a leader. He had a way with men which made them eager to work for him; and he was, outwardly at least, supremely confident, and he brought out in others that very same quality. If he exploited the men and women who worked for him, it was never, even indirectly, to his own advantage, but to the advantage of his and their supreme ideal, a free Ireland.

He sensed immediately whether a man was for or against him; and if he did not succeed in winning that man over, the man concerned was damned in Collins' opinion from then on. The great test of his personality and character came in 1922, during the Treaty debate, for the final count (when the vote of 'for' or 'against' the Treaty was taken) was determined to an important extent not so much by ideals, but as to whether a particular voter loved or hated Collins. As such, it was the supreme test of his strength and he emerged victorious.

This attitude by his former acquaintances of overlooking the faults which he undoubtedly possessed is perhaps best summed-up by a person who worked with him and who knew him in all his varying moods. 'You don't start analysing God,' she says; 'you don't criticize God; you just accept him.'[3] Some of his former acquaintances practically regard him as a supreme being, outside the pale of criticism. To be placed on such a ledge of hyper-esteem, deification almost, beyond the probe of criticism, is quite unfair to Collins. No man, however great, is beyond criticism—a fact which Collins himself readily appreciated. He had his faults and he made mistakes. To build a god out of the framework of a human being invites criticism; besides which Collins was the very model of humanity.

But while it is natural for those who loved him to regard him as the nearest thing to God, what is the critic and the biographer to make of the men who were once his sworn enemies: the men who were formerly convinced that Collins, in signing the Anglo-Irish Treaty of 1921, had turned traitor on his country and its people, but who now say: 'Collins? A lovely man,' or: 'Collins? A bloody great character.' Could it be that Collins' idea of Dominion Status for Ireland (which he accepted in 1921), followed by a process of gradual development to the Status of a Republic which he then envisaged, and which has since become fact, has after all persuaded many of his former opponents into thinking the same way? If that is the case, Collins' powers as a visionary have at last borne fruit.

Yet, even outside the Irish scene, the story is much the same. In 1921 a visiting American journalist cabled his editor: *No interview with Collins. Did not find the man. Found a god.*

The fact is: Collins was not a god; but he was a great man. His presence and his influence enlivened the Irish scene. He was adept at blowing away the cobwebs of inertia; he was ever thrusting for action. He gathered round him a band of men who willingly went into the greatest of dangers at the mere raising of his finger; and as Adjutant-General of the Volunteer army, he was worshipped by the men of the brigades, many of whom had never seen him. Such was the power of one man over his fellow men. Ireland in the years 1917 to 1921 was ripe for such a man as Collins: a man with boundless vitality, dynamic energy, confidence, brain, a man who had a way with other men. In the wilderness of hope alternating with despair, of chancy fortune, of the stalking of the terror in the streets of the cities and in the quiet country lanes, there was a desperate need for a man of such mettle; and Collins stepped into the gap. He did not choose his time; fortune and the times chose him; and for some considerable time fortune favoured him.

But even so, he was no stargazer; he simply knew the extent and the strength of his own abilities. These he mustered on behalf of freedom: and they carried the day. As a soldier, as the creator of a vast intelligence system, as a Government Minister, ability backed him to the full. It was only when he stepped, or was pushed, into the arena of diplomatic-political intrigue, that these self-same abilities became debatable assets.

Between Collins and Daniel O'Connell (the 'Liberator') there is a comparison of sorts. They had the same native shrewdness; certain physical similarities; O'Connell intellectually greater by far, more complex in mental make-up, but living his full life course (over seventy years of age when he died). Collins might have displayed latent and unsuspected powers had he lived.

There is one name associated with French history which

immediately suggests itself whenever Collins is discussed: the name is that of Danton, the French revolutionary leader. One may go even further and say that yet another comparison is suggested whenever the Irish fight for freedom and the French Revolution is discussed, for, even as Collins and Danton have certain resemblances, so, too, has the character of Eamon de Valera with that of Robespierre, another leader of the French Revolution. There are many comparisons between the characters of Collins and Danton: in their phrasing of words, for example. The present writer is indebted to J. M. Hone (Yeats' biographer) for the use of a letter written to him in 1942 by the late Mrs. Llewelyn Davies who was acquainted with Collins. In this letter Mrs. Llewelyn Davies points out that Collins could well be called the Danton of the Irish revolution.

> 'The myth of de Valera as the Incorruptible is now so firmly established that it will take as long to put Collins in his rightful place as it took to put Danton in his.
>
> Without knowing it, Collins used phrases almost identical with Danton. Compare "Since there must be a scapegoat, then let it be me . . ." [on the occasion of de Valera's refusal to go to London for the Treaty discussions—*see* page 115] with Danton's "*Que mon nom soi fletri*", when the Girondais would not give him the complete control necessary to stop the September massacres, and he decided to take the responsibility for them rather than let them be blamed on the whole nation. De Valera was weak, stupid, and treacherous and since that time he can do no good in my eyes and never will.'

Physically Collins' presence was commanding. He stood five feet ten inches in height but looked taller because of his build. He had an upright, easy, natural stance; wore trousers with a cross pocket into which he thrust his hand. A falling lock of dank hair which he tossed backward continually gave a hint of his boundless vitality and this vitality he was able to communicate instantly to others—not by any affectation but rather by the easiness of his manner. It is often remarked that Collins seemed to explode into a room rather than enter it in the normal way and, with his entrance, he appeared to communicate his dynamic energy to those present. His walk was not the sedate or steady pace of the scholar and the thinking man—it was a rolling, jaunty walk, in the style of a man of confidence; and the confidence which Collins possessed, in relation to his ability, was a completely alert sense-cohesion.

His features were mobile, every emotional change clearly showing there. Boyish-faced, frank and open in expression, a touch of lustiness, or perhaps coarseness, showing there; eyes small for his size and grey in colour; brown the colour of his hair. More than any other physical feature, the mouth betrayed his feelings: normally a sulky mouth, ill-humour was visible in the lips pressed tightly together and thrust out.

His handwriting, in the clearness of the script, plainly showed his early civil-service training; and showed, too, in the firmness of line, the strength of his character.

He had a rich, chuckling voice, in texture a light baritone, a very clear distinctive voice, a voice which one recognized, even among a crowd, as belonging only to Collins. A Co. Cork upbringing was obvious in the abrupt way in which he spoke, though his voice was that of a West Corkman as distinct from those of Cork City where the voices go up and down. He could speak for an hour without notes in an easy and relaxed manner. As a speechmaker he was forthright in expressing himself and although he left much of the speechmaking to those possessed of silvery tongues and the 'die-for-Ireland' flagwavers, he could, when the occasion demanded it, give ample proof of his abilities as a speaker. The way of his career was divorced from the platform and from public speaking and his personal preference was for the more subtle ways of conspiracy and man-to-man contacts—a boy of the back-room where the real power lay.

He was of a normally happy, if sometimes serious, disposition, acutely aware of the responsibilities which were his yet supremely confident in his ability to cope with them.

Judged by any standard, the outstanding feature of his character is that of humanity. He was recognized as being the most humane of men. Workers and fighters for the cause were sincerely considered by Collins; and, when they suffered, he suffered, too. The arrest of McKee and Clancy, in 1920, bears out this side of his character. His sensitive nature caused him great mental anguish in the realization of what they were undergoing as 'special' prisoners. Regarding Collins' humanity, Mrs. Llewelyn Davies, writing to J. M. Hone in 1942, comments thus:

> 'A man with a great and tender heart, who loved the beautiful in nature and in art as far as he had time or opportunity to find it. His friends who wrote about him have distorted him as much or more than his enemies.'

Many examples might be quoted to show how Collins went out of his way to alleviate the sufferings and the troubles of others.

On many occasions he worked night and day to effect the release from imprisonment of those who served him faithfully. He had every consideration for others without thought for himself.

The one thing which he could not and would not tolerate was failure, even though sound reason was given for such failure. Harry Boland, aware of this peculiar insistence of Collins', argued that circumstances often ruled the success or failure of a particular job. 'Not at all,' replied Collins; 'more often than not it is the slipshod handling of the job which brings about the failure.'[4]

In many respects he was a man of conflicting emotions though not excitable, as he was summed-up to be by the author of the advance 'biographies' of the Irish delegation to London in 1921.

He never dealt in theory; he had no time for it; and he refused to listen to anything which dealt only in the theoretical. He took the standpoint of a practical man whenever plans were submitted to him for approval. No one was quicker to realize the great gulf which yawned between the possible success of a theoretical plan and the more probable success of a practical plan. He was a realist, as distinct from the idealists who have numerously abounded in Ireland. It may be thought that his judgment on Padraic Pearse and the Easter Rising in general was a harsh judgment (Collins thought the Easter Rising a most inappropriate occasion for 'memoranda couched in poetic phrases'—*see* Chapter 4). For that same reason, it is so obvious that he should admire another leader of the Easter Rising, James Connolly, who was a down-to-earth realist. Similarly, there was a bridgeless void between Collins and Terence MacSwiney (who died on hunger strike in Brixton Jail in 1920). Nobility and high-mindedness counted for very little in Collins' estimation; a solid appreciation of matters of fact was, to him, a great asset. The idea of a map studded with markers, so beloved by the orthodox military men, appealed to him not at all. Personality was the thing which counted most to him. He liked to know the men with whom he was dealing; and nothing gave him so much pleasure as a few minutes of chat with the men of the brigades over a drink at Vaughan's Hotel or some other favourite rendezvous of his.

Collins was a realist to the point of bluntness. It was not that he lacked the finer points of etiquette—he himself was sprung from an ancient clan; but because of the conditions in which he spent the most fruitful of his years, he exorcised everything which might hinder quick, concise thinking. Shortly after his arrival in London (for the Treaty discussions) he sent a memorable note to Joe O'Reilly in Dublin, and he added this footnote: 'I have come here to call a spade a spade. It is the only name I know it by.'

(For full text of this note see page 121.) There was a wealth of meaning in the simple statement. The British delegation would be loth, he knew, to get down to such plain essentials. They would have to conform to a strict code which included the graces of political and diplomatic etiquette. They would call a spade by any other name except the real one. Collins knew he would be faced with this conformity to a code and the formalities and lengthy discussions it entailed.

Essentially the chief difference between Collins and most of the members of the British delegation was simply this: to them, Collins was unreal (the advance 'biography' supplied to the British delegates by their own officials is proof of this). In their eyes, he was experienced only in the use of a gun and in bloodshed. He did not measure up to their standard of diplomacy and round-table etiquette. What they failed to see, however, is that Collins' education during his formative years had been both intense and practical. The British thought his bluntness dangerous: the thought-process of a revolutionary almost. Only one of them was able to form a correct estimate of Collins' character. That man was Lord Birkenhead and he himself was a realist. It was natural that the two men should find common ground. In much the same way, because of like personalities, Griffith and Chamberlain took to each other. On the other hand, Collins distrusted Chamberlain and Griffith distrusted Birkenhead.

There was a touch of the Napoleonic in Collins' military brilliance. He used thorough, unorthodox methods to beat his enemy, giving tactical lessons which have not been lost since his time on other guerilla fighters in many parts of the world.

Being, by natural instinct, acutely aware of the possibilities attached to situations, this instinct or flair allowed of a thorough, but quick and accurate, assessment; and by this means 'on the spot' decisions were a matter of second nature to him. 'I have seen him,' remarked one of his former lieutenants, 'do no more than push his hand through his hair; yet in that quick action the decision was made.'

A general observation that 'Collins was forever wanting to get things done' fits well with the restless temperament of a man who had the idea that sleep was a waste of valuable time. The driving force of the energy within him was the reason for this while strong will-power kept his nerves under full control. Mr. Moylett (an Irish business man, and a friend of both Collins and Griffiths), speaking to the present writer, recalled that Collins appeared to be quite fresh, in contrast to most others, after a debate which had lasted for eighteen hours.

The tag of 'gunman' which became attached to his name was a title for which he had a personal loathing. Collins never killed a man in his life, except perhaps during actual fighting operations in 1916. It was given to him, principally, by the press chiefs of Britain, who sought to glamorize a 'wanted' man. The events of 'Bloody Sunday' provided a field-day for them, and they piled on the horror. Further attempts have been made in recent times to restore that old and untrue legend of 'Collins the gunman'.*

Collins was lacking in the patience which is necessary to a politician. A long-winded speaker bored and exasperated him, and he became impatient with anyone who did not come directly to the point. The plain truth is he was no politician, and when, in 1917, he gave his attention to the primary object of the Irish Republican Brotherhood (the building of a strong military force) it was with a sense of relief. For, although intrigue and conspiracy was a part of his daily life, it was so in the military sense and not the political. As a politician he was 'out of his depth', and he knew it.

First and foremost, he was an organizer and a strategist—a soldier 'out of uniform', the wearing of which, by some mystic means, reduced and retarded the natural dynamic qualities which he possessed. He had the good soldier's respect and tolerance for the enemy—if they fought fair. He has been described as being a man of 'unorthodox versatility': and that assessment pretty well sums up Collins the soldier.

On December 6th, 1921, Collins and the other four members of the Irish delegation signed the Anglo-Irish Treaty. For Collins it meant near disaster; his action in signing the Treaty literally stunned the whole of the Irish nation. That a man who had faced overwhelming odds and scouted death could willingly have put his name to what his critics described as an infamous document was unbelievable. There are, however, other points to the argument which, in many ways, form good reasons for Collins' action in signing the Treaty.

Looking beyond officialdom, beyond the despatches, the Cabinet meetings in Dublin, and the London discussions, looking, as it were, into Collins' private thoughts, what do we find? The utterances in letters, notes, and diaries of a man convinced that he is taking the only possible course: the only possible course, that is, for the good of his country, and under the circumstances ruling at the time.

From the letters quoted in Chapters 11 to 14, it will be seen that Collins understood his selection as a delegate to the London

* Maurice Headlam, C.B., C.M.G., in his book *Irish Reminiscences* (published by Hale in the 1940's), refers to 'the gunman Michael Collins' (pp. 149-50).

conferences as one forced on him and he regarded his position, and that of others, as being intolerable. In short, he was being made the scapegoat for the failings of the politicians. Also, a faction in Dublin plotted against him in an endeavour to bring his name into disrepute around the London conference table; and in the delegation party itself there were men unscrupulous enough to aid and abet the Dublin faction.

The point at issue, however, is this: Collins was not driven, by action taking place around him, into signing the Treaty, although the circumstances were set before the delegation party left Ireland for London. His signature came as a result of long discussions and after having, as he thought, obtained the best possible bargain, within the limits allowed him, from the British. He repeatedly thought of Dominion Status as being the best way for a 'young' country to stabilize itself. Some will say that Collins' idea of Dominion Status was a second-best, the argument for a Republic having failed; but this is not so. By tradition and temperament Collins was the most Republican of men. There are two reasons why he chose to give so much consideration to Dominion Status: (1) That the British would not entertain the idea of a Republic; and (2) that Collins was considerably influenced by Griffith's views and ideas, as Collins' articles in *The Path to Freedom* (Talbot Press, 1922) prove.

Following the signing of the Treaty, there came the clash between the realists, represented by Collins and Griffith, and the idealists, represented by de Valera and Cathal Brugha. Personalities, too, came into the clash; but essentially it was a matter of ideals as signified by the two fronts. Oddly enough, de Valera, although no doctrinaire Republican, to use his own words,* stood at the head of the Republican idealists; while Collins, although standing by his London signature, tended to lean over the opposite side of the fence. Indeed, it has been said that if victory had gone against the upholders of the Treaty (the Collins-Griffith front), Collins would not have hesitated to join the ranks of the anti-Treaty Republicans. Serious consideration of this point makes it clear, however, that it was for the sake of avoiding the coming 'split' which led Collins into making temporizing speeches.

Responsibility for the Civil War, which followed a state of no

* Quote from de Valera's speech on the occasion of his election as President of the Second Dail, August 16th, 1921.

'. . . Two and a half years ago . . . the question was put to the Irish people, what form of government they wanted, how they wished to live, so that they might have an opportunity of working out for themselves their own national life in their own way, and the answer that the Irish people gave was unmistakable. I do not say that that answer was for a form of government so much, because we are not Republican doctrinaires, but it was for Irish freedom and Irish independence . . .'

compromise between the two fronts, is difficult to assess. Many will have it that de Valera's speech at Thurles, on St. Patrick's Day, 1922, was a direct incitement to Civil War. It is true to say that this speech, and others made by de Valera, had a certain effect on the minds of the people; and that by being addressed directly to the army, they certainly excited that body into a state of action. One thing is certain: of all the leading men engaged in the talk and the war, Collins was the least responsible for the war. He was torn between two loyalties: to the Treaty, and to the men who had stood by him in the great contest for freedom. He worked ceaselessly for a compromise between the two fronts; and, in doing so, he aroused the ire of his great friend Arthur Griffith. Griffith, for his part, maintained that the Civil War had to come and the sooner the better for all concerned; but Collins thought otherwise and continued to think and say so. And there is the greatest tragedy of all: the fact that the Civil War, which Collins hated most of all, should in the end prove to be the destroyer of himself.

With the death of Collins, it seemed that the driving force which would consolidate the fruits of political freedom had gone and certainly there is something in the character of Collins which has never been replaced in Irish affairs. It is true to say that his personality captured the imagination of the general public; but his loss goes far beyond the range of mere personality. It is like the stage of a theatre on which all the actors except one are assembled, and if that actor is not the leading man, no one doubts that his presence and his talents will be sorely missed, both by his fellow actors and the audience. It may well be, in Collins' case, that the changing opinions of his former opponents provide the clue to his stature in Irish affairs; and that, after all, he has left his mark on the history of Ireland more as a man of vision than as a soldier.

Chapter 2

O Coileain—A Fateful Year—Birth of Michael Collins—Influences—Education—London—Employment—The I.R.B.

THE Collinses of West Cork are a branch of the O Coileain. Formerly the O Coileain were lords of Ui Conaill Gabhra; but in the year 1178 the main body of the clan were expelled from the territory, and eventually they settled in West Cork. Those who remained continued to be lords of Claonghlas, a district in the south-west of Co. Limerick, until towards the end of the thirteenth century, when they were dispossessed by the Fitzgeralds. It was from the West Cork branch of the clan that Michael Collins was directly sprung.[1]

The hamlet of Sam's Cross, in West Cork, stands almost midway between the market town of Clonakilty and Roscarbery bay. Its name perpetuates the legend of one Sam Wallace, a highwayman, who plied his 'trade' at the crossroads there. Hereabouts the Collinses are a majority. A cousin of Michael Collins, Jeremiah, keeps a tavern there and pride of place is given to the curious signboard on which is painted the following inscription: 'I Rule All, I Fight for All, I Pray for All, I Pay for All.' The tavern has been in the hands of the Collins family for generations; and it is the place where Michael Collins took his last drink on the day of his death. Also peculiar to West Cork is a curious ball game in which a heavy iron ball is hurled between two lines of spectators—much in the manner of putting the shot. This ball game is called 'bowling' and it is played on the public roads.

Across from the tavern is the cottage in which the mother of Michael Collins was born, and in which she lived until her marriage to Michael, father of the subject of this biography. On the slope of a hill is the ruined and grass-grown relic of the former home of the Collinses, built when Michael was nine years of age and destroyed during the 'Black and Tan' terror.

These were the surroundings into which Michael Collins was born and their influence remained with him to the end of his days. The quiet of the countryside, the cottages, the people who tenanted them, the small personal country circle of his upbringing, with a fixed way of life were, with their narrow limits, to be the personal background of a lad who was destined for history.

Historically speaking, Michael Collins was born in a fateful year and on a fateful day. The year of 1890 was a year of destiny for Ireland, for the star of Charles Stewart Parnell, the greatest advocate of the Home Rule for Ireland policy, was on the wane. It was, too, a year notable for 'outrages' committed by the 'Moonlighters': men whose activities were directed chiefly against harsh and unpopular landlords and land-agents, and were reprisalist in nature. Tenants who, scab-like, broke the rules of the Land League also incurred their wrath. The Land League had been founded by Michael Davitt in the year 1879; and although a number of prominent people, including Parnell as President, occupied positions, the Land League was really set on foot by a number of Fenians. Briefly, its main objectives were as follows: to bring about a reduction of rack-rents, to enable tenants to become owners of their holdings after paying a fair rent for a number of years, to promote organization among the tenant farmers, and to defend those who were threatened with eviction following refusal to pay unjust rents.

In Co. Mayo and other western districts the terrible threat of famine hung over the heads of the people. In Co. Tipperary John Dillon, M.P., and William O'Brien, M.P., together with three other M.P.s and seven other men, were arrested and charged with inducing the tenants of Mr. Smith Barry, landowner, not to pay their rent. They were eventually released on bail, the cases to be heard before Mr. J. B. Irwin and Mr. J. B. Shannon on the 25th September, 1890, at Tipperary. Neither O'Brien nor Dillon appeared at court to answer the charges on the day named for the case to be heard, nor again on the 10th October; but on the 16th October—the day on which Michael Collins was born—the Irish fugitives from the law were seen in Paris en route for America.

Michael was the eighth, and youngest, child of the marriage of two members of old-established families: the O Coileain (Collins) and the O'Briens. Michael Collins senior was sixty years of age when he married Mary Anne O'Brien, then aged twenty, the daughter of the deceased James O'Brien of Sam's Cross. Many of the characteristics of Michael senior were predominant in his youngest son, even at an early age. Young Michael had the same intensity as his father, the same determination, the same spirit of good fellowship, and his outlook was that of the born scholar.

Michael senior was seventy-five years of age when Michael was born and if his life had not been of particular note publicly, it had been a useful one. From a schooling of the most meagre kind, the teaching of a wandering 'hedge-schoolmaster', Diarmuid O Suilliobhain, a cousin on his mother's side, he had developed into a scholar of the 'dead' languages, Latin and Greek. He had a good knowledge of English, French, and his native Irish, while in the workings of mathematics he took a real pleasure. Even then the list does not fail, for he was one of those rare beings who have a great use for their hands as well as their head; and from Latin and Greek he could easily put his hands, the hands of a skilled carpenter and builder, to more essential things. It is not to be wondered that the lad looked up to his father, the possessor of so many talents. To Hayden Talbot (the author of *Michael Collins' Own Story*) Collins once said: 'Great age held something for me that was awesome. I was much fonder of old people in the darkness than of young people in the daylight'; and, indeed, throughout his life he had a great affection for old people, and any amount of patience in dealing with their problems, great or small. One may account for this reverence of the aged as being part of an innate sense of poetry which he possessed.

Through his father's teacher, the 'hedge-schoolmaster' O Suilliobhain, the young Collins first received knowledge of the Irish patriots of other days, for O Suilliobhain claimed a personal acquaintance with Wolfe Tone and had first-hand experience of the ill-fated rising of 1798. It is not difficult to imagine the impression made on the child by the knowledge that, however remote the relationship might be, he had a relative who had actually known the great Wolfe Tone, whose principle was:

> 'To subvert the tyranny of our execrable Government, to break the connection with England, the never failing source of all our political evils, and to assert the independence of my country—these were my objects. To unite the whole people of Ireland, to abolish the memory of all past dissensions, and to substitute the common name of Irishman in place of the denomination of Protestant, Catholic and Dissenter—these were my means.'[2]

The tender years of the young Michael are a record of influences, beginning with that of his father. All of these influences centred upon one thing: they created in him at his most impressionable age a rapidly awakening interest in Irish patriotic affairs. The fact that he was reared in a district famous for its allegiance to the Irish cause served further to guarantee a continuation of the interest aroused by these influences. In this connection of local allegiance, the names of two famous men come easily to mind: Jeremiah O'Donovan Rossa, born at Roscarbery, the famous Fenian leader, and William Thompson, a pioneer of Socialism, who preceded Owen and Marx, and died in 1832.

At the age of four and a half years, Michael came under an influence which was probably as strong, if not stronger, than any other which he encountered throughout his younger years. The influence which Denis Lyons exercised on his young pupil (Lyons was the schoolmaster at the Lisavaird National School) was that of a patriot. Lyons was an old member of the Irish Republican Brotherhood, the American counterpart of which was usually called the Fenian Brotherhood. Lyons was noted for his teaching ability and as a disciplinarian who meted out rough justice to his pupils. The effect which these attributes had on the young Collins was almost akin to hero-worship. Years later, when Collins was interned at Frongoch Camp in North Wales, he said of Lyons:

> 'In Denis Lyons and James Santry I had my first tutors capable of—because of their personalities alone—infusing into me a pride

of the Irish as a race. Other men may have helped me along the searching path to a political goal, I may have worked hard myself in the long search, nevertheless, Denis Lyons and James Santry remain to me as my first stalwarts. In Denis Lyons especially his manner, although seemingly hiding what meant most to him, had this pride of Irishness which has always meant most to me. . . .'[3]

Between Lyons and Santry (the other influence mentioned in Collins' letter) there was a great deal of difference: that between a schoolmaster and a blacksmith. Santry's forge was situated near the school and it became for the young Collins a haven of patriotic folklore. Santry was an inveterate story-teller and his own background provided a sound foundation on which to build stories thrilling enough to impress the lad. Santry himself was the son of a man who had forged pikes for the unsuccessful risings of 1848 and 1867 and he could proudly claim that his grandfather had taken part in the 1798 rising at Shannonvale.

Since Collins delivered judgment on Denis Lyons, it is the more interesting to note Lyons' assessment of his pupil. As a forecast of the future of a boy of ten, or possibly twelve, years of age—the date of its writing would be 1900 or 1902—it is amazingly accurate, showing that Lyons had carefully summed up the characteristics of his pupil:

'Exceptionally intelligent in observation and at figures. A certain restlessness in temperament. Character: Good. Able and willing to adjust himself to all circumstances. A good reader. Displays more than a normal interest in things appertaining to the welfare of his country. A youthful, but nevertheless striking, interest in politics. Coupled with the above is a determination to become an engineer. A good sportsman, though often temperamental.'[4]

The references regarding politics and engineering are bracketed, and a further observation is made: 'Either of these could possibly become finalised at maturity.'[5]

Away from the personal influences of Lyons and Santry, the lad read about his particular heroes, Wolfe Tone and Robert Emmet. He was thrilled by the words spoken by Wolfe Tone in 1795 and one can imagine the profound influence they had on him, this eager receptionist of Irish ideals:

'On the summit of Macart's Fort on Cave Hill we took a solemn obligation never to rest in our efforts until we had subverted the authority of England over our country and asserted our independence.'

In the main, his reading consisted of books with a core of politics: Thomas Davis, that sincere and thoughtful patriot; the books and poems of the brothers A. M. and T. D. Sullivan, the latter the author of a patriotic poem, 'God Save Ireland', which became the Fenian anthem; the novels of Banim and Kickham; O'Donovan Rossa's *Prison Life*, to name a few. Otherwise, the novelists Scott, Thackeray and Dickens occupied his attention, together with Thomas Moore's poems. He was an inveterate reader, and, for his age, always seeking out books of serious content as apart from the usual run of childhood literature.

At the age of twelve years, or thereabouts, the judgment offered by the young Collins on two men actively associated with Irish politics is particularly sensitive in its choice of furthering the Irish ideal in his mind. He expressed a strong dislike for the politics of John Redmond and the Irish Parliamentary Party—against, whom, later in his life, he was destined to play a major role. 'Slaves of England',[6] the schoolboy called them; and in a one-page essay, 'Freedom for Ireland', he refers to the Irish Parliamentary Party as 'chains around Irish necks'.[7] On the other hand, his admiration for Griffith is unbounded:

> 'In Arthur Griffith there is a mighty force afoot in Ireland. He has none of the wildness of some I could name. Instead there is an abundance of wisdom and an awareness of things which ARE Ireland.'[8]

Griffith at this time, 1902, had already been through the political mill; but only in the sense that he had been an active pro-Parnellite in Parnell's last campaign 1890-1. Griffith then, after Parnell's death (1891), withdrew from actual politics, preferring to be active in the Young Ireland League, the Celtic Literary Society, etc., which were largely cultural, educational, social, etc., but not affiliated to any political movement. About 1900-2 Griffith was active in Cumann na Gaedheal, a loosely-knit organization of youthful patriotic clubs, more or less hostile to the Irish Parliamentary Party, and already formulating the ideas which reached full development in Sinn Fein. W. B. Yeats, John O'Leary, and Maud Gonne, for example, were active in Cumann na Gaedheal. Behind the Cumann na Gaedheal was the I.R.B. which was giving that organization its separatist impetus. Griffith was almost twenty years the senior in age of the youthful Collins and it seemed inconceivable that not many years hence they would be linked together in what was to be the highlight of the most passionate phase in Irish history: the signing of the Anglo-Irish Treaty.

For many years the country around West Cork had been noted for the number of youths which it supplied to the British postal service. In many cases, after passing the necessary examination the youths were entered as boy entrants to the clerkships of the Post Office, usually to one or other of its branches: the Savings Bank division, for example. At Clonakilty School, where Collins was now a pupil, special civil service classes were conducted and at the age of thirteen and a half years Collins was enrolled as a pupil in those classes.

His elder sister, Margaret O'Driscoll—whose husband was the owner, editor, reporter and general factotum of the local newspaper—lived in Clonakilty and Collins stayed with them for the whole of the time that he spent at the school. He also helped her husband prepare the issues of the paper, did general reporting jobs, and made himself useful in a dozen different ways. Although he took no particular interest in reporting local events, the terse matter-of-factness of journalist's prose appealed to him and the directives which he issued in later years all bear the stamp of the part-time training which he received from his brother-in-law.

A momentary picture of him at this stage in his life reveals that the scholar could readily forsake his books and turn to sport. He was exceptionally strong, healthy and energetic; and he included among his favourite sports wrestling, running, jumping, and horse-riding. He is remembered by Sean Deasey, a former class-mate, as being 'powerful in figure for his age, and a veritable terror at the sport of wrestling'.[9]

Meantime, at the age of fifteen years he had passed the Post Office examination and he prepared to leave Ireland and go to London.

In comparison to the city which was about to receive him, the part of Ireland which he was leaving created an impression which never afterwards wholly deserted him. All his life he remembered with affection the remoteness of the hamlet of Sam's Cross and the countryside around—a land where the country customs died hard and where the political talk of its people was tinged with a mixture of pessimism and opportunism; where the regard was all for the patriots of the past, leaving little to spare for the newcomers, the men who, even at that moment, were busily re-creating the gospel of Irish freedom from British domination. It struck the young Collins as being rather odd that he should be leaving this idealism behind and exchanging it for the life of the capital city of the oppressors.

In July, 1906, he began employment as a boy clerk at the Post Office Savings Bank, West Kensington, where his sister, Johanna, was already established as a clerk. During the whole of the time that he spent in London he lodged at the one address: in rooms at 5 Netherwood Place, West Kensington.

At first, a natural feeling of loneliness assailed him. For many weeks he desperately longed for his home countryside and its more staid way of life when compared to the bustle of the capital city. 'Loneliness,' he said to a chance friend, 'can be of two sorts: the delighted loneliness of the traveller in the country; and the desperate loneliness of the stranger to a city.'[10] For many weeks he was thoroughly miserable.

Soon, however, he found companionship in the company of other Irish youths of his own age and gradually the yearning for his homeland gave way to the more exciting and revealing life of the city. The migrants from West Cork and from other parts of Ireland formed a separate community; and many of them, such as Collins, being only as yet of tender years and in a strange city, a group of Irish business men interested themselves in the welfare of the youths. As a separate community they also had their own sports teams; and Collins had not been long in London when he joined the Geraldine football and hurling club. He also took up the secretaryship of the Gaelic League and the Gaelic Athletic Association. As a sportsman he played games with the same intensity of purpose as that which he devoted to his learning. One who knew him in those days recalls that Collins' temper often got the better of him during a game. But essentially he was the cheeriest of companions.

The dreary routine of his work at the Post Office Savings Bank was something for which he had no especial liking. His life was governed by a series of restless impulses and he found it very difficult to curb them. But although the monotony of his work went against these restless impulses and ambitions, he began attendance at the evening classes held at King's College, with a view to sitting for a further examination when the required age permitted him to do so. There is one sound reason—two, possibly—which account for both the ambitions and the restlessness. In learning, especially in mathematics, he was far in advance of his years; and his general outlook was also in advance of the youth still only in his teens.

Wherever Irish communities were to be found outside Ireland, in the big cities of England and Scotland, the Gaelic League flourished. Originally established by a group of scholars, of whom Dr. Douglas Hyde and Eoin MacNeill are best known, it was founded to encourage the extension of Irish as a spoken language. The Constitution of the Gaelic League was non-political, and during the presidency of Dr. Douglas Hyde (i.e., up to 1915) it uttered officially no opinions of a political nature. Hyde's purpose was to have it cultural, popular and non-political. On the other hand, it is true that it possessed strong latent political influence, and its members, by their actions in other organizations, gave a stimulus to republican separatist ideas. In Collins the political germ was already established; his interest in the native language was simply a furtherance of the political ideal.

At the age of eighteen years he took two steps forward in search of a goal to curb his restlessness. The first step was his appointment to the Treasurership of the London County Board of Joint Athletic Clubs. But of far greater significance is the fact that he was now a member of the Irish Republican Brotherhood, having been sworn in at the Barnsbury Hall on a night in November of the year 1909. For the remainder of his comparatively short life the I.R.B. was his chief interest, even after the reorganized Sinn Fein began its rapid rise to power in 1917.* But even when Sinn Fein became the 'popular' party and the recognized power in Irish politics, and though it overshadowed the I.R.B., the latter movement still had a great deal to say in the political arena. It is a mistake to assume that the I.R.B. ceased to exist, or to have any say in the affairs of a nation progressing towards its ideal from the time when Sinn Fein took over the political reins in 1917. As late as 1921 the I.R.B. was still in the picture at the London Treaty discussions. It is significant, also, that a great deal of distrust and even open animosity towards it existed. The secrecy and intrigue of the I.R.B. were resented by non-members.

A paper prepared by Collins for reading before a meeting of the I.R.B. is interesting as showing the development of his mind in

* Sinn Fein had already been established as a political organization in November, 1905, by Arthur Griffith. What took place in 1917 was its reorganization on a far wider basis, namely, to include the evolutionary (1905) element and the revolutionary (1916) wing. The economic programme of the original Sinn Fein was retained in its entirety, but the following was made the first aim of its political purpose:

> 'Sinn Fein aims at securing international recognition of Ireland as an independent Irish Republic. Having achieved that status the Irish people may, by referendum, freely choose their own form of government.'

This political formula was de Valera's.

The Irish Republican Brotherhood was established by James Stephens in Dublin in 1858. About the same time its American counterpart, the Fenian Brotherhood, was organized by John O'Mahony. On both sides of the Atlantic the organization lived through several generations, the key to its permanent character being found in a resolution of the Chicago Fenian Convention (1863) that the Fenian Brotherhood was a fixed and permanent institution in America which would continue its labours until successful. The I.R.B. lasted in Ireland down to Collins' time and after, at times flourishing, at times not, but it inspired and organized the 1916 Rising. In America the functions of the Fenian Brotherhood were taken over, in Collins' time, by the Clan na Gael, of which John Devoy, an old Fenian, was head.

political matters; and, of far greater significance, the stress which he laid on organization, proving that even in his youth the awareness existed which was to find answer in his own activities not many years hence. This extract is a fair sample of the work as a whole:

> '. . . In Ireland, from time to time, there have been a number of organisations and movements, one gradually coming into force as the power of another gradually waned. Our own re-established I.R.B. is a case in point, as with the decline of the pre-I.R.B. movement, so did ours come into prominence.
>
> But, by comparison, this revitalised I.R.B. is a vastly different proposition to former movements. In, for example, organisation. Organisation, a lack of it, was chiefly responsible for the failure of several risings of recent times. It is, therefore, of great significance—and of some urgency also—that, if and when the occasion should demand it, the I.R.B. should be even better organised, and so better prepared to meet such an emergency. A great deal of the organisation will, of course, have to be theoretical—that is the danger. Whereas in practical organisation there is no danger for the element of luck and chance does not enter into it. A force organised on practical lines, and headed by realists, would be of great consequence. Whereas a force organised on theoretical lines, and headed by idealists, would, I think be a very doubtful factor. . . .'[11]

In a little more than six years' time from the date of Collins' election to membership, the I.R.B. was destined to write its policy in blood in the streets of Dublin and elsewhere in Ireland. But it is significant that the force which attempted the insurrection was—as against Collins' desire—largely organized on theoretical lines and was headed, in the main, by idealists.

Most of his spare time, energy and brain he now devoted to the I.R.B. After barely one year of membership he was promoted to the rank of Section Master and in 1914 he became Treasurer for the London and South England district of the I.R.B. As an organizer he was rapidly coming into his own and also showing some of the dynamic energy which was to be his personal gift in the years to come. So, too, it seemed, he had achieved a purpose, and reached a temporary goal: a goal mainly achieved by reading and study and by way of the influences already named.

Aside from political and sporting activities, he paid attention to the theatre, where the current plays of Synge, Barrie, Yeats, and Padraic Colum attracted him. There was a great deal of the lover of the arts in Collins' character. Because of other more pressing activities, the art lover was rarely allowed to show itself, but on the other hand, he enlarged the scope of his reading, taking in such subjects as philosophy and economics, and, for relaxation, poetry.

Previous to achieving some status in the I.R.B., he had left the Post Office Savings Bank and had gained employment in another branch of the Civil Service, the Board of Trade. But although he successfully passed the higher grade examination, he left the Board of Trade and secured employment with a firm of stockbrokers, Horner and Company. He was a good worker and keen on his job; but he could hardly have foreseen, at this early stage, that dealing with finance would stand him in such good stead later in life.

Yet even though he was living a full and varied life, the old bouts of restlessness kept cropping up, causing him much mental anguish. In reply to a letter which apparently commented on this uneasiness of mind, he wrote:

> 'However happy I happen to be in a particular job, the thought is always with me that my future is otherwise than among the facts and figures of money. Yet I do not really dream of greater things . . . only the thought is always there.'[12]

Knowing the course of his life subsequently, it is easy now to account for these continual bouts of restlessness; for like the poet, the painter and the musician, he was subject to that bottled-up feeling, knowing instinctively that he was not yet set on the true path: he was forever searching for it, but some time would pass before he found himself on it. But even so his future encompassed, and was much concerned with, the 'facts and figures of money'.

He enjoyed good companionship; and others of his age found in the young man a certain attractiveness of character. Kevin O'Brien (no relative), who knew Collins well in those days, comments (in a letter to the present writer, dated 18th June, 1955) thus:

> 'A later realization as to the quality of Collins' character prompts me to write and say that, even in his London days, his earlier days, he had any amount of personality. His character was such that I, at least, found him to be absolutely dependable. There was nothing of selfishness in him. A certain air about him —call it magic if you will—drew many of us into his company. We used to say that he was "game", that he shirked nothing, and this was certainly true of him. But he was never reckless with his gameness. As one facet of his character I particularly recall an

occasion when, after Michael had been in a boisterous mood, he went suddenly silent. He had a book of poems in his hand. He started to read aloud, and we started to laugh. He went white with temper, stormed and raved at us. We only laughed the more. He then lunged out at me, and I was so full of laughter, I could do no more than fall over helplessly. He struck me—I have the mark today. We parted on the worst of terms. At five o'clock the next morning, my mother (we resided in London permanently) was awakened by someone knocking at the door. It was Michael. Overcome with remorse at what he thought had been a cowardly blow on his part, he had been unable to sleep, and so had come round to my home to apologize to me.'

To two other companions Collins was especially devoted: Joe O'Reilly, the man who was destined to be by his side through most of the great days of the fight for independence, and Sean Hurley. More than once in letters Collins remarked on the adaptability of Hurley as a companion:

'He has the sharpness of wit to see my own particular mood. We think the same way in Irish matters. We have walked London's streets on many a night, silently, because our thinking was elsewhere. . . . I appreciate him because his mind seems compact, whereas mine fritters away hours in idle thought. At worst he is a boon companion, at best there is no one else I would have as a friend.'[13]

Still more of his time was now being devoted to the I.R.B. But while his enthusiasm was unbounded, his thinking shows the mark of the untrained mind in politics. At fifteen years of age he had held the name of Charles Stewart Parnell in respect but now he thought the statesman's attitude that of 'an old mother': 'old mother' because Collins was of the opinion, along with many others, that independence would only be gained by the use of force and never through the medium of debate and discussion. As a theory it was shortly destined to be fully tested in a practical way.

He possessed a brain which was capable of a searching enquiry into details, he had a certain ability in the marshalling of facts, and as a speaker he found favour with those who liked to get down to a quick summary of the details. But these assets were offset to some extent by a lack of patience—a thing which proved to be a trait of character throughout his life. He could not sit at I.R.B. meetings listening to a speaker rambling on and on. When such a thing occurred, he would get up from his seat, walk out of the building, and tramp the streets until such time as he thought the wordy speaker had finished his say.

Towards the end of 1915 he turned his attention to the probabilities of a future in America. While it would seem idle to speculate on what his future might have been had he pressed the matter of America more closely, there are certain points in the American way of life which would have been agreeable to Collins. America is a land which had claimed, still does claim, so many of Collins' compatriots. It is peopled by a nation renowned for their energy and enthusiasm and, in all probability, Collins would have made good in the land in which so many of his fellow-countrymen have left their mark of genius.

A letter to Sean Deasey, dated January 5th, 1915, explains to some extent his feelings with regard to his position in England and also offers a reason for his wanting to go to America:

> 'This unhappy position in which I find myself. Not wanting to be part of an army which, in the past and now, has pledged itself to the oppression of Ireland. Yet not wanting at the same time to seek the murky honour of being a conscientious objector. America would seem to be the best solution to a pressing problem.'[14]

Admittedly, his position was a difficult one, and one which also, as the letter indicates, brought to his conscience a great deal of troubled thought. As much as he abhorred the idea of fighting for an authority for which he had an intense dislike, and against a people (the Germans) with whom he had no quarrel, the idea of cowardly action went even more against his character.

The schoolboy ambition to be an engineer reasserted itself and this, together with a natural bent for mathematics and an apparent enjoyment in the working of figures, made thoughts of an engineering career in America a distinct possibility. He wrote: 'Spent the day (Saturday) at the docks. Walked about debating my future. Should it be America?'[15] This was probably the most troubled phase of his youthful years. One can picture the young man walking among the dockside workers, alongside the ships, some of them bound for American ports, with his future weighing heavily on his mind as the impatience with himself increased, attempting to imagine the land across the ocean and what it might hold for him in the way of a future; and at the end of the day, with the problem still unsolved, returning dispirited to his Netherwood Place lodging. He had not as yet found the road for which he was seeking.

In the meantime, he had changed his employment again. On the 26th April, 1915, he commenced working for the Guaranty Trust Company of New York, at their London office in Lombard Street. He spoke afterwards of this period in his life in the friendliest of terms. Although employed in the general run of clerical duties, he nevertheless devoted to his work all of his ability and energy. Members of the staff found Collins to be a very likeable young man, quick in temper, but easily forgiving, and unable to nurse a grudge to the point where it became menacing. A late member of the staff, speaking to the present writer, recalled that 'Mick', as everyone called him, had abilities, 'though not, as we thought, in the direction into which he eventually channelled them! I do not think it possible that anyone, least of all among ourselves, could possibly have sought enmity with him. It is true he had a temper. Equally, though, the smile or the laugh of forgiveness was just as quick in coming to the fore. We had no real idea of how he spent his spare time apart, that is, from the sporting life of hurling, etc., which seemed to come so naturally to him. I once asked him, in fun, if hurling was a civilized sport. "Yes," he replied quietly: "It is a part of the most civilized race on earth." His death, in 1922, came as a tremendous shock to me, and to others also, I daresay.'

No doubt in this particularly restless phase of his career the job with the Guaranty Trust Company meant nothing more to him than a temporary stop-gap. He still hankered after America, still visited the docks and returned to his lodging more dissatisfied than ever. After such a day, and in a mood of impatient despondency, he asked Kevin O'Brien, 'Will anything ever happen?'[16]

Indeed something was happening: something which he himself knew had been contemplated as long ago as the previous year, though not in London but in Ireland. In London there was the talk and the rumour, the rumour a little more convincing than mere gossiping for talking's sake. Collins' friends were drifting back to Ireland one at a time, and with their going Collins linked the rumours. Chafing at being without something definite in the way of fact, he journeyed to Dublin, determined to find out for himself the true state of things. There he met Tom Clarke, Sean MacDiarmada, and others, and, from their talk, was convinced that something was about to happen. Happier in mind, he returned to London, but only for a brief spell. The capital city, after the excitement of Dublin, seemed stale and empty, his job even more drearily monotonous. He came to the conclusion that it would be Dublin or nothing, for in Dublin he would be on the doorstep waiting. There was also one other understandable reason for his wish to quit England: the threat of conscription into the British

Army: and there is no doubt that this fact hastened his departure from London, as against waiting to receive definite word from MacDiarmada. On the 14th January, 1916, he terminated his employment with the Guaranty Trust Company. On his saying that he was going to 'join up', he was congratulated by the manager, and given an extra month's salary-cheque which he changed into gold for the future use of those in Dublin who were preparing for a new insurrection.

Whatever dreams he had held of a career in engineering in America were now ended. His reading of the books of Hardy, Bennett, Wilde, and others was brought to a halt. Whatever was to be his fate in the future, the restlessness of mind which had troubled him for so long was now ended. The decision, one which was destined to alter the whole shape of his career, was made. On the 15th January he sailed for Ireland.

Chapter 3

THE EASTER RISING

IN DUBLIN CITY, at least, opportunity beckoned to the force of Irish revolution and pessimism was brushed aside. The disappointments of '48 and '67 were left behind for history. The physical force movement was on the upsurge once more, quietly at first, gradually becoming bolder as day succeeded day. No one can say that the British Authority in Ireland did not receive sufficient warning of what was about to happen. That they chose to ignore those warnings will be a subject for debate for many years hence; as it must also have been a matter of bitter regret to Chief Secretary Augustine Birrell.

There was the Howth gun-running exploit of the 26th June, 1914. It is an incident which has been much discussed by historians and biographers and it brought into fresh prominence Erskine Childers, ex-British officer, novelist, and former member of the 'Magpie and Stump Debating Society' of Trinity College, Cambridge, a cousin of Robert Barton, one of the Irish signatories to the Treaty of 1921. At the time of the landing of the arms from Childers' yacht, the *Asgard*, at Howth pier (and the subsequent march of the rifle-carrying volunteers into Dublin City, followed by the clash with soldiers of the Scottish Borderers* and police at Clontarf and when, later, the soldiers were returning to barracks they were jeered at by a crowd in Bachelor's Walk alongside the river Liffey) it was reckoned a great thing that authority could be so openly flaunted. It was only when the fever of excitement at having done so bold a thing died down that the true value of the gun-running became apparent. Half the total of the arms landed proved to be of no use, and the remaining half, so far as ammunition is concerned, proved to be of like value: one round for each rifle.[1]

There was, naturally, a certain awareness on the part of the British authorities in Ireland regarding both the undercover work and the more open activities of the Irish Volunteers, but whether or not the authorities garnered from these activities the true state of affairs is a matter of doubt. John Redmond, leader of the Irish Parliamentary Party, had, in July, 1915, scoffed at the idea of an insurrection being of any importance, and as his opinions were usually accepted by authority, this may be one reason why the situation was not looked at in a serious light.

The army of the Irish Volunteers actually came into being on the 25th November, 1913, after a meeting held on the 11th; and, in fact, its founders took example from the tactics of Sir Edward Carson and the 'Ulster Volunteers', a body which had been formed to resist a proposed Act to set up a Home Rule Parliament in Ireland which was then only at the proposal stage. Some of the founders of the Irish Volunteers, like Pearse and MacNeill, did not withhold their admiration for Carson, whom they looked on as defying the British Government in arms and accordingly a man to emulate. The leaders of the Irish Republican Brotherhood reasoned that if the British Government were prepared to tolerate the volunteers in Ulster, they could hardly interfere with the activities of volunteers elsewhere. This assumption proved wrong, chiefly because of the political trickery which was behind the formation of the volunteers in Ulster, but which was, also, against similar activities of other Irishmen. From this time (the formation of the Irish Volunteers) onward there was a constant succession of incidents.

From August, 1914, the British were fighting a war with Germany, which was proving to be a heavy drain on the man-power resources of the nation. A percentage of the British Army in Ireland consisted of soldiers who had been wounded in the war and of battalions who had been sent to Ireland for a period of

* There is a Dublin street-song which goes:

'Show, show yer petticoat, yer petticoat, yer petticoat,
Show, show yer petticoat,
Yeh dirty Scottish Borderer. . . .'

rest after the fierce fighting on the Western Front. The members of the I.R.B. and other organizations were of the opinion that if a move for independence was to be made now was the time for it. Plans were accordingly drawn up and the first preparations made.

Prior to the commencement of the Easter Rising, Collins divided his time between a job at Craig Gardners, an accountancy firm in Dame Street, Dublin, the camp at Kimmage which housed his London friends and other volunteers from across the Irish Sea, and in a constant change of lodgings, first with Patrick Belton, next with his aunt, Mrs. Donovan, at Inchicore, and finally at 16 Rathdown Road, N.C.R. A great deal of his spare time was also spent at the premises of the Keating Branch of the Gaelic League, 18 North Frederick Street.

The Branch President was Cathal Brugha, a fiery idealist, a scholarly speaker of Munster Irish, and a director of Lalor Limited, church candle makers, of Ormond Quay. In later times he and Collins were to clash frequently on opinions, and Brugha for his part would look on Collins with barely concealed hostility ; but, for the present, Collins was made welcome at the branch, receiving the nod of recognition from Brugha. Against the hostility which was later to come, Collins' assessment then of Brugha was that

> 'B. is a strange man. Not unfriendly but oddly remote. He will, I think, be capable of rising to the occasion if it should ever come. I don't doubt his courage but his remoteness puzzles me.'[2]

Others whom Collins became acquainted with at the Keating Branch included Diarmuid O'Hegarty, Richard Mulcahy and Con Collins (no relation), all of whom were destined at a future date to take a very active part in the fight for independence.

From across the Irish Sea came a steady stream of volunteers, many of whom had never before been on Irish soil ; for others, still, it was a homecoming ; for all concerned it was a time of waiting.

Books have been written, explanations given about the leaders of the forthcoming Rising. Yet, when all these assessments of the characters of the seven leaders have been made, have been accepted, or rejected, and then rescrutinized, the basic fact about them is that they were probably the strangest mixture of idealists and realists ever to grace the historic pages of revolution. That their names have gained a noteworthy honour in the history books of Ireland and in the hearts of the people should not be allowed to disguise the fact that the Rising was an ill-managed affair, and that they alone were responsible for its failure. To this statement a note of explanation must be added to the effect that in many other parts of Ireland the promised support was not given, owing to MacNeill's countermanding order the day before the Rising, and therefore, in the main, the brunt of the fighting was borne by the men in the Dublin area.

The proclamation announcing the setting up of a Provisional Government was drafted by Padraic Pearse and revised by James Connolly. Pearse was barely thirty-seven years of age at the time of the Rising. His birthright was of mixed stock, an English father, James Pearse (or Pierce), who was a native of Devonshire, and an Irish mother. Brought up in Ireland, he acquired the Gaelic tongue as a youth, and in the language he proved himself a master. He adopted the profession of barrister; and his name appears in one celebrated reported case, that of McBride *v.* M'Govern (1906. 2 Irish Reports, page 181). He appeared with Timothy Healy, K.C., as his leader; and Lord O'Brien, L.C.J., paid a tribute to Pearse's argument. Except for this one case, he never practised as he despised the profession. He devoted all of his time and energy—apart from his work for the independence movement—to the experiment of a bilingual school, St. Enda's, which was educationally a remarkable success. Its organization was suggested to Pearse from a study of Belgian bilingual schools. He was also a poet in the native tongue; and when, in 1914, he published a book of poems, *Suantraidhe agus Goltraidhe* ('Songs of Sleep and Sorrow' or 'Lullaby and Lament')—which is thought by some to be by far the best of his work—it contained a poem, 'Ideal', in which occurs this startling predication regarding his future:

> I set my face
> To the road before me,
> To the work that I shall see,
> To the death that I shall get.

Pearse, it is true, was a poet of some achievement, but he was not a soldier; and even a revolution demands a commander-in-chief with at least a rudimentary knowledge of the arts of war. Two other men, Major John MacBride and Ned Daly, were far more qualified to act in the capacity of commander-in-chief than was Pearse, and James Connolly had fully prepared for the Rising by making a special study of the tactics of street and house-to-house fighting. To admit so much is casting no doubt on the character or the integrity of Pearse, but it is a simple statement of fact that he was not qualified to lead men against experienced soldiers acting under the orders of experienced leaders.

Pearse and James Connolly were the leaders of the Rising; and they were as different from each other as chalk is from cheese, in birthright, education, thought, action, and in the differing ways of the lives they led. Connolly was the man of strength behind the Rising. He had threatened the more cautious elements that in the event of their failing to start an insurrection, he would start one with only two hundred men of the Citizen Army at his back, and it was no idle threat.

He was the son of a labourer, and was born near Clones, Co. Monaghan, on June 5th, 1870. In 1880 the family emigrated to Edinburgh and James worked in a bakery until his health failed. He then took up other work, in a tiling factory, for example. He was widely read and he loved books. John Leslie, the Socialist, urged him to return to Dublin in 1896, which he did, and there founded the Irish Socialist Republican Party. In 1903 he emigrated to America, and advocated Socialist teachings there. In 1910 he returned to Ireland. He was a close friend of Arthur Griffith, who disagreed with him in almost everything; none the less, they had great admiration for each other's characters and qualities. In speech, appearance and character Connolly was more of an Ulsterman. At birth a Catholic, he later often clashed with the Catholic leaders in Ireland but he nevertheless died a believer in that faith. He found his material for revolution in the city of Dublin. The Citizen Army men were in the main Dubliners. Above all, James Connolly was a man of the people, a great democratic leader and a fighting philosopher who hated injustice. He spent his talent, energy and life in elevating the anonymous, inarticulate, povertied workers of Dublin and Ireland. He was the one man among the leaders with his feet planted firmly on the ground, grimly philosophical, and fully aware of the repercussions which would follow their action.

The first signature to appear on the Proclamation is that of Tom Clarke (Thomas J. Clarke) and it was an honour wholly deserving of the man. More than any other, Tom Clarke had suffered for his ideals. Aged fifty-nine, sixteen of those years had been spent inside English jails, and under conditions of misery which would not be the unhappy lot of even the humblest of animals. At the time of the Rising, he kept a newsagent and tobacconist shop in Great Britain Street, which also served as a convenient rendezvous for the insurrectionists. One wonders how, when the time came, this man of iron viewed the failure of the Rising, which was to be his last act in a lifetime's toil and cruel suffering for the ideal which he cherished.

In Sean MacDiarmada there was an enthusiasm of ideal of such strength that no argument would prevail against it. A native of Co. Leitrim, he was one of the founders of the Volunteer movement and he had suffered imprisonment for the cause which he served so faithfully, so nobly, and so well. To MacDiarmada the cost meant nothing. He was a Sinn Fein and I.R.B. organizer, tramping through Ireland, spreading the gospel of independence. Illness (said to be polio, but doubtful), brought on by overwork in the cause, had changed him from a fine athletic figure of a man to that of a cripple, walking with the aid of a stick. But the physical change affected in him by illness in no way served to diminish the cheeriness of his outlook on life or altered the course to which he had destined himself. He viewed the Rising with a great intensity of spirit. It was MacDiarmada, more than any of the other leaders, who caught the imagination of Collins, such was the former's magic of personality.

The personal view of Thomas MacDonagh was for moderation: a show of arms madness without German aid.[3] MacDonagh was born at Cloughjordan, Co. Tipperary, in the year 1878 and later worked as a tutor at University College, Dublin. He was a colleague and helper of Pearse's in many educational projects and literature was his chief joy in life. But though he was on occasion a remarkable poet, he did not then belong to the illustrious company of Yeats, Russell and Stephens. Yeats, in his poem 'Easter, 1916', couples his name with Pearse's:

> This man had kept a school
> And rode our wingéd horse;
> This other his helper and friend
> Was coming into his force;
> He might have won fame in the end
> So sensitive his nature seemed,
> So daring and sweet his thought[4]

It says something for the character of MacDonagh that, even though the German aid was not forthcoming, he chose to suppress this opinion and take a leading part in the Rising, in which he proved himself a very able commandant.

Eamonn Ceannt was an intellectual, a native of Galway, where he was born in 1881. At heart a fiery gospeller for independence, his actual manner was reserved, almost aloof. He had great enthusiasm for the cause, but outwardly it was shown only to a few. His working hours were spent as a clerk in the City Treasurer's office while every moment of his spare time was devoted to the great ideal of independence for Ireland. He was recognized as one of the best teachers of Irish and he had music, his native music especially, in his soul. He was also a good athlete and in the year 1908 he was a member of a party of Irish athletes visiting Rome for the Jubilee celebrations in honour of His Holiness Pope Pius X. While there he was invited, as a piper, to play before the Pope. Ceannt had an impressive military bearing, and as Commandant of the Fourth Battalion during the Rising fully displayed his military abilities.

The seventh signatory to the Proclamation was Joseph Plunkett, and he was responsible for the planning of the Rising, his plan being loosely based on the 1803 insurrection. He was a son of the Papal Count and Countess Plunkett. For a time he was editor of the *Irish Review*, showing a fine literary judgment in his selection of contributors. He was the author of a book of poems, *The Circle and the Sword*. Outside the Volunteer movement he was not thought of seriously as a man of action but events were to prove those wrong who assessed his character as one of the literary world only, when, in fact, Plunkett was chiefly responsible for the military planning. At the time of the Rising, he was seriously ill with consumption, but it did not deter him from taking part. On the evening before his execution, he married Grace Gifford, sister-in-law to Thomas MacDonagh.

These are brief histories of the seven men destined to lead a revolution of major importance. As a military effort it was foredoomed to failure, chiefly on account of the odds. But the stupidity of the British in executing the leaders brought about a change in public opinion which hastened the tempo of revolution. It is beyond argument to say that the British, by executing the seven signatories and eight others, did more for the cause of independence than could have been achieved by Irishmen in years of gospelling or fighting.

The Rising was fought, in the main, by members of the Irish Republican Brotherhood and the Volunteers of the Citizen Army, while most of the nurses and the women helpers belonged to the movement of Cumann na mBan. Various estimates have been put forward from time to time regarding the numbers who actually engaged in the Rising. A figure generally accepted is of not more than three hundred men in the Dublin area, and approximately three thousand men over the whole of the country. A more accurate figure, however, is of one thousand (later one thousand eight hundred) men on the Irish side, and two thousand five hundred (later five thousand five hundred) on the British side.[5] It is extremely doubtful whether, at heart, any man among the Irish contingent had any great hope of success. Collins himself was of the opinion that, after the Rising, Ireland would be a 'free country', and in this view he was correct—though more than five years were to pass before his prediction came true.

More than any other term, the word 'if' could be applied to the failure of the Rising. If the Casement expedition of Good Friday, 1916, had not failed in its task of bringing sorely needed arms and ammunition to the insurrectionists; if the countermanding order against the manœuvre which was to be the opening move of the Rising had not been given by Chief of Staff Eoin MacNeill; if the country as a whole—instead of isolated instances in the counties of Dublin, Meath, Louth, Galway, Wexford, Clare, and Kerry—had turned out and fought, things might have taken on a different aspect. As it was, the circumstances enabled the British to pour men, arms and ammunition into Dublin City. While on the subject of failures, it should be added that the amount of arms, ammunition and general equipment was considerably less than the number of men (volunteers) who took part in the Rising.

The original idea of a rising had been one which would concern the city of Dublin alone; and it was to be a sacrifice for a principle. As early as May, 1915, Sean MacDiarmada had disclosed plans and intentions to the late P. S. O'Hegarty, who was then in exile. Sometime after this disclosure, the plans were altered to include the provinces as well as Dublin.

It should not be presumed that all the members of the Supreme Council of the I.R.B. were in favour of a rising; indeed, Bulmer Hobson, a stalwart of the movement, had resigned because he considered that a defensive insurrection (independence by peaceful means) would serve a better purpose in the long run than would an open offensive insurrection.

Knowing that Hobson would never retract from his views about the intending rising, the other leaders, chiefly Clarke, MacDiarmada and Connolly, sought to keep their plans from Hobson; and, indeed, on Easter Monday, they went to the extraordinary lengths of kidnapping Hobson—who had, in the meantime, counselled Chief of Staff MacNeill to put a stop to the impending insurrection—and thereby deprived MacNeill of the views of the one most likely to influence his actions.

Nevertheless, at 1.20 p.m. on Easter Sunday, April 23rd, 1916, the Chief of Staff issued the following order:

'To Commt. Eamon de Baileara [Eamon de Valera].

As Commt. MacDonagh is not accessible, I have to give you this order direct. Commt. MacDonagh left me last night with the understanding that he would return or send me a message. He has done neither.

As Chief of Staff, I have ordered and hereby order that no movement whatsoever of the Irish Volunteers is to be made today. You will carry out this order in your own command and make it known to other commands.

Eoin MacNeill.'[6]

He followed this message with another:

'Easter Sunday.
Woodtown Park,
Rathfarnham.

The order to Irish Volunteers printed over my name in today's "Sunday Independent" is hereby authenticated. Every influence should be used immediately and throughout the day to secure faithful execution of this order, as any failure to obey it may result in a very grave catastrophe.

Eoin MacNeill.'[7]

Both these messages had been preceded by demonstrations at Tullamore on the evening of March 20th; at a hurling match in aid of the Wolfe Tone Memorial, on Sunday, March 19th, and at the Sinn Fein Hall in William Street, on the same evening, a mêlée ensued, in which revolvers were fired at the police, and as a result of which Sergeant Ahern was seriously injured and taken to Steevens' Hospital, Dublin. On Sunday, April 9th, a motor car, containing a quantity of shotguns, revolvers, bayonets and ammunition, was seized by the British in College Green, Dublin.

Between the hours of Wednesday, April 20th, and Thursday, April 21st, occurred the Casement expedition failure. An Admiralty message stated:

'During the period between p.m. April 20th and p.m. April 21st, an attempt to land arms and ammunition in Ireland was made by a vessel under the guise of a neutral ship, but in reality a Germany auxiliary, in conjunction with a German submarine. The auxiliary sank, and a number of prisoners were made, amongst whom was Sir Roger Casement.'[8]

The arrangement with Germany for the shipment of arms had been made through John Devoy and the revolutionary directory of the Clan na Gael in New York. In October, 1914, Sir Roger Casement obtained the sanction of the Clan na Gael to proceed to Germany, there to enlist the aid of Germany in forming an Irish Brigade from prisoners-of-war held in Germany. This brigade was to be equipped by the Imperial Government of Germany as a gift to aid the Irish fight for independence.

The cancelling of manœuvres for the Volunteers, signed by MacNeill, which appeared in the *Sunday Independent* of April 23rd, was as follows:

> 'Owing to the very critical position, all orders given to Irish Volunteers for tomorrow, Easter Sunday, are hereby rescinded, and no parades, marches, or other movements of Irish Volunteers will take place. Each individual Volunteer will obey this order strictly in every particular.'

In the week preceding the Rising a very curious incident had occurred. It concerned Eamon de Valera, and his dislike of what he termed secret societies, among whom he listed the I.R.B., though for a time de Valera had been a member of the I.R.B.* Sean MacDiarmada, by some means, managed to convince de Valera of the absolute necessity of his attendance at an I.R.B. meeting to be held on the evening of Thursday, April 20th. The last that MacDiarmada saw of de Valera was of the latter waving a cheery 'goodbye' from the step of a tram. But de Valera did not attend the meeting[9] at which, no doubt, the final decision for the Rising to commence on a given date was made; a decision which afterwards ignored the orders of MacNeill.†

No convincing reason has ever been given for MacNeill's countermanding order. By some it is said that at the last moment MacNeill became appalled at what he thought would be nothing short of a massacre of which the Volunteers would be the victims. Another story has it that MacNeill had disagreed violently over a matter of policy with the other leaders; and that he thought to show his strength by issuing the countermanding order.

The Rising commenced at about midday on Easter Monday, April 24th, 1916, and the infiltration of the various groups of the Volunteers caught the British totally unprepared. How such a thing could have happened is beyond belief. Under the noses of the military, the Volunteers had been preparing for this event. The camp at Kimmage was run on strict military lines with guard duties, drill, and all the rest of military paraphernalia. It should have been obvious to the British that something out of the ordinary

* MacDonagh had, on a previous date, asked de Valera to become a member of the I.R.B., and de Valera consented to do so only on condition that, as MacDonagh had promised, he be given his orders at the appropriate time.

† Later, in 1917, de Valera 'confessed' that he had not believed in open rebellion; and that he had been in favour of MacNeill's attempted postponement. (Mary Bromage, *Sunday Independent*, December 9th, 1956. *See also* Miss Bromage's book on de Valera, published by Hutchinson.)

was about to happen. That they chose to ignore the rapidly developing situation will always be a cause for speculation.

At midday the Volunteers passing along the streets to take up their appointed positions were ignored by the police and the military.

At the G.P.O. in Sackville Street (now O'Connell Street), the clerks were ordered out of the building along with about twenty civilians. The Volunteers then proceeded to cut the telegraph wires which gave communication to England and Scotland. From now, until the surrender, the G.P.O. became the headquarters for the Volunteers. It may be added that the selection of the G.P.O. building for their headquarters later proved to be a bad decision because of the comparative ease with which it was isolated, by the British, from the other strongpoints.

Houses and buildings adjacent to the G.P.O. were commandeered and garrisoned by snipers hidden behind sandbags. Kelly's ammunition shop at the corner of Bachelor's Walk, and Hopkins' jewellery shop at the corner of Eden Quay, were seized, along with many other buildings which commanded the approaches.

This methodical seizure of buildings failed in a few instances. The telephone exchange in Crown Alley—which later proved to be of great advantage to the military—was one failure ; and another failure occurred at Dublin Castle, although at that hour very few men garrisoned it. The importance of the telephone exchange in Crown Alley cannot be overstressed, for it provided the military in Dublin with their one remaining link with the rest of the country.

A bitter struggle for the possession of the *Daily Express* building in Lower Abbey Street took place. The staircase leading to the upper rooms was the scene of a ferocious hand-to-hand encounter between a group of the Volunteers and a detachment of the Fifth Royal Dublin Fusiliers under the command of Lieutenant O'Neill. The building was finally won by the military.

The various battalions of the Volunteers and the Citizen Army were eventually placed as follows:

G.P.O. Headquarters: Supreme Commandant—Padraic Pearse ; Commandant General—James Connolly.

First Battalion, under the command of Ned Daly: Four Courts, North Brunswick Street, Church Street, North King Street.

Second Battalion, under the command of Thomas MacDonagh: Jacob's Biscuit Factory and outposts.

Third Battalion, under the command of Eamon de Valera: Boland's Mills, and outposts from Westland Row Station to Ringsend, and at Mount Street Bridge.

Fourth Battalion, under the command of Eamonn Ceannt: South Dublin Union, Marrowbone Lane Distillery, and adjacent posts.

Combined Citizen Army and Volunteer force, under the command of Countess Markievicz and Michael Mallin: St. Stephen's Green and the College of Surgeons.

A force under the command of Sean Heuston ably garrisoned the Mendicity Institution on the South Quays, likewise one under M. W. O'Reilly at the Imperial Hotel in Sackville Street, and another under Jim Sullivan at positions at North Circular Road and Cabra Road.

The British plan—when they finally awoke to the seriousness of the situation—was to cordon off the north side of the River Liffey, from Parkgate to the North Wall, and on the south side from Kingsbridge to Ringsend, and to strike at the centre of the Volunteer stronghold, the G.P.O.

British reinforcement troops were marched in from Dun Laoghaire, and eventually they came up against de Valera's Third Battalion, suffering heavy casualties, losing approximately half their number. At Mount Street Bridge over the canal most bitter fighting took place. Granted that many of the British dead were only partially trained soldiers of the Sherwood Foresters and that their officers, in marching them into the city instead of infiltrating, committed an act of folly, yet nothing can detract from the way in which de Valera handled the troops under his command.

Probably the greatest individual display of courage was that of Cathal Brugha, fighting with Ceannt's Fourth Battalion. Although suffering from no less than twenty-five bullet wounds, he insisted on carrying on; and it used to be said of him after 1916 that, as he walked, 'you could hear the bullets rattling in him'. Such an act of courage was typical of the man, noted for his hot-headedness, recklessness, courage, and obstinacy.

British reinforcements summoned from the Curragh, Belfast and England began to arrive in Dublin on Tuesday the 25th. Owing to the cutting of the rail communications by the Volunteers, the troops were finally forced to infiltrate slowly into the city and many individual battles took place in and around various positions held by the Volunteers.

The force under the command of Countess Markievicz and Michael Mallin in St. Stephen's Green was subjected to the fire of machine-guns and snipers stationed in the houses overlooking the Green. But it was not until towards the end of the week that the Green was evacuated under cover of darkness and from then the fight was carried on from the College of Surgeons, its garrison being one of the last to surrender.

Trinity College in the hands of the militia territorials commanded the heart of the city. Nassau Street, Grafton Street, Dame Street, Great Brunswick Street (now Pearse Street) and the south end of Sackville Street all came under fire from the College. It was a strongpoint which proved a great embarrassment to the operations of the Volunteers throughout the week of the Rising.

Almost immediately following the Volunteers' seizure of the G.P.O., they were in action against a party of Lancers who were escorting ammunition wagons to the magazine in the Phoenix Park. Taken completely by surprise, the Lancers retreated in the direction of the Parnell monument, leaving four dead comrades behind.

All over the city the battles for the strongposts were being fought and the shambles of wrecked buildings, demolished by shellfire, became worse as day succeeded day. On the arrival of further British reinforcements, the G.P.O. was quickly isolated and subjected to a heavy bombardment while machine-guns on the roof of Trinity College concentrated their fire-power on Sackville Street and Westmoreland Street.

By the evening of Friday, April 28th, the G.P.O. was a mass of flames, as were other buildings such as the Hotel Metropole, Eason's, and the entire block of adjacent buildings. At the time of the surrender, the fires had done so much damage that in Sackville Street alone only the block of shops from Elvery's Elephant House to the O'Connell Bridge were left. The whole of the street from the Nelson Pillar to the bridge was thick with debris. Yet one of the odd facts about the Rising and the damage wrought is that looters made daily raids into premises which were considered to be danger spots because of gunfire and that people seated on the parapet of the O'Connell Bridge had a front-seat view of the fighting.

The part played by Collins was one of a minor nature and yet a part which he played with conspicuous successes of ability and efficiency. 'The most efficient officer in the G.P.O. building,' said one eye-witness.[10] His rank was that of a Staff Captain, and he served as A.D.C. to Joseph Plunkett. He also attached himself to the leaders guarding them, and commiserating with Pearse when the fight seemed lost. But his pity for the defeated leaders was not without an edge of scorn.

He was near the front rank of the group who seized the G.P.O.

It is recorded[11] that his first act on entering the building was to pour two tierces of porter down the canteen drain and to take the names and addresses of those who served under Plunkett's command. At the last, when a tunnel had been blasted from the G.P.O. into Henry Street, and in response to the curses and entreaties of the wounded Connolly (who was shot in the thigh on the Thursday), Collins led the charge, revolver in hand, from the G.P.O. and through the gauntlet of fire set up by the British. He suffered no hurt, although his uniform was badly scorched and burned. Writing later to a friend, he said:

> 'Although I was never actually scared in the G.P.O. I was—and others also—witless enough to do the most stupid things. As the flames and heat increased so apparently did the shelling. Machine gun fire made escape more or less impossible. Not that we wished to escape. No man wished to budge. In that building the defiance of our men, and the gallantry, reached unimaginable proportions.'[12]

Collins went into the Rising with the light-hearted abandon of a schoolboy playing a game of sport and from the beginning he was out to enjoy himself in this his first taste of war. He was the military man personified, efficient, cool, and sometimes ruthless. He had set himself a test and he was determined to acquit himself with honour. The Rising shaped and moulded his character, and from it he learned to accept the humiliation and bitterness of defeat. He had come to Dublin as a young and immature idealist. He left the city, for internment in England and Wales, as a seasoned warrior and a man of more mature judgment.

The men of the Easter Rising were just as great and illustrious as those who had gone before them: they were of the stature of Wolfe Tone and Emmet. Sean MacDiarmada, who had worked himself into ill-health in freedom's cause; Tom Clarke, his face lined with years of prison, a slight, indomitable figure, one of the great of the century before; and that hard man of the nation, James Connolly. Among the great, Connolly has found a place. The Rising was something which he had been working towards for twenty years. It set the seal on the grand achievement; it was a success, even as it was failing. It was the cry of a nation, beggared and oppressed, seeking a long-lost crown, and laying down its blood for the greatest of all causes: freedom.

And, among the ruin and the spilled blood, there began to germinate the seeds of final success. In death the leaders of the Rising struck their greatest blow of all for honour and for freedom.

Chapter 4

Prisoner—Stafford and Frongoch

AT 3.45 p.m. on Saturday, April 29th, 1916, Padraic Pearse issued his note of unconditional surrender:

> 'In order to prevent the further slaughter of Dublin citizens, and in the hope of saving the lives of our followers now surrounded and hopelessly outnumbered, the members of the Provisional Government present at Headquarters have agreed to an unconditional surrender, and the Commandants of the various districts in the City and Country will order their commands to lay down arms.'[1]

This was followed by two further notes of surrender: those of Connolly and MacDonagh. It is interesting to observe, as a characteristic of the man, that Connolly's note stipulated '. . . for the men only under my command . . .'[2] i.e., the men of the Citizen Army, whose Commandant was Connolly.

At once the round-up of the prisoners began. In isolated instances surrender was refused and fighting continued until well into the following day.

While the prisoners were being gathered together, the fire brigades were doing their best to cope with the superhuman task which faced them. Not until now, late on the Saturday, had the military given them the 'all clear' to commence operations. The centre of the city was a smouldering ruin and rolling clouds of smoke blotted out the blue of the sky.

The British chose for the final collection of the prisoners the green in front of the Rotunda Hospital, and here they were assembled, batch after batch, wounded and unwounded, in a seemingly endless flow, surrounded by a ring of fixed bayonets. The officer in charge, Captain Lee Wilson (afterwards shot dead in Co. Wexford), an Irishman by birth, a member of a British Regiment by inclination, then proceeded to distinguish himself by mocking, taunting, and insulting the prisoners. Watched by the nurses from the windows of the hospital, Lee Wilson had men brought before him for stripping, and when they were in the nude he vaunted his own particular brand of sadism on the unfortunates. Night came with a steady drizzle of rain and still the torture continued.

Early on the Sunday morning, the apparently indefatigable Lee Wilson chose as fresh victims for his mockery the persons of Tom Clarke, Sean MacDiarmada, and Ned Daly, Clarke's brother-in-law. He had the three men stripped and in the process Tom Clarke suffered the most. An old wound in the hollow of his arm made it impossible for him to flex the elbow without feeling pain, but Lee Wilson, in a fury of impatience, forced Clarke's arm into a straight position in order to get the jacket sleeve off, and the action of doing so at once reopened the wound. But if Lee Wilson sought to humiliate the three men in the sight of their fellow prisoners and the watching nurses, he was unsuccessful; all bore their trial without utterance.

The overall picture was much the same. Men were pounced on for the most trivial of offences, if they can be called such; Collins himself, while feeling in his pocket for malted milk tablets, found himself subjected to a round of curses from a British N.C.O.

Eventually an order arrived, and the prisoners were marched off to Richmond Barracks, there to undergo yet a further trial, but this time of greater seriousness than the 'game' played in front of the Rotunda Hospital.

Crowded into one end of the barracks gymnasium, the prisoners were subjected to close scrutiny by the detectives of the 'G' (Political) Division of the Dublin police, the object of this scrutiny being the selecting of victims for courtsmartial, to be followed by either the death sentence or penal servitude. Those selected—and many of them were already known to the detectives—were taken across to the other end of the building and there herded together to await further orders. Collins was one of those selected but the reason for it remains an obscure one, as he was, at this time, comparatively unknown to all except to his immediate associates, so that one is driven to the conclusion that many other hapless victims were chosen in a like manner, perhaps to serve as examples to the rest of the prisoners. After Collins had been some time with the batch of selected prisoners, he heard his name being called from the further end of the building. Looking, he could not see who was calling him. After two or three attempts to locate the caller he grew impatient and decided to risk a walk across the room. And once there he stayed. It was for him probably the luckiest escape of his whole career; and the soldiers and the police, in unknowingly allowing him to wander away from the special batch of prisoners, lost from their clutches the man who was destined to be their chief enemy as well as the main thorn in the side of British authority.[3]

Later the same day (30th April), Collins, together with two hundred and thirty-eight other prisoners, left Richmond Barracks for the docks and the boat which was to carry them into internment in an English jail. On the 1st day of May they arrived in England and were placed in Stafford detention barracks. From time to time further batches of prisoners were added to the original total: two hundred and three on the 8th May, and a further fifty-eight on the 13th.[4]

Collins now appeared in the prisoner list as 'Collins, M. 16 Rathdown Road, N.C.R., Dublin. Irish Prisoner 48F'—a fact which caused him great amusement. 'Is one expected to lose one's identity, one's humanity, to become instead a numbered nonentity?' he asked in a letter.[5] Such a thing was entirely alien to his nature; humanity was his most striking characteristic, and to those who had his close personal acquaintance it was an endearing quality.

For all the change in his character which the Easter Rising had wrought in him, one thing never changed: the ability to keep his youth, his boyishness, which made him capable of switching from the serious to the gay lighthearted in a matter of seconds. Through all the desperate times which the future held in store for him, he stubbornly held on to this characteristic. At Stafford he could be, at almost one and the same time, the serious scholar and the sportsman enjoying a kick-about with a make-do football of brown paper tied with string. It was because of the football that his fierce, almost uncontrollable temper often gained the upper hand of him. The other prisoners, knowing this, and also aware of how far they dared torment him (sitting aside from the play, reading a book), deliberately kicked the football at him. He would then rise up in a great wrath and attempt to belabour the offenders of his peace. All in the spirit of good fun, it usually ended in a wrestling match.

It was at Stafford that he recommenced his study of the Irish language. It seemed alien to him, of such pure Irish birth, not to know the true language of his country. But then again there is perhaps a double meaning in a remark which he made in a letter, to the effect that 'this place gives me an opportunity of learning Irish'.[6] His language study cost him no great mental effort, and brought him a great deal of pleasure; and the time devoted to it, 'As valuable as I shall ever spend.'[7] Yet here again the realism in him reared up, questioning the use of Irish—a language secondary to English in Ireland at the time—as a language of means, needing on many occasions a translator. He never interested himself in the language to the same extent as did Cathal Brugha, who was the idealist supreme. Nor could Collins, in later days, ever come to a complete understanding with those who used Irish exclusively.

Writing on the 24th June, he discussed the coming move to Frongoch, a move which he viewed with mixed feelings. It was a phase in his life which only those who are naturally restless and who have undergone prison life will fully appreciate: how to keep one's self from stagnating, from succumbing to the weariness of the life. A moment of depression; and in another moment it is gone; and he is writing: 'They tell me that the Pears [soap] has improved my complexion.'[8] And thereby hangs a story.

In Frongoch—as at Stafford—Collins contrived to make a good personal appearance. He was essentially a clean-shirt man, always fastidiously neat and tidy, his face never showing any trace of blue chin or even the beginnings of a beard. For this almost superhuman effort of cleanliness in the conditions of internment, he became the butt, much to his disgust and rage, of the other internees, who invariably looked like brigands. 'D'you pull 'em out, Mick?' they jeered at him, referring to his lack of hairy growth on face and chin. No doubt Collins had thought the matter over, coming to a conclusion that the lack of growth represented a slur on his masculinity. For this reason, he sought to enforce a certain show of bombast on the other prisoners, many of whom early came to know that lack of hairs on Collins' features did not also mean a lack of strength.

The area in which the camp was situated was rough moorland country, agreeable country, but void of any particular distinction; a countryside suitable, because of its wildness, for the sports of shooting and fishing. To many of the internees, however, it recalled the situation of their homes in Ireland, with its background of mountains, and rich, full growths of heather, scattered trees and ferns.

Wooden huts formed the North camp and disused distillery buildings the South Camp, the whole area being surrounded by barbed wire. German prisoners had formerly occupied the camps but they were removed, and the Irish internees installed.

Proof of the part played in the Rising by many of the Frongoch inhabitants was sadly lacking: hence the occasional definition 'internees' instead of 'prisoners'. They could not, unless specifically charged, be called prisoners. Collins himself said:

> 'I grow more wondrous every day, for here at Frongoch by my own count at least a quarter of the men in the North Camp know very little about the Rising. One man, a former labourer of my acquaintance, said that he was just forced off the street in the round-up. His only crime appears to be that he was walking the streets.'[9]

Which was true, for the British military—and no one could lay special blame on the soldiers—had collected men on sight during the round-up, and, furthermore, protestations had been of little avail. Because of this doubt regarding the Frongoch internees, the British were extremely wary in the way in which they handled the men. No doubt the instruction came from a higher authority; but, at the same time, many of the guards were in sympathy with the plight of the internees. One example will serve to illustrate this sympathy: letters which the internees did not wish the censor to see were given to the friendly guards, who afterwards posted them.[10]

On the whole, the internees faced their imprisonment with an air of dourness; though some of them (mostly those who had been caught in the round-up, and who were innocent of any part in the Rising) gave way to despair. 'It is pitiable,' said Collins in a letter,[11] 'to see those who have given way to imprisonment now enforcing on themselves the extra burden of loneliness. Many of them are family men.' Between the two groups of internees there existed an unseen barrier, which could not be broken down. Those innocent of taking any part in the Rising blamed, naturally, the others whom they considered responsible for their own present predicament.

As leader of number ten hut, Collins came directly under the command of M. W. O'Reilly, the former Vice-Commandant of the Dublin Brigade. As a leader O'Reilly was an outstanding example of dour cheerfulness and his greatest strength lay in his determination not to yield in any protestations which he made on behalf of the internees. In much the same way, though in conditions far worse than at Frongoch, Eamon de Valera was adding further laurels to a name already known for the part he had played in the Rising. (De Valera was serving a sentence of penal servitude for life first at Dartmoor and then at Lewes Jail in the county of Sussex.) The British, however, fully appreciated O'Reilly's attitude, and he was removed to Reading Jail.

All the time there was a gradual exodus of internees from Frongoch camp. Men were taken in batches to London for interrogation and many were afterwards released. In an undated letter of this period, Collins remarked that there were no Kilkenny men left 'but lots of Wexford men'.[12] By the end of August, 1916, only about six hundred and fifty men remained, and as a consequence, the men in the North Camp were moved into the South Camp.

The occasional route march was a thing which found Collins tremendously enthusiastic. It was now late summer and the countryside was looking its best. Later, in winter, it was to assume the air of desolation common to this part of the country. But for all that, he was quick to appreciate his luck—if such a word might be applied to the circumstances—of being interned at Frongoch, instead of the prison of Wormwood Scrubs or some other such establishment. In many respects the wild unspoiled beauty of Wales reminded him strongly of County Cork, yet in such a way that he was never plagued by homesickness, or any kind of desperate futile longing. He had the happy knack of making a 'home' of any temporary habitation whether he was there for only a few hours or a few months, and although he would not say that he was totally happy as a Frongoch internee, he did say:

> 'I'm here and that's the thing that matters. Prating about home, friends and so on doesn't alter the fact that this is Frongoch, an internment camp, and that I'm a member of the camp. There's only one thing to do while the situation is as it is—make what I can of it. . . .'[13]

He interested himself keenly in the Welsh tradesmen who came to do jobs in the camp and who spoke their native language with the pride of the undefeated. Hearing them speak, seeing them at their work, determined him yet again to seek out the true value of his native language. It was something for which other Irish patriots had worked in the past: the idea of a native language as a means of stimulation towards freedom. And even now, at Frongoch and in other places of internment and imprisonment, the idea of a native language was being rapidly fostered. It was in such places that the tremendous surge of nationalism was really begun, which was, later, to sweep to victory over the British, politically and otherwise.

Coupled with this resurgence of nationalism in the camps and jails was the stupendous blunder made by the British Authorities in executing the leaders of the Rising and others also; those executed became martyrs to people who might otherwise have ridiculed them. The action of the British set the whole population of Ireland into a seething, simmering rage, thereby making the work of the later workers and fighters for independence a much easier task. It required little or no exploitation on their part to convince the population of the rights of the cause for which they stood. Where, for example, was the justice, and where, from the British point of view, the reasoning, behind the act of executing William Pearse, the brother of Padraic Pearse? Because he was the brother of the leader of the Rising? It is significant enough to say that even to this day and year (1958) no official documents of the courtsmartial have ever been made public and any attempt on the part of a biographer or other interested person to get permission to see the appropriate documents is most carefully waved aside. Instead, at the time of the executions, the people of Ireland were treated to the following laconic *communiqué*:

> (Wednesday, May 3rd.) 'Three signatories of the notice proclaiming the Irish Republic, P. H. Pearse, T. MacDonagh and T. J. Clarke, have been tried by Field General Courtsmartial and sentenced to death. The sentence having been duly confirmed, the three above-mentioned men were shot this morning.'[14]

People were bound to compare two cases, in the light of the executions: (1) The executions of the Easter Week men (fifteen in all), and (2) the acquittal of Captain Bowen-Colthurst, a British Army man, on a plea of insanity, for the murders of at least three civilians, Francis Sheehy-Skeffington, Thomas Dickson, and Patrick MacIntyre, during the week of the Rising. From the evidence available the case of Bowen-Colthurst represents an appalling miscarriage of justice, to the benefit of the accused, and in being so, it served, even at the time, to add fuel to the fire of resentment which was all too apparent among the population.

The following letter, dated May 10th, 1916, from George Gavan Duffy to M. Fitzgerald, accurately describes post-Rising sentiment in Dublin:

> '. . . I have just returned from Dublin, where the feeling even among Redmond's people is intensely bitter. They were, of course, strongly against the Rebellion while it lasted, but hundreds have veered completely around since the military atrocities began; in fact nothing could have been better calculated to revive the spirit of the "Jail Journal" than General Maxwell's performance.
>
> The bar to conciliation at present is that Redmond called out for blood from the first and everybody believes that he was fully aware of the intentions of the military. He has received urgent messages from Ireland reporting that he and his party are done if they do not change their tune and hence you have the appeals for clemency of the last two days.
>
> But I think it is felt that for the "Leader of the Irish Race at Home and Abroad" nothing could excuse the first speech he made and that his present attitude is unconvincing.
>
> If we had a General Botha, he would have got up in his place in the House as soon as Asquith announced that three of the

leaders had been shot after a military "trial" *in camera* and deprived of legal aid, and would have denounced the indecent haste with which these people conduct their secret proceedings, trying, convicting, sentencing and shooting the rebels first and making the fact public afterwards, for fear decent opinion in this country should have intervened.

The military, largely composed of young and raw recruits, were in a panic at first and now they are out for revenge.

A committee has been formed to help the unfortunate dependents. . . .'[15]

About the middle of September, Collins established contact with his former friend of the London days, Kevin O'Brien. O'Brien was a Londoner, born and bred, although of Irish parentage, and he had taken no part in the Rising, refusing to believe it otherwise than the work of fanatics. Collins chided him on his decision to abstain from ever leaving London.

'I wouldn't say your decision was a proper one. Hundreds of men in similar circumstances thought differently. You're as much Irish as I am. Had I been in your place native instinct would have made me stand up and fight.'[16]

But in a letter, written from Frongoch on the 6th October, 1916, Collins went to great pains to give O'Brien a personal impression of the men of the Rising.

'It is so easy to fault the actions of others when their particular actions have resulted in defeat. I want to be quite fair about this —the Easter Rising—and say how much I admired the men in the ranks and the womenfolk thus engaged. But at the same time —as it must appear to others also—the actions of the leaders should not pass without comment. They have died nobly at the hands of the firing squads. So much I grant. But I do not think the Rising week was an appropriate time for the issue of memoranda couched in poetic phrases, nor of actions worked out in a similar fashion. Looking at it from the inside (I was in the G.P.O.) it had the air of a Greek tragedy about it, the illusion being more or less completed with the issue of the before mentioned memoranda. Of Pearse and Connolly I admire the latter the most. Connolly was a realist, Pearse the direct opposite. There was an air of earthy directness about Connolly. It impressed me. I would have followed him through hell had such action been necessary. But I honestly doubt very much if I would have followed Pearse—not without some thought anyway.

I think chiefly of Tom Clarke and MacDiarmada. Both were built on the best foundations. Ireland will not see another Sean MacDiarmada.

These are sharp reflections. On the whole I think the Rising was bungled terribly costing many a good life. It seemed at first to be well organised, but afterwards became subjected to panic decisions and a great lack of very essential organisation and co-operation.'

Apart from a deal of homely truths contained in the letter, it brings out the realist in Collins. The opinions expressed are those of the realist looking at the idealists. The favour which Connolly gained in Collins' estimation is that which one realist accords another, whereas Pearse, poet, dreamer, supreme idealist, is looked on with much less favour.

From time to time a spirit of stubbornness asserted itself in the camp such as when the internees refused to empty the ash-bins situated around the soldiers' quarters. For this refusal they were punished. Day by day, in batches of eight, they were removed to the former empty loneliness of the North Camp and all privileges were stopped. For a time, although they missed their letters, newspapers and cigarettes, they would not accept what they considered to be an injustice. A case parallel to that at Frongoch occurred immediately after the Rising, at Richmond Barracks. There the prisoners had refused similar duties and, although it was the cause of much dispute, they won their point.

At Frongoch, in this time of trouble, the personality of Collins began to assert itself. He became one of the leaders in a system of smuggling the forbidden things to the men in the North Camp. And he noted that, 'This game of smuggling and communication is one for which there is no definite end. In its present form it could go on for ever. Daily the British grow more weary of attempting counteraction to it. As one of them remarked, "If you were bloody Jerries we'd know what to do. But you're not." Besides,' added Collins cheerily, 'it gives some spice to the usual monotony.'[17]

He became aware of the usefulness of a dogged persistence. 'Sit down—refuse to budge—you have the British beaten. For a time they'll raise war—in the end they'll despair. Method, but unorthodox, has them beaten the whole time.'[18]

Even as he had forecast, the struggle was soon over. By October no more bins were emptied.

It was in this atmosphere of struggle and conspiracy that the real Collins was born. Apart from the fact that he was rapidly coming into his force as a man whom others looked to for leadership, the smuggling and the methods used to beat the ban appealed to his nature. He was having a happy—the word is his[19]—foretaste of the atmosphere of conspiracy which was to be part of his daily life in the years to come and it was an atmosphere which was in complete tone with his character: the man-to-man contacts, in preference to the leader who organized from a distance, unseen and unknown to those whom he commands.

The next event of importance was one of refusal to answer roll call and for this the internees had a very good reason. Men, such as Collins, were, if identified, liable for conscription into the forces of the United Kingdom, or, if they refused, to punishment in jail. At this time the British were extremely cautious. Past mistakes in the identification of internees had made them so and they did not wish to press the matter too closely. They decided that a system was necessary. Forthwith, they confined the 'unidentified' internees, among them Collins, separately from the rest and again all privileges were stopped. Even so, the move was not at all successful, for the system of smuggling and communication began all over again.

There were, of course, a batch of the internees who gave no thought to the future, or to the present, except that of getting home and into work again. They were the moderates, with their counsel of any government providing we are home. Collins poured scorn and ridicule on this idea of moderation; and the moderates, in their turn, named him a 'crank' and a 'firebrand'. Truth was, his self-assertiveness did not appeal to those inclined to moderation. But with the exodus of the moderates, who had not generally added to the morale of the other internees, it left a core of sound nationalism, fixed in its determination, calculating every move, and, above all, certain of itself. Collins was one of the shrewdest of this core of indomitables, a man certain of his every action, and recognized by the others as a man of some consequence.

For the British the situation was becoming even more complex. Their action in executing the leaders of the Rising had met with opposition in America and now that same opposition began to question why men, against whom no definite charges had been made, were compelled to suffer prolonged imprisonment at camps such as the one at Frongoch. In the camp itself, there was a never-ending agitation against their imprisonment. The truth is that the men who had fought in the Rising were not crushed in spirit, nor had they ever been. The position had been badly miscalculated by the British, who thought that, following the failure of the Rising, the men who had taken part in it would be a broken force. But the flame which had very nearly died in the ruins of Dublin was kept burning, and ready for future action, in the prison camps.

The man who had really lit the flame of nationalism in Collins was Sean MacDiarmada. Many times in the future he was to speak of MacDiarmada in terms of affection and reverence. Collins himself was too much the individualist ever to model his thinking and his actions on those of another person, but he said of MacDiarmada:

> 'He is not dead. Today he is as much alive in this camp as if he were here with us. If I have one quarter of the strength of Sean MacDiarmada I am satisfied. Wherever he walked there went with him all the shades of the great Irishmen of the past. He was God given. He was humble in the knowledge of his own greatness and in the task which he had chosen to do. He did not seek glory as a personal investment but as a National investment. He was not Sean MacDiarmada, he was Ireland.'[20]

In this note there is nothing of the sentimentalist for when he spoke of MacDiarmada in other times it was always said in the same way. After the signing of the Truce in July, 1921, the remark was passed: 'Well, Michael, this is a great day for you.' Collins rounded on the speaker, saying with great heat, 'We are only the reapers; MacDiarmada and the others were the sowers.'

Winter came, drab and cheerless, the desolation, the remoteness and wildness of this part of Wales underlying the loneliness which was in the hearts of many of the internees. Nor did the thought of spending Christmas in the camp, and away from their homeland, in any way serve to illuminate what was, to many, a day-long darkness, with sleep the only means of compensation.

It was a time of rumour—home for Christmas was the favourite one, the disappointment being felt more keenly as day succeeded day without any sign of the rumour becoming a fact. For Collins it may have been mere speculation on his part which caused him to write, on the 8th December:

> '. . . This state of affairs can't last much longer. While many of the men are looking forward dismally to the prospect of spending Christmas here, I would not be surprised to find myself at home for that event.'[21]

Speculation, observation, or otherwise, it proved to be true. On the evening of the 22nd December, the Adjutant of the camp informed the internees that all would be released: prisoners from the north, south and west of Ireland would go that night; the rest would leave the next day. He asked for the names, addresses, and home rail stations of the two batches of men. At once the internees were suspicious, thinking it to be the bait of freedom dangled before them in an attempt to identify the wanted men. Collins outspokenly condemned the move as a trap. There followed an uneasy silence. Then, a little wearily, the Adjutant explained that this was no trap. He suggested, as they were still suspicious, that the internees write out their own lists. To this suggestion Collins agreed.

There was nothing more to it. The internees left Frongoch camp to, as one suggested, 'stew in its own desolation'.[22] And for Collins yet another phase in his career had come to an end.

Chapter 5

National Aid Association—Bye-elections—The I.R.B. and Sinn Fein—Death of Tom Ashe—Sinn Fein Convention, 1917—'German Plot Round-up'—Collins and Boland

THE Ireland to which Collins returned already showed a marked difference from the country from which he had departed as a prisoner of the British.

The aftermath of the Easter Rising proved to be a challenge from the dead, the horror of the executions having had a great effect on the feelings of many of the population. Consequently the hold exercised for so long by the Irish Parliamentary Party had been considerably loosened and anything which had the slightest semblance of British about it now stank in the nostrils of the majority of the people.

Politically the country was in a wilderness. The people were muddled and restless, keen in their hatred of such men as General Sir John Maxwell, the British Commander-in-Chief in Ireland. In turning away from the authority of the Irish Parliamentary Party, the people had as yet no definite party on which to anchor their political feelings. It was a time ripe for whatever could be done in the way of getting a political foothold in the fortunes of the country, a time ripe for the work of the zealous idealists of independence.

Collins was quick to appraise the situation. A letter written early in 1917 indicates a keen appreciation of the position.

'Consider the situation. It is ripe for whatever one may wish. Both British Authority and the I.P.P. are in a corner, driven there by what they have done and by the will of the people. There now exists a wilderness—ripe for any advancement along the road to salvation. Will any Irishman stand and wait and let this opportunity pass?'[1]

But, first, Collins had to get a job. He was now in Dublin meeting daily with some of those who had been his fellow internees at Frongoch and by whom he was now considered to be a man of some consequence.

He became Secretary to the National Aid Association, a body set up to alleviate the distress caused by the Easter Rising. In this position he succeeded Joseph McGrath, with whom he had worked at Craig Gardners in the weeks prior to the Rising. McGrath had done the secretarial work as a volunteer, but when Collins succeeded him, it was at a salary of £2 10*s*. per week.

When he gained the interview necessary for further consideration for the position, the women members of the trust did not view him in too favourable a light. He seemed to them to be altogether too cocksure, seated on the edge of a desk, swinging his legs. But he created, nevertheless, an impression of a certainty of manner, of someone able to grasp the detail, quick in action, and trustworthy. He himself has said with regard to the interview:

'I was regarded with a certain amount of suspicion. I was young and would therefore be almost certain to be irresponsible to the importance of the position. More, I had been active during the Rising. All these things had been carefully calculated by the members and more especially the ladies. Certainly the salary of £2 10 0 weekly was not to be sneered at. In the end chiefly by good fortune the job became mine.'[2]

It was not, however, so much the 'good fortune' as the active canvassing of his friends of the Frongoch era which had got him the job. As several of them stated to the present writer:

'We worked like hell; though we were careful to keep any knowledge from him of what we were doing. Mick would have taken a very sour view of our part in the affair.'

Collins did not hold the position for very long. Other work of far greater importance was in urgent need of being done and the secretaryship of the Association hampered these other activities. In 1918 he resigned and was glad to do so.

Others, besides Collins, had recognized the importance of the political wilderness and with many of these men Collins had made contact through his secretaryship of the Association. They were the men of the I.R.B. and Sinn Fein. Both parties were dedicated to the one ideal: the overthrow of British Authority in Ireland; but it was a dedication resolved on the differing principles of military force (the I.R.B.) and political force (Sinn Fein).

How best, then, to achieve this ideal? First, by testing the reactions of the people to the Irish Parliamentary Party, who, according to the Sinn Fein spokesmen, were the slaves of British Authority, for the Irish Parliamentary Party was little more than a mouthpiece for the doings of the Westminster Parliament.* Such was the scheme advocated by the more daring elements of the I.R.B. and Sinn Fein. One imagines the more thoughtful members of the two parties thinking the matter over very carefully, assessing the risks involved against the rewards of a possible success. North Roscommon was the constituency chosen, the vacancy being caused by the death of James J. O'Kelly, formerly a leading Fenian. The candidate ultimately nominated to oppose the I.P.P. was the Papal Count Plunkett with whose son, Joseph, Collins had served as A.D.C. during the Rising. The choice of candidate was a shrewd one, for, it was calculated, the circumstances attached to an incident connected with Count Plunkett would further influence the opinions of the voters. Plunkett had lately been expelled from membership of the Royal Dublin Society, and it was generally understood that he had been expelled because of his sympathy with the actions of his sons during the Easter Rising; Joseph had been executed, while George and John were serving terms of penal servitude.

No formal policy was put before the electors. Plunkett was chosen and supported by a co-operation of Sinn Fein, the I.R.B., the Irish Nation League, and the Irish Volunteers. Between these elements there was, as yet, only a loose cohesion, and they had no unified policy, except opposition to England and the Irish Parliamentary Party, which they regarded as being subservient to the British Government. They were, of course, united by a devotion to the memory of the executed Joseph Plunkett so that the election was fought mainly on an emotional issue.

None worked more ably and more willingly than Collins to

* Historically speaking, this opinion of the Irish Parliamentary Party by the Sinn Fein spokesmen is untrue. Men like John Dillon, John Boland, and individualist Parliamentarians like William O'Brien, M.P., were certainly not mouthpieces for the doings of the Westminster Parliament. The propaganda of Sinn Fein was in certain aspects narrow and ungenerous, and particularly on the death of John Redmond early in 1918. No credit was given to the sincerity and labours of the Irish Parliamentary Party in the aftermath of 1916. Only in method did the aims of the I.P.P. differ from those of Sinn Fein.

ensure victory at North Roscommon. The election leaflet put forward to aid Plunkett's fight was a carefully worded six-point masterpiece. The sixth point illustrates the general tone of the address:

> 'Because he will not associate with the Irishmen who cheered in Parliament when his son was shot against a wall for loving Ireland.* Will you insult him in North Roscommon, as the Dublin Society did, and tell the British Government that he is not the man you want? No. There are Irishmen in North Roscommon yet.'[3]

In the three-sided contest which followed Plunkett emerged the victor, by a clear majority of more than thirteen hundred votes, polling 3,022 against the I.P.P. candidate's 1,708 and an Independent Nationalist's 687.

With the consequent elation which followed the victory of their candidate, there was also a note of caution. Collins and others recognized that, in reality, Count Plunkett was as yet an unknown quantity; more, he had had a measure of power suddenly thrust into his hands, as being the only representative of the movements dedicated to independence. Much depended on Plunkett's reactions to what the party of Sinn Fein proposed, and in particular to what Arthur Griffith had had in mind for a long time, namely, the refusal by the candidate to attend the Parliament of Westminster. It was a point of vital importance, since in the Count there rested the nucleus of a native government.

Judging by Plunkett's subsequent attitude, it was a fear well realized. At a meeting held at Boyle, Plunkett announced his intention to abstain from the Westminster Parliament only after he was certain that a majority was in favour of his abstention.

Even so, any hope which they held that Plunkett would toe the party line soon received a shock, for Plunkett announced his intention of forming a new party with himself as its leader and, in the process of doing so, to scrap the I.R.B., Sinn Fein and other nationally minded bodies.[4]

Arthur Griffith, now back in Ireland after serving a term of imprisonment in Wandsworth and Reading Jails, was against the new move by Plunkett. Instead, Griffith proposed that a joint executive should be formed consisting of members of the interested parties. But with the defeat on vote of Griffith's proposal things

* This is a mistaken impression, circulated by Laurence Ginnell, M.P. (an individualist member who was a strong critic of Redmond and Dillon). It does not seem to be supported from any other source. However, it wreaked havoc with the reputation in Ireland of the I.P.P., and Sinn Fein made devastating use of it.

took a dangerous turn. After a great deal of controversy, however, an almost similar proposal to that of Griffith's was accepted.

There next occurred a second victory at the polls and, from the point of view of those responsible, a more sound one than that of Plunkett's at North Roscommon. This was the election of Joseph McGuinness to the constituency of Longford County.

At the time of his election McGuinness was a prisoner in Lewes Jail and this peculiar circumstance was made the theme for the forthcoming election. Posters showing a man in convict garb carried also the inscription, 'Put him in to get him out.' On the 9th May, 1917, McGuinness, against his personal wishes, was elected on a narrow majority of thirty-seven votes, polling 1,498 against his opponent's 1,461—proof again of the value of an emotional appeal to the electors.

Before October of that same year, two more resounding victories were recorded by independence candidates. The first brought back into the picture the person of Eamon de Valera—if it can be said that he was ever absent.

De Valera's conduct during the Easter Rising had given some indication of the possibilities of the man in the matter of leadership. A death sentence commuted to penal servitude for life in no way served to alter his personal convictions. From the time he was imprisoned, the qualities which he had shown during the fighting became further obvious. The standard of character set by de Valera while a prisoner is beyond reproach. A character of strength coupled with an almost monkish isolationist outlook which allowed of no weaknesses—such was the example he set for the rest of the prisoners to follow. He frustrated any attempt by the British, either of favour or otherwise, which did not accord to the standards of prisoners of war—which right de Valera said was due to them. Small wonder that when the released prisoners arrived back in Dublin on the 18th June, 1917, they were greeted by many of the populace as heroes, and de Valera as the hero-in-chief—much to his surprise, it may be added.

Major William Redmond, M.P. (brother of John Redmond), had been killed in the battle of Messines and a vacancy was created at East Clare. De Valera, although expressing doubts as to whether he was suitable as a candidate, was elected to stand; and the result of the election, de Valera 5,010 votes against Patrick Lynch's 2,025,* left no doubt as to the popularity of de Valera. So began his sensational climb to power and the making of his name in the world.

* Patrick Lynch subsequently became a supporter of de Valera and was later made Attorney-General under the Fianna Fail administration of the 1930's.

The victory of W. T. Cosgrave (by 772 votes against his opponent's 392) at the Kilkenny bye-election gained another foothold for Sinn Fein in the fortunes of the country.* Coupled with this victory went the decision of Laurence Ginnell, Irish Parliamentary Party M.P., to refrain from attending at Westminster. This decision was of supreme importance. For some time Ginnell had had no dealings with the I.P.P. and his had been the only dissenting voice raised in the Westminster Parliament against the executions of the Easter Rising leaders. Nevertheless, it was almost unthinkable that a member of the supposedly powerful I.P.P. should refuse, along with the newly elected 'rebels', to attend at Westminster. But the days of the I.P.P. were numbered: the warning light had been shown at North Roscommon, Longford County, East Clare, and Kilkenny.

In the midst of this apparent political clover, a clash occurred. It was a clash of enthusiasms and ideals between the old-established I.R.B. and the comparatively new, but none the less considerable, force of Sinn Fein.

To remuster and reorganize the I.R.B. was, in the opinion of a former stalwart, Cathal Brugha, a waste of time because the I.R.B. had outlived its usefulness. It was an opinion which had considerable backing. De Valera, although formerly a member of the pre-1916 I.R.B., declined to have anything to do with the reorganized Brotherhood on the grounds that it was a secret society, and as such was condemned by the Catholic Hierarchy. Collins, who was now a member of the Supreme Council of the I.R.B., stated:

> 'There are many things to be said in favour of Sinn Fein, many of whose ideals are but the re-weighed ideals of the I.R.B. But the things to be said in favour of Sinn Fein do not outweigh the uses of the I.R.B. which is respected and acknowledged by many who will think twice about the prospects of Sinn Fein. This is a time when to be united is to have the strongest asset. Instead of which there is a growing undercurrent of unrest.'[5]

It is possible, indeed most probable, that the I.R.B. gave way to some extent to the demands of Sinn Fein in order to preserve unity.

Cathal Brugha's remarks on the I.R.B. have been noted, and Collins' also. The words of a man of the I.R.B., who was shortly

* The Kilkenny Nationalists, unable to agree on the selection of a candidate, appealed to Sinn Fein headquarters, 6 Harcourt Street, Dublin, to propose a suitable man. The Standing Committee of Sinn Fein selected W. T. Cosgrave; and he was, in fact, the first official Sinn Fein candidate to be put forward after 1916. (A Sinn Fein candidate unsuccessfully contested North Leitrim in 1908.)

to die for the cause of independence, are also worth noting. The man was Tom Ashe.

> 'Have we yet reached the state of power when we can afford to cast aside a proven ideal for a barely proven one? Are we so great that we can afford a quarrel among ourselves, oblivious to the common enemy? Men and movements should be as nothing in this time of great test; country, our country of Ireland, should be our main thought.'[6]

The outcome of it all was that the I.R.B. remained a force on the councils, but the title seemed gradually to fade from everyday use. None the less, the ideals of the I.R.B. have never really been forsaken, just as they were apparent at the Treaty discussions in 1921.

This undercurrent of trouble between the two parties was the primary cause of what was to be the first of many clashes of opinion between Cathal Brugha and Collins, and which was later to develop into an open hostility, though chiefly on Brugha's part. Brugha distrusted Collins with a barely concealed suspicion. On the other hand, Collins did not for a long time really appreciate the barrier which had come between them. There is no doubt that jealousy on Brugha's part towards his younger 'rival' was one of the reasons for this state of friction. Still another reason was one which had previously caused a certain amount of friction between the men of the various movements: the differing opinions of the idealists, such as Brugha, and the realists, such as Collins. Brugha's stubbornness had already been mentioned, and this aspect of his character he often carried to the point of enmity—as with Collins. But at this stage (1917) Collins could not possibly have foreseen how this enmity of Brugha's was later to become an efficient net of intrigue with himself as its victim.

The public, unaware of this undercurrent of trouble between the two parties, solved the problem in its own way. Irrespective of whichever party the members belonged to they were dubbed 'Sinn Feiners'.

Despite this setback to its title and reputation, the I.R.B. determined to forge ahead and revise its Constitution. The Committee appointed for this task consisted of Tom Ashe, Diarmuid Lynch and Con Collins. The name of Michael Collins was not officially mentioned, but most of the work was done by Lynch and Michael Collins. Lynch was not slow to appreciate the hard-working capabilities of Michael Collins, nor was Tom Ashe. The friendship of Ashe and Collins, although of very short duration owing to the former's death, was, nevertheless, of great importance to Collins and he felt the loss of Ashe far more than he ever cared to show outwardly.

The arrest of Ashe, Austin Stack and Fionan Lynch in August of 1917 was destined to prove more than ever where the sympathy of the people lay. But, to make the point, it involved the death of Ashe, who died in circumstances of extreme cruelty and misery. In Mountjoy Prison the three men were treated as ordinary criminals and against this treatment they protested. Their protestations being ignored, they decided to go on hunger strike and on the fifth day of the hunger strike Ashe was removed to the Mater Hospital where he died a few hours later.

At the inquest the coroner's jury came out with a direct verdict, laying the whole of the blame on the Dublin Castle authorities.

The bed, bedding, and the boots belonging to the prisoner had been taken away from him. He had been left lying on the cold floor of his cell for more than fifty hours. Following which cruelty, an assistant doctor, without previous experience, had attempted forcible feeding. The jury went on to say:

> 'We censure the Castle authorities for not acting more promptly, especially when the grave condition of the deceased was brought under their notice on the previous Saturday by the Lord Mayor and Sir. J. Irwin.'[7]

Many thousands of people visited the Mater Hospital where Ashe's body, clad in the Volunteer uniform, lay in state. His funeral was a demonstration of public mourning and at the graveside Collins spoke the short funeral oration.

The character of Ashe was one of faith and endeavour, and a will to do things in a quiet and unassuming way. Handsome and tall, he was a former National teacher, a poet and a singer of ballads, and a fine speaker of his native tongue. In the Easter Rising he had commanded a detachment at Ashbourne and had personally distinguished himself in the fighting there. With de Valera and others, he had later been a prisoner in Lewes Jail. From a position of second-in-command to de Valera at Lewes, Ashe later often clashed on points of opinion with his former leader, especially in regard to the I.R.B., on whose councils he was a force of some consequence. For Collins the death of Ashe was a blow from which he only slowly recovered:

> 'I grieve as perhaps no one else grieves. And yet our comradeship had not been of long duration. He was a man of no

complexes. Doing whatever he did for Ireland and always in a quiet way.'[8]

That was written in 1917. In 1922, when the Treaty storm burst about the heads of Collins and Griffith, Collins bitterly remarked, 'At least Ashe was spared this final degradation.'

At the Annual Convention held on October 25th, de Valera was elected to the Presidency of Sinn Fein, the title under which sections of the new movement were grouped. This Convention is significant for one thing relating to de Valera's election: that of Griffith's standing down from election of President, though in all probability he would have carried the vote even against I.R.B. canvassing for the newly-elected President. Instead, Griffith was elected Vice-President. Austin Stack and Darrell Figgis became joint Honorary Secretaries with W. T. Cosgrave and Laurence Ginnell as Honorary Treasurers. The Executive Council consisted of twenty-four persons, of whom Michael Collins was one. Harry Boland, for some time a particular friend of Collins, was also elected to the Executive.

The Sinn Fein Convention of 1917 involved a great deal of preliminary discussion between Griffith's followers, the Irish Nation League (Conservatives chiefly), the I.R.B., the 1916 Revolutionary wing (Brugha, Collins, de Valera), and Count Plunkett's followers. The difficulties involved meant hammering out a common platform between the moderates and revolutionaries.

It was highly successful in uniting these hitherto diverse national forces which were opposed to the Irish Parliamentary Party, in agreeing on the question of leadership, and in presenting a constructive and positive policy. From this date Sinn Fein, now a broad-based organization, gathered momentum.

The programme was finally agreed on by accepting the old Sinn Fein (Griffith) programme of industrial and economic development (itself based on the economic nationalism of the nineteenth-century German economist, Friedrich Liszt), its programme of abstention, together with the political formula devised by de Valera of aiming at 'securing international recognition of Ireland as an Independent Irish Republic'.[9]

De Valera's skill in negotiation was seen to considerable effect in these preliminary negotiations. He dominated the 1917 Convention. Griffith always regarded this and subsequent Conventions as being in lineal succession to the pre-1916 Sinn Fein Conventions. He achieved his desire by having his economic and abstention programme accepted by a nation-wide organization, instead of the extremely limited one with which he had worked in the years before 1916.

On October 27th, 1917, at a Convention of the Volunteers, de Valera was again elected President. The most significant point, however, to emerge from this Convention was its instigation of a policy empowering the Executive to declare war should the British Government press their plans for military conscription in Ireland.

Here again the I.R.B. was the dominating influence, for Collins became Director of Organization, and was also elected a member of the Executive of the Volunteers. Cathal Brugha was appointed to the position of Chief of Staff.

In the drafting of a new constitution for the Volunteers, Collins did a first-rate job. By nature fastidious and methodical, perfection was his aim in all things; anything which fell short of this high standard aroused his wrath.

The position at the end of the year 1917 was that a great many points had been straightened out, a certain amount of success achieved, and the name of Michael Collins was beginning to be known as a name of consequence.

The year 1918, contrary to many expectations, opened on a sombre note for Sinn Fein. Three successive defeats were recorded against their candidates. On February 1st, at the South Armagh bye-election, Dr. MacCartan was defeated. On the 22nd March, at the Waterford bye-election, Dr. Vincent White was defeated, though there was little hope of success here, the seat being retained by John Redmond's son. And on the 2nd April, at the East Tyrone bye-election, Sean Milroy was defeated.

However, the balance was more or less maintained by the success of the anti-conscription campaign. At the Mansion House, Dublin, an event of historic importance occurred. Leaders of Sinn Fein, the Irish Parliamentary Party, and the Irish Labour Party met, and passed a resolution against conscription, and in this they had the assistance of the Catholic Hierarchy. Enormous crowds signed a pledge in furtherance of the resolution. A National Defence Fund realized a huge sum of money against the efforts of the British Authorities who sought to suppress any support of the resolution and the fund by the newspapers. Finally, the Irish Labour Party called a one-day strike in further support.

Aside from the primary object of this meeting of the three parties, the chief topic of interest was the fact that the Irish Parliamentary Party had at long last recognized that others were also entitled to speak for the country as against the days when the I.P.P. had done all the speaking. So far as the I.P.P. was concerned, their power was nearing its end.

Yet in the month of May, the Republican movement was dealt a crushing blow by the authorities. Between midnight and dawn of the 18th, the British instituted a gigantic round-up of persons known to them as being prominent in the Sinn Fein movement. Thereafter the round-up became known as the 'German Plot Round-up', the 'existence' of such a plot being the excuse offered by the British for the arrests; though, in fact, the truth was that the British, wanting to arrest these people, desired an excuse of sorts in order to blind American eyes to the true facts. Those arrested included Arthur Griffith, W. T. Cosgrave, Eamon de Valera, Count Plunkett, Dr. Richard Hayes, Dr. Brian Cusack, Sean Milroy, Joseph MacGuinness, and Countess Markievicz. All, without exception, were of importance to the movement. The captives were herded off to a waiting gunboat at Dun Laoghaire.

The capture of this hard core of the movement need not have happened. Many had ample warning but preferred to await events. The first warning was given by Joe Kavanagh, a detective in the 'G' Division, who had been for some time also active in the National cause. He gave a list of the 'wanted' men who were to be arrested that night to Gay, the librarian in the Public Library in Capel Street. Gay, recognizing the importance of Kavanagh's list, rushed it away to Harry Boland, who kept a tailor's shop in Middle Abbey Street. From Boland the list went to Collins at his office in Bachelor's Walk and at once Joe O'Reilly was sent out with the appropriate warnings. At a meeting of the Volunteer Executive that same evening, Collins again repeated the warning. Still yet another warning was given by O'Keeffe to the Sinn Fein Executive.*

* The present writer is indebted to Sean O Luing for the following translation from his biography of Arthur Griffith (Art O Griofa). It will be seen from this translation that the Sinn Fein leaders had foreknowledge of their impending arrests.

> 'I.R.B. intelligence discovered that the coup had been planned and a list of the most prominent men made. They obtained a copy of the list and despatched the knowledge to the Sinn Fein leaders. Griffith, de Valera and other members of the Executive met at 6 Harcourt Street on the evening of the 17th May to discuss what had best be done. Three courses were open to them: to go into hiding, to meet the arrests with resistance, or to let the Government take them into custody. They proposed to let the Government take them, as this course would be of most advantage to Sinn Fein since enough personnel would be left to direct the movement and also because their arrests would be an advantage in the (forthcoming) Cavan bye-election.' (Griffith was subsequently elected.) 'They named a new Officer Board to take their places, and hid away papers.'

According to Darrell Figgis (*Recollections of the Irish War*) the arrests had a curious sequel. The removal of the diplomatic and statesmanlike section of Sinn Fein (notably de Valera and Griffith) at a critical time, left the militant section, personified by Cathal Brugha, in complete control of the organization. The result was that the tactical error was made, on the opening of Dail Eireann, of declaring a Republic in unequivocal terms. The declaration was found to present extreme difficulties, as, once proclaimed, the difficulty of going back on it was apparent; whereas, if the status had been left undefined, it would have been possible to work gradually towards it, untrammelled by any previous definition and affirmation. The position can be related in fact to certain (later) celebrated statements made by de Valera, e.g., 'We are not Republican doctrinaires' and 'Get me out of the strait-jacket of the Republic.' (*See* Chapter 10.)

As for Collins, that same night he came, by accident, into the centre of the operation and again he rushed around delivering warnings. Finally, he slept the night at the house of Sean McGarry which had previously been raided.

Even accounting for the fact that the Sinn Fein Executive had planned carefully, the position in general on the morning following the arrests was little short of disastrous. Most of the leaders had gone; and consequently a situation of near crisis was produced, in which more than one man was all for calling an end to the fight. Collins and Boland worked desperately to heal the threatened breach. It was a case of make-do with both men shouldering more responsibility than would normally have been the lot of ten men.

It was from the added responsibility at this stage that Collins proved his abilities to face a crisis and to organize to advantage. For Harry Boland, too, it proved to be a time of selfless energy and determination. Yet, to read accounts of this particular period and after, the figure of Harry Boland more or less passes unrecognized across the pages of Irish history. He is given a description which makes of him little more than a foil for Collins: Collins in boyish good humour, Collins in a rage, and so on; and always Boland is there, but with very little recognition of the man he actually was. The fact is, when Harry Boland was killed, in 1922, a man of tireless energy, a man of brain, a statesman, and a diplomat was lost to the nation. And at this time, in 1918, it is more than possible that the whole organization on the political side would have faltered and failed had it not been for his matchless energy.

By 1918 he had already been through the phases and punishments of his beliefs. His father was a member of the Dublin I.R.B., his uncle a Fenian organizer in America. Harry Boland himself was in the Gaelic Athletic Association and a member of the Volunteers in the pre-1916 era. He took part in the Rising and was afterwards imprisoned in Dartmoor Convict Prison and Lewes Jail. His character—like Collins', who was his bosom friend—was such that it could never be spoken of in neutral terms, for behind the gaiety and the kindness was a brain of force and power.

Together with Alderman Tom Kelly, Boland (they were joint Secretaries of Sinn Fein) now strove his mightiest to piece the crumbling framework together; while Collins, who had forsaken politics in order to organize the Volunteers, did likewise on his side. For both men it proved to be their time of triumph.

Chapter 6

Adjutant-General—Director of Organization—Minister of Finance

IT IS chiefly because of his work as Adjutant-General of the Volunteers and as Director of Organization and Director of Intelligence that Collins became famous, almost, as it seemed, overnight. With these positions, he later accepted another: that of Minister of Finance in the Government of Dail Eireann. All these offices were accepted, organized, and administered by Collins at more or less one and the same time and the major portion of the work was done during a time when Collins headed the list of men 'wanted' by the British Authorities. It was a strain to which he was subjected to for almost the whole of the four years 1917 to 1921. In the end it proved, and rightly so, to be a major triumph for him. This chapter is wholly concerned with Collins' work as Adjutant-General, Director of Organization, and Minister of Finance.

In the reorganization of the Volunteers, Cathal Brugha held the position of Chief of Staff and for the moment he concentrated on meeting the threat of conscription. Because of Brugha's pre-occupation with the one objective, Richard Mulcahy was appointed Deputy Chief of Staff, taking over a great deal of the work which would have normally been done by Brugha. This is not to say that Brugha neglected his duties as Chief of Staff. It can never be said of Brugha that he neglected anything. He did, however, believe in tackling things in a more forthright way than others were prepared to accept, and some of the measures which he formulated in the event of conscription were extreme ones, including the possible shooting of British Cabinet Ministers.[1]

M. W. O'Reilly (formerly Collins' commandant at Frongoch internment camp) held the position of Director of Training. Michael Staines was Director of Equipment, in which position he came into contact with Collins a great deal. Diarmuid O'Hegarty occupied the key position of Director of Communications. Dick McKee was appointed Commandant of the Dublin Brigade, in which position he was responsible, along with Collins, for the events of 'Bloody Sunday', November 21st, 1920 (*see* pages 105-

107). Piaras Beaslai filled the later position of Editor of *An t-Oglach*, the official journal of the Volunteers. Both Beaslai and McKee were members of the Headquarters Staff.

There were times when Collins took on a number of extra tasks, and, consequently, extra burdens: for example, that of the distribution of *An t-Oglach*. He was probably the most overworked leader of them all.

To say that the Volunteer Army, including Executive and Headquarters, was a ragtime outfit, formed hastily from the more lawless members of the population, is to do it a grave injustice. Yet such was its assessment by the Chief of the Imperial General Staff, Field-Marshal Sir Henry Wilson. In fact, the code of efficiency of the Volunteers was as high, if not higher, than that of its enemy, the British Army and its subsidiaries, the Royal Irish Constabulary, the Auxiliaries, and the 'Black and Tans'. Disciplinary matters were dealt with, first, by the local brigade commanders or, if proving to be beyond their measure, by the G.H.Q. in Dublin. As its continued success was entirely dependent on strict discipline, nothing was allowed to contaminate efficiency and morale. In this way a highly efficient, reliable, and soldier-like atmosphere pervaded even the smallest task which the local brigade commanders were called upon to perform.

It was the failure of the British commanders to appreciate the efficiency of the Volunteers which went a long way towards the ultimate failure of the forces of British Authority. From Field-Marshal Sir Henry Wilson in London to the various army commanders in Ireland, all were guilty of not assessing at face value the efficiency of the Volunteers. The contempt often voiced by Sir Henry Wilson, in which he named the Volunteers as 'rats', 'gunmen' and 'murder gangs',[2] is wholly undeserving of the men engaged in the fight for independence and on whose very existence as a capable fighting force so much depended.

The method of warfare employed by the Volunteers was, at the time, unique, and was preceded only by the tactics of the Boer Army of 1899-1901, though not as efficiently. Nowadays it is called guerilla warfare. The pattern of guerilla warfare as practised by the Volunteers from 1918 to 1921 proved its value as a means whereby a limited number of soldiers, although lacking in arms, can yet, by tactics which take into account certain inferiorities of the enemy, eventually prove themselves superior to an officially trained army.

In the four years 1918 to 1921, the Volunteers rarely engaged in any action of greater extent than local skirmishes. The rare occurrences were those such as when the Cork No. 1 Brigade ambushed seven lorry-loads of the enemy near Macroom and only one lorry-load got back to barracks. In all these engagements the element of surprise was the factor which made for victory because the Volunteers were invariably out-manned and out-gunned. This type of action was something not governed by the British Army handbooks.

Nor did the Royal Irish Constabulary fare any better than the military. Their garrisons, dotted about the length and breadth of the land, were subject on innumerable occasions to sudden attack by the Volunteers. In open country the story was the same, though, more often than not, less than a third of the Volunteer force was armed, which arms encompassed anything from the most ancient of rifles to a modern revolver.

It was never contemplated that the Executive, G.H.Q., or the army itself should be of such rigid structure as not to permit of a certain amount of flexibility in the exchange of duties among its members. For this there was good reason: since it was, on British judgment, an outlaw organization, its members were liable to arrest at any time. It was, therefore, essential that the organization should be both adaptable and also of far-reaching compass. That this state of affairs—entirely unorthodox by recognized standards—should function with a minimum of trouble is a cause of wonder to those familiar with orthodox methods. But the explanation is a simple one. In practice, none of the departments of G.H.Q. kept religiously to its own sphere of work and every man was possessed of a reasonable knowledge of the workings of departments other than his own. Therefore, in the case of an arrest being made involving the loss of a particular member of the staff, the vacancy was filled with the minimum of trouble.

It would be unfair to say, as has been said, that one man alone (Collins' name is often mentioned) was responsible for the re-charged and revitalized army of the Volunteers, from the broken and disorganized element which it had been following the failure of the Rising. One man alone could never have achieved the setting up and the administration of the new force. But neither is it true to say, as Cathal Brugha later said, that Collins was a mere departmental head under Brugha's leadership. That he may nominally have been, but if one man deserves special mention for what was accomplished that man is Collins. He bore his manifold burden with cheery acceptance, working eighteen and often twenty hours each day—a man 'on the run' for all of the hours of almost four years.

His offices were, at best, of a temporary nature only and liable to a visit from a raiding party at any time of day or night. Often he received warning of an impending raid; sometimes he was actually on the premises when a raiding party arrived. Whatever happened was never allowed to interfere with his daily work. On one occasion his office—one of four which he had in use at the time—was raided. The raiding party were coming up the stairs, when Collins, a bundle of important documents in his hand, met them and brushed past them. He was out and walking down the street before the raiding party had time to think.

Into quite a few of the establishments used by Collins, his devoted friend, Batt O'Connor, a master builder, had built secret cupboards and sleeping quarters, adapting for the purpose a cupboard or a room and cunningly altering it. Often Collins would be in the secret room listening to the raiders searching for him in the house.

From his headquarters in Dublin Collins ruled the officers and men of the brigades, not so much by iron-fist rule as by a judicious mixture of ruthlessness and humanity. It has been said that he exploited them and this he would not have denied; but it was exploitation with a difference: not for self, but for country—and surely no man was exploited more than Collins himself. He had a way with men and women which made them his devoted followers. He demanded from them perfection, as he himself tried to give it.

It is impossible within the compass of one chapter to do more than hint at the many thousands of directives issued by Collins in his positions of Adjutant-General and Director of Organization or, for the same reason, to deal, except in a brief way, with the many thousands of queries (all of which were answered) which literally cascaded into Collins' headquarters. The majority, if not all, of these directives, queries and replies, are contained in thousands of feet of microfilm, safely housed for posterity in the National Library of Ireland. These are only the known sources; many others are in private hands, and others still have vanished without trace. But the microfilms give some idea of the total number of these documents, and also the amount of paper work involved in running the Volunteer Army.

These directives, queries and replies, are an illustration of the times, and the stress of the times, in which men fought and laboured during the years 1917 to 1921. They vary from a quarter sheet of note-paper, handwritten, to a typed or printed issue, 18 inches by 12 inches. They vary again from a blood-stained scrap of paper torn from a diary to a hastily written note penned by Collins himself. There is no uniformity whatsoever, except in the case of the issues of *An t-Oglach*. They are a study of the character of man: the scholar fighter, the literary ignorant fighter. It was not that Collins counted good spelling as a necessary asset to a brigade (in fact it was often the reverse). What he did count as an important asset was brevity in the reports which reached him. In this he set a good example. If his directive had more than one subject in its contents, he then numbered the paragraph which contained the subject, thus:

'(1) Enclosed is order re bail . . .'
'(2) I have been expecting a reply to my letter of . . .'

In his work as Adjutant-General and Director of Organization, Collins was both fastidious and methodical, as, indeed, he was in all things. It is an assessment contrary to the general impression as created by the press of Great Britain, which liked to describe Collins as a dashing and romantic gunman. Today, in England at least, that impression still holds, of Collins the gunman, Collins the murderer. He had, instead, the trained civil servant's hatred of loose ends, and anything which at all resembled untidiness. More than one brigade commander and more than one intelligence officer knew the strength of Collins' wrath on account of a seemingly small detail overlooked by the person concerned.

One example will suffice to illustrate Collins' demand for orderliness. In a directive issued from G.H.Q. Dublin, and dated August 31st, 1918, to Michael de Lacy of the Mid-Limerick Brigade, Collins wrote:

'There are one hundred copies of the September number of *An t-Oglach* allotted to your Brigade, so that the amount due is 16/8, please forward this sum without delay. By attending to this at once you will greatly facilitate matters.'

Within the next ten days he made at least two requests for the sum of money mentioned. Eventually, on the 15th September, he wrote:

'16/8 not to hand, after numerous requests. A small sum of money—agreed. Yet multiply this apparently trivial amount by, say, one hundred—what have you? A largish sum. I do not request, I insist.'

He had all manner of men to deal with. Of some he spoke very highly, of others he said nothing at all. For the former he was always at great pains to disguise from them anything which might have the look of too much praise but he did not spare his feelings for those whom he considered to be valueless to the fight. More than one brigade commander found himself being chased down the steps of the irate Adjutant-General's office. It was of no use attempting to pull the wool over Collins' eyes; he carried around in his head a mass of information regarding the doings of every brigade, as the following account well illustrates.

> 'I had arrived in Dublin from the country [says a former brigade officer], the purpose of my visit was to see Collins, re arms and ammunition for my brigade.
>
> It was late at night when I arrived and I had little hope of seeing him until the following morning. On being directed to his office, I found that he was still hard at work reading and commenting on a mass of papers in front of him. "D'you know . . .?" he asked me. I didn't. "Well," said Collins, "he's an idiot and the sooner someone tells him so the better for us and for him." That was my introduction to the man who was universally admired by the men of the brigades.
>
> It seemed that his manner changed in a moment. He told me to sit down, gave me cigarettes, asked me the purpose of my visit. I told him: "Arms and ammunition in great shortage." To my amazement he began to reel off a list of skirmishes which my brigade had had with the enemy. "Not bad," he commented, and there was a friendly growl in his voice as he said it. He began to pace about the room. "See here," he said, "if I had a few more brigades of the quality of yours I'd be happy. Luckily the good ones outnumber the bad by a fair majority. Would it surprise you to know," he went on, "that in some brigades there's never a damned shot fired except at a bird?" "It would surprise me a great deal," I said. He cocked his head on one side and pushed his fingers through his hair. "Well, it's a fact," he said.
>
> "What did you make of that last job which was given to you?" "It went fair," I said. "Haven't got the stuff to hand yet," he said in some explanation of the fact of his not knowing about it. "How about the boys?" he asked. "No losses," I informed him. He was all enthusiasm. "Grand," he said. "It deserves a drink." And off we went to Vaughan's Hotel.'[3]

The subjects dealt with by Collins were multitudinous in their variety, embracing practically everything, from issues of *An t-Oglach*, to the following brigade report:

'Wireless station Falcarragh. No person to work it'; from affiliation forms, such as the following:

'County. Brigade. Company (Exact name)
Give exact name of Company, district and direction from nearest town, etc.

Name of Captain:	———
Name of Lieutenant:	James Bradley
Name of 2nd Lt.:	Thomas McKenna
Name of Adjutant:	Charles Cassidy
Name of Quarter Master:	Edward Hagan.

Signed: John Walsh
Medical Hall,
Maghera'

to this report:

'Parcel of "An t-Oglach" addressed to B. Connolly instead of J. P. Coughlan.

Letters to Miss Murphy instead of Mrs. Julia Murphy at our Blarney Street address.'

There were, of course, the apparently insurmountable difficulties always associated with a new and striking venture. Chief among these was a lack of trained men to instruct the raw recruits. It is significant that a brigade, the Cork No. 1, which boasted two ex-British Army men, Tom Barry (later Commandant-General Tom Barry) and Sean Murray, became famous for its fighting qualities as well as for its discipline. A scheme was put forward at Headquarters, and afterwards abandoned, whereby men should be encouraged to join the British Army, and, when fully trained, would be recalled home to Ireland, there to serve in the brigades.

Occasionally matters got out of hand in a brigade, a thing which could not at once be overcome since many of the Volunteers were civilians also. On occasions Collins was driven to administering a sharp lecture, such as this addressed to Michael de Lacy:

'Document number A52 (continued)

(3) The remedy is very clear. It speaks poorly for the discipline and loyalty of men if they cannot work together in these times.

Do Chara.
Michael O Coileain.
A.G.'[4]

The following directive from Collins to de Lacy also bears reference to the above-quoted document:

'Headquarters. Dublin. 15th May, 1918. To: M. de Lacy, Mid Limerick Brigade.

It was not until this moment that de V [de Valera] gave me D. Hannigan's despatch with your note attached. The course of a particular Coy or Battalion detaching itself from its own local Headquarters is most irregular. You might get all the local details from Con [Con Collins].

The matter is coming up at the next meeting of the Staff. It is unlikely that the Ballylanders crowd will be allowed to do as they like. A Brigade election was held in that area (East Limerick) recently and all parties agreed to abide by the decision for two months (from about 1st May) at the end of which a new election will be held. . . .'[5]

Lack of arms and ammunition provided Collins with one of his biggest headaches, for although Michael Staines was the Director of Equipment, it was Collins who had to bear the brunt of the grumbles which issued regularly from the brigades. Collins recognized the futility of a working basis of seventeen rounds of ammunition for a unit consisting of fifty men, only half of whom were armed. In a note to a Brigade Commander, dated October 6th, 1919, Collins deplored the lack:

'. . . The question of armament and of course ammunition for same is a chancy business. Captured equipment of this kind is a mere one thousandth of what we really need. Purchase of arms is difficult and also dangerous to those engaged in this vital task. I will worry them all I possibly can, but at the moment your allocation must remain as it is.'[6]

One month later he is still writing in the same terms, adding:

'Lives are important, but so are guns. Without the latter, you may as well be dead. Guard what you have and guard it well.'[7]

Some idea of the detail and the planning may be gained from the following document, numbered B.9, and dated 5.9.19.

'H.Q.
Dublin.

M. de Lacy
Limerick.

1. Yours of the 30th which was laid before the staff last night. Sorry to say I cannot go down. It was decided however that Dick Mulcahy* would go. He has recently been appointed Dep.

* Now General Mulcahy, T.D.

Chief of S. He will travel by the 7.30 train on Tuesday Sep. 10th arriving in Limerick 11.20. Leave word at Dalys where he will find you and have Con [Con Collins] somewhere for him without fail. The idea is to hold the Brigade Election on about Sunday but this can be definitely arranged after you've met him. He wants to meet Council of the First Battn. on Tuesday night—that of the Second on Wednesday night. Meeting with the others can be arranged for . . .

Michael O Coileain
A.G.'[8]

Loose ends again attracted his attention and his rage. He complained about the lack of answers to the following questionnaire:

'(1) Various houses which were to be raided.
(2) Various barracks which were to be demolished.
(3) Number of raids carried out successfully.
(4) Number of Barracks demolished.
(5) Cause or failure of raids.
(6) Cause of Barracks often being untouched.
I have to forward it to the Chief of Staff

By order.'[9]

Whilst he recognized that many of the brigades were doing magnificent work, others he knew were doing very little or nothing at all. A characteristic note reads:

'When you ask me for ammunition for guns which have never fired a shot in this fight, my answer is a simple one. Fire shots at some useful target or get to hell out of it.' [Note to a Brigade Commander, dated May 17th, 1919.][10]

Failure was a word which aroused in Collins a ruthlessness which, on occasions, he was quite capable of producing to effect. If the recipient of his anger was not dealt with in a disciplinary way, the brigade, of which the offender was a member, felt the lash of Collins' tongue in the shape of a sharply worded directive:

'I take it as said. No need to apportion out the blame. It was badly organised and could be faulted in a dozen ways. Therefore—

(1) You, the Brigade Commander, are responsible for the failure.

(2) As much discredit should be lavished on your I.O. [Intelligence Officer].

(3) The raiding party Commander was at fault in not withdrawing his men at once when the situation was a hopeless one. See that it does not happen again.'[11]

The failure of the ambush party to kill Lord French, the Lord Lieutenant, at Ashtown Cross (while French was on his way from his country residence to the Vice-Regal Lodge) enraged Collins. On this occasion no sharply worded directive was issued. Those whom Collins considered to be responsible for the failure were brought to him, and he then delivered a stormy lecture on 'stupidity and clumsiness'.[12]

When a brigade commander committed what, to Collins, was a cardinal sin, in allowing his intelligence officer to go out with a mail-bag raiding party, the following directive was sent out:

'Provided orders given are carried out in a satisfactory manner, there should be no mistake.

My orders do not permit an Intelligence Officer to go out on mail raiding parties.'[13]

The crime in Collins' eyes, though evidently not so apparent to the brigade commander concerned, was that it involved the possible loss of a specialist.

He could be both ruthless and aggressive; but he could also show intense humanity. He worried about the welfare of his 'boys', his 'lads', as he called them. So far as he was concerned no one was insignificant. Anyone who came to Dublin to see 'Mick' Collins was sure of a hearing. He was never too busy and nothing was more important to him than the man waiting to see him. What could be done was done. Sometimes the almost impossible was achieved. If, by attending to a particular want, it made a man or a group of men happier, Collins saw that it was done. By these personal attentions Collins endeared himself to the men of the brigades. He was especially considerate to those in trouble, and in particular to the relatives of men killed or captured. Thus:

'The Irish Volunteers Headquarters. 23rd July, 1920. Ref: A/G. To: Brigade Commander, South Tipperary.

A Chara, Would you let me know if Patrick P—, Cashel, Co. Tipperary, is a volunteer. I understand amongst those arrested in the last round-up.

What is his financial status?'[14]

Collins often saw a humorous side to things, but in this case it was a humour tinged with irony. For a long time he had been annoyed by useless pages of memoranda from a particular intelligence officer. He determined to teach the I.O. a lesson. In answer to a summons from Collins the I.O. arrived in Dublin and there met Collins. Pointing to a trunk, Collins explained that it contained the 'very important documents which you have sent me from time to time'. He went on to explain that the documents were of such a confidential nature as to warrant a special hiding place. 'We're going to take the trunk there,' he announced.

Choosing a time of day when he knew the Military, the 'G' Division and the Auxiliaries would be out in force, and a route which went through the most crowded part of the city, they staggered along bearing, often under suspicion, the heavy trunk.

When the I.O. was almost in a state of collapse—for Collins had forbidden rest, saying that it would only increase suspicion—they arrived at their destination.

Up three flights of steep stairs they dragged the trunk. Finally, Collins unlocked the door of a room, and the trunk was dragged inside. Then, with a grim expression on his face, Collins unlocked the trunk and threw back the lid. It was filled with lead! It is said that Collins' wrath haunted the man for many weeks afterwards.[15]

As near as possible, though in a flexible way, the organization of the Volunteers was run on sound military lines, with a manual of instruction, disciplinary courts and the like. The manual of instruction, entitled 'Organisation Scheme', was a noteworthy production covering almost every phase of the organization. Collins often quoted from it:

> 'Document number A.11. To: M. de Lacy, Adjutant and Brigade Quartermasters.
>
> (2) Please therefore have a meeting called with all possible despatch, as laid down in para b, part 3, Organisation Scheme, to elect these officers.'[16]

Printed forms detailed the setting up of the disciplinary courts:

'Court: Commandant The Deputy Chief of Staff.
The Director of Engineering.
The Director of Organisation.
Presenting Officer: Commandant The Quartermaster General.
Date of Court: To be advised in a day or two.
Time: " " "
Place: " " "'[17]

Orders for bail, orders for men 'on the run' were also fully covered by set instructions.

Anything regarding documents from the brigades which had a touch of the out of the ordinary about it was viewed by Collins with a certain amount of suspicion. It was natural that he should adopt this attitude since he was dealing with men many of whom he had never seen plus the fact that enemy agents were roaming the country and were out to trap him. Therefore, in an undated note, but numbered B.57, Collins expresses mild suspicion over a brigade despatch which was not in the writing of its Commandant, Michael de Lacy.

> '(1) Thanks for money. Two receipts enclosed for £8 each. One amount of £8 came with a note saying it was part of 1st Battalion Levy. Writing was not yours but I suppose you know of it.'[18]

Collins' early civil service and business training is in evidence through most of the dealing with, and handling of, matters regarding the organization. But the efficiency of Collins and those who worked directly with him was one which lacked the fussiness usually associated with civil service departmental work. It was a practical way of handling affairs, but one which, nevertheless, entailed piles of paper work.

Prior to the return of Liam Mellowes* from America, Collins also took on the job of Director of Purchases. He counted it as just one of those jobs which were, literally, heaped around him and always demanding his attention. Privately, he viewed the transactions of arms purchase in a very unfavourable light, and it was probably, through no fault of his own, the least efficient of the departments which he ran. It was viewed unfavourably by him simply because of its inefficiency: there was too much of the often misplaced trust attached to it. Men were entrusted with sums of money in order that they might be able to purchase abroad the arms and ammunition required by the Volunteers and in more than one instance the money disappeared along with the bearer, and no arms appeared. Thus the accountancy side of the business was often in a shambles. Later, the state of this particular department provided Cathal Brugha with further 'evidence' with which to discredit Collins.

* From his early youth Mellowes had been active in the Fianna and the Volunteers; and although he was later expelled from Ireland, he returned secretly and commanded the Volunteers in the west of Ireland during the 1916 Rising. He was one of the chief organizers of de Valera's American tour. He was shot in Mountjoy Prison, Dublin, on December 8th, 1922.

On the other hand, Collins appreciated the trust of a particular Volunteer, as asked for, and given, in the following memoranda:

'To: Adj. Gen. From: Commandant—Feb. 2nd, 1919.
Volunteer —— insists that *you* witness the enclosed will form. Sorry to trouble you.'

To which Collins replied on the 4th:

'Will form enclosed, signed. Appreciate trust. But would rather Volunteer —— had left me the money!
M. O. Coileain.'[19]

. . . . .

As Minister of Finance Collins took on his shoulders a task for which he received very little credit. He got the kicks, but not the ha'pence. Here again, at a later date, he earned the personal animosity of Brugha, for it was he who questioned, with obvious implication, the finances which Collins handled.

In this capacity Collins was instrumental in gaining for the Government a vast amount of very necessary money. The sums aimed at were £250,000 in Ireland and $1,250,000 in America (where de Valera handled the loan). The latter amount, by request of de Valera, was later raised to $5,000,000.

From the offices of the Finance Minister at 6 Harcourt Street, bonds were issued to the value of £1 and multiples. As a precaution against investigation by the British Authorities, the loan money was banked in the names of various citizens.

Up to and including the 4th August, 1920, the amount raised in Ireland alone was more that £357,000 (*see* Appendix C).

The attention of the 'G' Division of the Dublin Police and of various private investigators employed by the British Authorities was a constant handicap to the venture. The offices of the Finance Minister were changed on at least four occasions: 6 Harcourt Street, 22 Henry Street, 29 Mary Street, and 3 St. Andrew Street. It needs little imagination to realize the strain to which Collins, as the responsible Minister, was subjected.

Unfortunately, also, Collins and de Valera crossed swords over the matter of the Irish loan. At the time of the argument, de Valera was himself undergoing a period of great stress in America, where he had succeeded in earning the animosity of a section (a very important one) of the Irish-American public. Throughout almost the whole period of the National Loan, de Valera went out of his way to point out to Collins what he considered to be irregularities in the drawing up of the scheme for repayment, stressing the difference between Collins' method of calculating the interest on the certificates from the time when they were fully acknowledged as regards payment, and his own method of dating the interest as from the day of issue. In this encounter with de Valera, Collins had the support of Griffith because his impression was the same as Collins'. But de Valera's quibbling stung Collins into writing to Boland in such a straightforward manner as to leave no one in doubt as to what he thought of de Valera's action.

Chapter 7

General Election—Dail Eireann—Lincoln Jail Escape—de Valera—Griffith—Cathal Brugha

ON THE 11th November, 1918, the Great War in Europe ended. Almost immediately the attention of the British Government focused on Ireland. With the German war off their hands it appeared as if they were ready now to sweep the Irish board clean of what they called the 'unruly elements'.

But first there was another task, at home, to occupy their attention. On the 25th November, Parliament was dissolved and the date 14th December was fixed for a general election. It was now that the 'unruly element' sprang its biggest surprise to date, causing the British Government to have second thoughts about sweeping the Irish board clean.

The election in Ireland resulted in what *The Times* called an 'overwhelming victory' for Sinn Fein. Out of a total of one hundred and five seats for Ireland, seventy-three went to Sinn Fein, the remainder consisting of twenty-six Unionists and six Irish Party members, including the well-known Joe Devlin. In effect, Sinn Fein had almost swept Ireland clean of British political influence.

Among the Irish leaders, Collins gained the seats for West Cork and Armagh, Eamon de Valera for East Clare and County Down, and Arthur Griffith for East Cavan and Tyrone-Fermanagh.

The next step for the men who were set on independence for Ireland was the formation of a native government and on the 21st January, 1919, an Irish Parliament (Dail Eireann), consisting of those elected in the recent election for Westminster, was summoned to meet at the Mansion House, Dublin. Despite the fact that both the Irish Party members and the Unionists were invited to attend the opening ceremony, none of these did so. The Dail itself was a sadly depleted assembly, for out of the seventy-three seats gained, thirty-six of the victors were at this moment in prison, four were out of the country, and five were unable to attend. Yet for all its lack of representation the Dail provided a heart-warming sight for those nationally minded enough to care about a native government. Cathal Brugha delivered the opening address in Irish.

From this historic occasion both Collins and Harry Boland were absent. They were in England, concentrating on the possibilities of releasing Eamon de Valera from imprisonment in Lincoln Jail.* And events seemed to be running against them.

A key concealed in a cake, having been smuggled into the jail, proved to be too small. A second key was then made, but again it proved a failure. The third attempt, however, was successful—chiefly because the key was smuggled in rough-casted and afterwards made suitable by one of the prisoners with the aid of tools which had been smuggled in.

Even so, the attempt seemed doomed to failure. On the night (3rd February, 1919) fixed for the possible escape, Collins, Boland, and Frank Kelly approached the prison. At a point near the prison Frank Kelly was left to keep look-out for anyone approaching while Collins and Boland went on to the outer gate of the prison, to which Collins had the key. He proceeded to fit it into the lock while, on the other side, de Valera and two other prisoners, Sean Milroy and Sean McGarry, waited impatiently. Then disaster occurred: the key partly turned in the lock and then broke, leaving a half jammed in the lock. On being informed of the circumstances, de Valera, in a fury of impatience, thrust his key into the lock. He was successful: the broken half of the other key fell out, and his own key opened the gate. The prisoners were free.

Meantime, Frank Kelly had become alarmed by the sight of some British soldiers and their girl friends occupying the stile through which the escaping prisoners, Collins and Boland, would have to come. He felt his way in the darkness along the wall, endeavouring to find another stile or a part of the wall which had tumbled down. Unaware of this new turn in their fortunes, Collins, Boland and the prisoners came along towards the stile, and saw the soldiers and the girls blocking their way. But Boland was equal to the occasion. Wishing them a pleasant 'Good night', he brushed past them

* When the escape plan was first mooted, Sean McGarry, a fellow prisoner, said that he would have to get in touch with Collins, but de Valera expressed a preference for Brugha. (Told to the present writer by Sean McGarry.)

followed by the rest of the party. Of Frank Kelly there was no sight; and so he was left to make his own way back. It is from the fact of Frank Kelly being absent when the party returned that a story got about to the effect that Kelly lost himself in the fields. As has been seen, he was not lost, but was endeavouring to find a safer way for their escape.[1]

From Lincoln the prisoners proceeded to Sheffield, thence to Manchester, there to stay for a time in the houses of friends. Eventually on arrival in Ireland, de Valera was given shelter at the home of Cathal Brugha.

Meanwhile, on the 22nd January, 1919, the Dail had met in private session, and Cathal Brugha was appointed Acting President until de Valera's return. Collins was appointed Minister for Home Affairs, Eoin MacNeill Minister for Finance, Count Plunkett Minister for Foreign Affairs, and Richard Mulcahy Minister for Defence.

On March 8th, 1919, the British Government released all political prisoners, chiefly because of the result of the ravages of a disastrous outbreak of influenza, which resulted in the death of one prisoner, Pierce McCann, in Gloucester Jail on March 6th.[2]

On the 1st April, the Dail, in private session in the Mansion House, Dublin, appointed de Valera as Priomh-Aire (First Minister), a term translated in the official report as President.

At three private meetings held on April 1st, 3rd, and 4th, the President appointed a Cabinet of seven which included Collins as Minister for Finance and Griffith as Minister for Home Affairs.

At once a policy was put to the test. In defiance of both British Authority in Ireland and the Government in London, the native Government of Dail Eireann literally took over the governing of the country by the setting up of its own courts of law and by other measures, such as its own departments, Home Affairs, Finance, etc. The Dail, in fact, put into operation Griffith's plan of Sinn Fein (lit. 'Ourselves'—Self Reliance) which he had evolved between 1900-1905. It was a composition of passive resistance and self-reliance.

With the reappearance of de Valera on the scene there were now three men of outstanding ability in the Dail Cabinet: de Valera, Arthur Griffith, and Michael Collins. There was a fourth to be reckoned with: an indomitable character of a man, whose opinions, although at times misguided, were of immeasurable influence; the man was Cathal Brugha.

At first sight there appears to be no link whatsoever between the four but on closer scrutiny one may establish that there was a link of sorts between Collins and Brugha, despite the fact that there was bitterness between them. Both had the adventurer spirit, though, of the two, Brugha was the more headstrong.

Arthur Griffith was far and away the man of experience in political theory. For a long time, Griffith had been the man in the background, quietly formulating his ideas, working out a policy, and now he was putting it to the supreme practical test, all without the blaze of glory which surrounded de Valera and, later, Collins. Griffith was the father of the independence movement, he and William Rooney, who died in 1901. It has been said that Collins was a 'backroom boy', but undoubtedly Griffith was the chief 'backroom boy'.

He was born on the 31st March, 1871, and from the first, literature, especially literary journalism, was in his blood. His father was a printer by profession, and Griffith himself served his apprenticeship as a compositor and worked for a short time in the printing trade.

From a very early age he associated himself with national movements—the I.R.B., Young Ireland League, Celtic Literary Society, Gaelic League, etc. In his teens, he was a follower of Parnell.

In 1896 he went to South Africa, to the Transvaal, and was there employed by the J. B. Robinson Mining Co. in a diamond mine at Landlaagte, near Johannesburg. He spent a year in Middelburg where, with a fellow countryman, he published a small newspaper, the *Middelburg Courant*. While in South Africa he travelled a good deal; met Kruger, Olive Schreiner, and other people, but he was never cut out for this sort of life, an existence away from the country which was life to him.

In January, 1899, at the request of his friend William Rooney, he returned to Ireland, and there edited (again at the request of Rooney) the paper *United Irishman*, which was first published on the 4th March, 1899, and which was to have I.R.B. backing. Griffith was editor of this paper until 1906.

In this same year Griffith resigned from the I.R.B. The publication of a pamphlet written by him, *The Resurrection of Hungary, a Parallel for Ireland*, was, in a much elaborated form and as applied to Irish conditions, the germ of Sinn Fein policy.

In 1914 Griffith opposed the idea of Irishmen joining the British Army. From the Boer War period, Griffith had actively opposed the enlistment of Irishmen into the British Army. In October, 1914, there was formed the Irish Neutrality League, with James Connolly as President and a committee which included Griffith, Countess Markievicz, Sean Milroy, Francis Sheehy-Skeffington, and William O'Brien. Major John MacBride, who was executed after the Easter

Rising, was connected with it also. On December 4th, 1914, military and police dismantled the printing machinery of *The Irish Worker* (Acting-editor James Connolly). At once the printers of *Sinn Fein* and *Eire* (both edited by Griffith) and the I.R.B. paper, *Irish Freedom*, refused to go to press—an action for these papers which was tantamount to suppression.

Although he was opposed to, and took no part in, the Easter Rising, Griffith was arrested on the 3rd May, 1916, and imprisoned, first at Wandsworth, and then at Reading, from which he was released on Christmas Eve, 1916. In actual fact, when the Rising commenced, he wanted to take an active part in it but the offer was declined on the grounds that his services might be required in the future as publicist and national philosopher.[3]

In the general election of 1918, Griffith, although rearrested in the 'German Plot Round-up', was elected for the constituencies of East Cavan and Tyrone-Fermanagh. Released in the following March, he was appointed to the position of Minister for Home Affairs in the Cabinet of Dail Eireann. Then, as de Valera was away in America, Griffith was appointed Acting President.

On the 24th November, 1920, he was arrested again and detained in Mountjoy. But with the signing of the Truce on the 11th July, he was released.

A dour, often silent man, Griffith possessed remarkable gifts as a journalist. In the year 1901 he refused an offer of £1,000 to work on a New York paper. It was typical of the man, with his great strength of character, to refuse riches, and, instead, to live in near poverty and to found the national ideal.

In contrast to the 'backroom' influence of Griffith and the steady plodding towards a certain goal, the rise to power of Eamon de Valera was dramatic.

In the character of de Valera a combination of three nationalities finds voice: Irish, Spanish, and American. He was born of Irish-Spanish parentage in Manhattan, America, and he came to Ireland at the age of five.

It has been recorded just how dramatic was his rise to power, founded, as it was, on no political experience at all. Indeed, he had previously shunned politics and had only consented to membership of the I.R.B. on terms. But if he lacked political experience, he had ably demonstrated his willingness and devotion to the cause in the uncompromising attitude which he adopted towards the British.

The character of de Valera is that of a man capable of rousing in others feelings of great emotion, both of love and of hatred. As an orator he is the least emotional of men, yet he speaks with an apparent sincerity.

Between de Valera and Michael Collins there was one great difference of character: humanity. With the former it is an apparent lack of warmth towards his fellow beings; with Collins it was the direct opposite: an excess of humanity, leading, as it did later, to a split loyalty.

Against the apparent sincerity of de Valera and his devotion to the cause must be measured a failing which is a characteristic of his alone. From that moment, in 1917, when he became famous in the eyes of the populace, he adopted the kingly attitude. He became sacrosanct even in his own mind and could not bear to think that anyone could honestly differ with him. This attitude, the measure of his mind, was later displayed to the full immediately before and after the signing of the Treaty in 1921.

In July, 1919, after the escape from Lincoln Jail, de Valera went to America. In going there his task was threefold: to raise a loan to provide financial backing for Dail Eireann; to persuade either or both of the major American political parties (Democrats and Republicans) to include in their election platform a plank recognizing the Irish Republic—in effect, this would practically mean recognition of the Irish Republic by the American Government; and to oppose Article 10 of the League of Nations Covenant, which was construed as being opposed to Irish National demands.* In the first and third objects he was supremely successful, in the second, and most important, he was not.

From that journey a misrepresentation has arisen. It is to the effect that de Valera went to America, where it was safe, while Collins stayed at home to carry on the fight. In view of subsequent happenings in America, where de Valera earned the animosity of two prominent Irish-American leaders, Judge Cohalan and John Devoy, the story gained weight, with the added fact that de Valera outraged Irish-American sympathy there. Perhaps he did commit a few gaffes, one especially of major importance; but there is still no foundation for assuming that de Valera shirked his responsibility in Ireland.

Although not bigoted or narrow-minded in the sense that Brugha was, de Valera has, or had, a singleness of purpose, an unshakable ideal of a Republic, more or less divorced from Britain and her Empire. In his own words (Dail Speech of July 17th, 1945): 'We are an independent Republic, associated as a matter of our external policy with the states of the British Commonwealth.' It was this

* Article 10 reads: 'The High Contracting Powers undertake to respect and preserve as against external aggression the territorial integrity and existing independence of all States members of the League. In case of any such aggression or in case of any threat of danger of such aggression the Executive Council shall advise upon the means by which this obligation shall be fulfilled.'

ideal which, together with certain other facts, eventually made the flashpoint for the tremendous repercussions which followed the signing of the Anglo-Irish Treaty in 1921.

De Valera is precise to the point of fastidiousness. In those days, 1917 to 1921, the care with which he considered things often aroused the ire of Collins, who complained that de Valera took days in mulling over the issue of a minor press statement. But de Valera early recognized that words are dangerous things, especially when being used as political matter. The substance of a word with its various shades of meaning made a ready trap for the unwary and de Valera refused to be rushed into making statements. That is another substantial difference between the characters of de Valera and Collins, for the latter, overflowing with restless impatience, termed de Valera's word fastidiousness 'word bandying'.

How near or how wide of the mark one can be in assessing the character of Cathal Brugha is proved by the two following quotations, both by men well acquainted with their subject:

> 'My own conviction is that except for war he [Cathal Brugha] is not worth a damn for anything else. . . .' (W. T. Cosgrave.)[4]
>
> When many of us are forgotten, Cathal Brugha will be remembered.' (*Michael Collins—see* page 193).

The puzzle is made greater still when one remembers that of the two, Brugha did far more harm to the name of Collins than to that of Cosgrave.

Cathal Brugha was one of the greatest patriots ever to breathe the air of his native land. His character may be summed up in three words: idealist, defiant, obstinate. There is a closeness of meaning between the three terms.

He was more the isolationist than even de Valera. He was an isolationist in one particular aspect, that of Cathal Brugha. As a critic he was merciless and he pounced on anything which, in his opinion, looked like a betrayal of the trust given to himself and to others by the people.

His mind was a formula, a strict pattern of ideas and ideals, and should anything occur which was at all inconsistent with this rigid formula, he became a bitter critic of both the idea and the person who had expressed it. He reasoned in a narrow-minded way.

It is generally accepted that Brugha belonged to the group headed by de Valera which also included (to name only two) Austin Stack and the Countess Markievicz. Nothing could be further from the truth. For if Brugha could be a bitter critic of Michael Collins, equally he could be, and was, a bitter critic of de Valera also. The following is a case in point; and one which also proves the power of Brugha behind the scenes in the making of a government. At a full meeting of the Ministries, held at the Mansion House, to discuss future policy in relation to the agreement arrived at between de Valera and Lloyd George regarding the possibility of further discussion, de Valera asked the secretary to read the Lloyd George proposals and the draft reply. He then asked the members present for their opinions.

Griffith was in agreement with the draft reply; Joseph MacDonagh was keenly critical; Austin Stack expressed himself as being very dissatisfied; Robert Barton was both dissatisfied and critical; Erskine Childers was hostile to the offer; MacNeill welcomed it; J. J. O'Kelly recommended that the document be circulated; Countess Markievicz agreed with O'Kelly; Collins said: 'You all know my opinion. . . .'; Kevin O'Higgins declined to speak because his chief (Cosgrave) was present; Cosgrave expressed the view that it was a better offer than many had expected; and Count Plunkett gave a masterly review of the cause for which they were fighting.

Finally, it was the turn of Cathal Brugha. 'I have left you to the last, Cathal, because of the position you have taken at the table,' [Brugha was at the foot] remarked de Valera. 'I haven't much to add,' replied Brugha, 'except to say how glad I am that it has been suggested that we circulate these documents and consider them fully before we meet again, if for no other reason than to give you and the great masters of English you keep at your elbow an opportunity of extricating us from the morass in which ye have landed us.'

'We have done our best,' said de Valera, 'and I have never undertaken to do more than my best.'

'We have proclaimed a Republic in arms,' said Brugha; 'it has been ratified by the votes of the people, and we have sworn to defend it with our lives.'

'The oath never conveyed any more to me than to do my best in whatever circumstances might arise,' said de Valera.

'You have accepted a position of authority and responsibility in the Government of the Republic,' Brugha replied, striking the table, 'and you will discharge the duties of that office as they have been defined. I do not want ever again to hear anything else from you.'

At which de Valera made the startling admission, 'I think I can promise, Cathal, that you won't have to complain again.'[5]

In his single-minded way, Brugha was responsible for a great many points of policy. Often his solitary voice of dissent on the councils of Sinn Fein and the Ministries caused other members to think twice before adopting a particular course. He was implacable, a far from easy man to deal with.

He was prone to hot-headed outbursts, and was full of the wildest schemes, but in balance against these faults of character was his great asset of sincerity—whether in friendship or in enmity.

Together with the idea that only the bullet would show the enemies of his country the way that he and others had chosen, there also went a deep-rooted mistrust of those who considered themselves statesmen. Statecraft never appealed to him. He ridiculed both the technique and the finer points of diplomacy. More than anything else he was a true dyed-in-the-wool strong-measures man, an ardent idealist, a great patriot, a fanatic.

Notwithstanding the bluntness of his approaches and his caustic tongue, he was also a fierce champion of what he considered to be the rights of the people: to hear the future of their country—their destiny—discussed openly in the Dail. He would not tolerate anything which smacked of secrecy when, in his opinion, it was the right of the people to know the full circumstances.

The characteristic of Brugha's which stands out above all else is independence. The opinions of others did not have the slightest effect on this wayward man. His character has been described as composed of only 'sheer cussedness'. To so underrate Brugha's capabilities was to play dangerously, for he was adept at discovering the weak places in other people's characters: and playing on those weaknesses he became a power in his own right.

. . . . .

For a time it appeared as if the British Government was prepared to accept Dail Eireann, even allowing for the fact that the native Government was ridiculing the British in the eyes of the population. But here there is another reason for the apparent British lack of decision. With the constant boasting about its democratic ideals it had also the confusion of having on its own doorstep the country of Ireland, which it had ruled by oppression for the past seven hundred years—a fact which other countries were not slow to recognize.

Yet it was American refusal—President Woodrow Wilson's—to support Ireland's plea for entry to the Peace Conference that changed the British attitude. They now resorted to force, as being, in their misguided opinion, the only means of subduing those who stood for independence in Ireland. They suppressed Dail Eireann on the 10th September, 1919; but the actual effect of this move made little change in the general situation.

Chapter 8

'Wanted' Man—Intelligence and Counter-intelligence—'Bloody Sunday'

IT IS said that on the 25th January, 1920, a considerable reward was offered for the body, dead or alive, of Michael Collins. There is some doubt about this, but none about the man-hunt that was sparked off, the proportions of which have rarely been seen since those days. It was proof enough, though in a particularly gruesome form, of the value of Collins to the Irish cause.

Collins answered this threat as he had answered all others: by behaving as his natural self, riding his cycle as if he owned the city, and by attempting no camouflage.

Twice he had been in the hands of the authorities. The first was immediately after the Rising; the second in 1918, when he served a three months' sentence in Sligo Jail for making a seditious speech. On the 6th February, 1919, the following notice appeared:

> 'At the Hilary Sessions, Longford.
> The King v Michael Collins.
> Application by the Crown Solicitor to forfeit Recognizance entered into by Michael Cox and Michael Doyle at Longford, dated 20th April 1918.
> £25 each.'[1]

Now, however, following notice of the large reward offered, Collins became the prey of hired spies, informers, and investigators.

The Military and Auxiliaries, not to be outdone, ran a jackpot among their members, the total contributions destined for the man who 'got' Collins. Hence this item from the torn page of a notebook, the former property of an Auxiliary officer:

> 'Michael Collins. 76, Harcourt Street. On Friday and on Monday. Otherwise no reports of any appearance there. £60. 5. 6.'[2]

A further note and a letter proved beyond doubt that Collins was the ace in the Irish pack as far as the Auxiliaries were concerned. The note 'Unit fund now £150' is contained in a pocket-book, the former property of an Auxiliary named Spence.[3] And on the 20th June, 1920, an Auxiliary nicknamed 'Jacky' wrote to a friend of his in Cork, stating:

> 'Here's a puzzle—which you lot in the south don't have—find a will o' th' wisp by the name of Collins. A modern Robin Hood or his Irish equivalent. Wish I could. He's worth a couple of hundred to me.'[4]

Bail, unit funds, a Government award—all because of one man—a man encompassed, because of his work, within a few square miles of city streets, a tallish, well-proportioned figure, speaking with a strong West Cork accent, carrying in his pocket nothing more lethal than a fountain pen: a man named Michael Collins. The same man who discussed with an Auxiliary officer, in Farrelly's pub at the top of Grafton Street, 'that man Collins. Wish I could nail him,' he said ruefully. 'Don't you worry,' answered the Auxiliary officer, 'his days are numbered.' In his office the next morning, Collins retold the conversation with many a shout of laughter. He was holding a calendar in his hand. 'See here,' he said to Joe O'Reilly; 'how many days have I got to live?'

It is from the 'wanted man' phase of his career, coupled with the incidents of 'Bloody Sunday,' that Collins earned the purely newspaper titles of 'glamorous gunman' and 'romantic gunman'. The *Daily Express* carried this farcical notion a stage further when it referred to Collins as a 'murderer' (*see* page 120). All but the latter title amused him, though he took no personal pride in being thought of as a 'cloak-and-dagger' man. But the power of the press is such that even now (1958), in England, Collins is still thought of by many as a 'terrorist and murderer'.

The many stories told about him tend to create the impression that he was reckless, openly flaunting his person before the eyes of those who were determined to get him, dead or alive. In fact, there is a world of wisdom in the way Collins chose to 'flaunt' his person, for by behaving naturally as a collar-and-tie worker, he assumed the best of 'disguises'. It was not in keeping with his character to be of a reckless disposition. He seldom, except in the most extreme emergency, took risks. While it is true to say that he had the adventurer spirit, he nevertheless kept it strictly within the bounds of prudence. Sometime in the year 1920 Harry Boland, who was then in America, wrote Collins a cautionary note, and in answer Collins said:

> 'I am in love with life as much as the next man. The escapes of others often chill me to the marrow. But for myself I take

a logical view of things and act in accordance with what would seem to be a supersensitiveness."[5]

Collins did not reserve his humanity for those under his command and for his own particular friends. The following eye-witness account, by a former British officer, as well as illustrating the rewards offered for the capture or killing of Collins, gives point to his humanity.

'My own judgment of Collins [Captain Maynard wrote to the author] is based on an incident which concerned myself.

In the Rathmines district I was in charge of a party conducting a house-to-house search for hidden arms. We had been on this task for about one hour. We entered a house, and a corporal and two men were searching the upstairs rooms, when I found myself in the company of three other men. I say "in the company of three other men"—and so it seemed, so silently had they entered. I was instructed to call down my men from the upstairs room. This I refused to do. Whereupon one of the men—they were dressed in civilian clothes—produced a revolver with which he threatened me. I called down my men. Others now entered the room. A few minutes later, bound and blindfolded, I was taken outside the house and marched away. Not more than ten minutes later (or so I would guess) I was pushed inside another door, and my blindfold was removed. We went along a passage to a door on which one of the men knocked. It was opened; and there seated at the table was a man whom one of the party addressed as "Mick". This, then, I thought is the man, the Collins. I emphasize "the" because of the fact that his doings were so well known to us.

My immediate impression—bolstered up by his courtesy in telling me to take a seat, and his offer of a cigarette—was of a man of strength: nervous energy and strength. I asked him what his intentions were towards me. He laughed and remarked that it depended on how useful I proved to be. I then remarked on the fact that search parties would no doubt be looking for me at this moment. "They have been looking for me a long time, Captain," he said. He then asked me a series of questions, including, I remember, unit strengths and so on, all of which I refused to answer. He then asked me how much I thought his life was worth. "A great deal," I said, "judging by the offers of certain officers to their men." "How much?" he persisted. "Anything from £5 to about £50," I answered. He laughed and said it was "poor value" that was put on him.

I think I smoked about three of his "Three Castles" cigarettes before he ended the interview. I was again blindfolded and ushered outside. Any moment I expected to be shot. But no shot came. Instead, I found myself in a side street close by College Green.

Despite what has been said about Collins, my own impression of him is of a man perhaps ruthless, but nevertheless extremely considerate, understanding and fair. One thing struck me at the time of my release—my revolver was still in its holster. I could so easily have earned £50 or even one of those supposed astronomical amounts often mentioned in connection with Collins.'

How close the pursuers were at times to achieving their objective may be seen in this note from Collins to Dick McKee, Commandant of the Dublin Brigade.

'. . . The fellow you named as safe is far from being thus. My own experience of last night makes it quite clear that he is not to be trusted. For the future the rule should be guilty until proved innocent. M.'[6]

This note was probably written at a time when Collins had become extremely wary of the Quinlisks, Jamesons, and Molloys.* In the case of the second named, Jameson, Collins had trusted too far—much to the disgust of others in his immediate circle who had distrusted the man from the very beginning.

The year 1920 was for Collins the most dangerous of all his career. That he survived the attentions of spies, informers, and investigators proves in some measure the state of his supersensitiveness; it proves also how faithful to him were those of his immediate circle.

When in trouble it was invariably his policy to seek the most effective, yet simple, means of bluff. When such a course failed him, it was sheer audacity that won him through.

One night, late in the year 1920, he was on his way, together with Joe O'Reilly, to Vaughan's Hotel. They had almost reached Parnell Square, where Vaughan's is situated, when they spied a party of Auxiliaries approaching. Acting on impulse O'Reilly turned to run, but Collins caught him by the arm, and together they walked towards the oncoming Auxiliaries. In a moment they were surrounded, a revolver was pushed into the pit of Collins' stomach and the bright light of a torch glared into his eyes, blinding him.

* Informers, investigators, spies—*see* books by Beaslai and O'Connor.

But he was equal to the occasion. Putting on a rich accent, and at the same time indicating that his companion was deaf and dumb, he asked the way to a certain street. He said they were in Dublin from the country and were lost. To Joe O'Reilly's immense relief the bluff succeeded. From the officer in charge they received a sharp lecture on walking the streets and were then given directions to get them to their 'destination'. Collins then apologized for himself and his companion. He could not, however, resist a parting shot, bidding the officer a cheery 'Good night'.[7]

On another occasion when trouble threatened him, his audacity seemed so great as to practically court trouble. On pretence of being a drunk he made so much noise that the embarrassed military, more by way of ridding themselves of a nuisance, placed him in the temporary care of the police. There, in their hands, he became still more noisy and aggressive, singing and shouting, until they, in turn, felt compelled to rid themselves of their troublesome 'visitor'. He was forthwith pitched out into the street.[8]

He always had this ability of openness. A disarming grin and a cheerful smile were often the only means he had of diverting suspicion.

An ex-soldier, McCallum, then serving with the military in Dublin, recalls that on a January night in 1921 his party were suspicious of two men whom they had stopped in the street. 'What's your name?' they asked one of the men. Collins (for it was he) said in a cheery tone, 'Could be "Mick" Collins.' 'Be glad it's not', said the corporal in charge of the military. For the rest of the patrol, says McCallum, we argued about the identity of the man, but it was not until after the signing of the Truce that I saw the same man again and learned that it had indeed been Collins.[9]

The intelligence and counter-intelligence section which Collins had created, and which he looked on with all the pride and joy of a creative specialist, was the real reason why the forces of British Authority desired to eliminate him. Instead, he virtually destroyed the British spy system in Ireland. All the planning of Dublin Castle made not the slightest difference to Collins for he knew of their plans almost before the ink was dry on the appropriate document. His intelligence network extended as far as London, into the post offices and even into Government departments.

In Dublin, he gathered together a handful of picked men, including Liam Tobin, Tom Cullen, and Frank Thornton. Tobin was set up in an office in Crow Street (within two hundred yards of Dublin Castle) and there was located the 'brain' of the intelligence organization: files, dossiers of men, ranging from military officers to Government leaders, captured documents, and so on.

And there Tobin, a natural expert at decoding cipher documents, carried on work of inestimable importance to Collins.

His agents in Dublin Castle included Ned Broy (later Colonel Broy, who afterwards became Commissioner of the Garda Siochana), Kavanagh, Neligan, and MacNamara. Apart from the value of the copies of documents which they brought to Collins, it would not be stretching a point to say that Collins' continued freedom from arrest was, to a large extent, dependent on the activities of these four men.

There were other agents the identities of whom Collins kept secret from even such trusted men as Tobin. And it is at this point that one of many mysteries is encountered: the identity of a mysterious 'Lieutenant G'.

So far as the present writer can ascertain, 'Lieutenant G' was a member of the British Military Intelligence in Ireland. He was also one of Collins' chief agents as well as being a particular confidant of his. The odd clues reveal that the two men were the greatest of friends, with a mutual trust and a liking for each other.

When this confidence between them originated is not known, nor the manner of its arrangement, though it is possible that one of Collins' Dublin Castle agents provided an introduction. Notes sent by 'Lt. G' to Collins give no clue to the date when the friendship ripened into something more; while the earliest entry in any diary of Collins' is for June 3rd, 1920—'Bailey. 8.G.' (Bailey restaurant, at—presumably—8 p.m.) 'Lt. G' is mentioned nine times in this particular diary.[10]

In all, about seventeen notes are initialled by the letter 'G', of which the following is a good example:

> 'Don't overdo. The road to Parnell Square is too well trod. Fifteen men, including you, went there [to Vaughan's Hotel] last night between 9 and 11 p.m.'[11]

The handwriting is small and neat and most of the notes concern the movements of troops, their strength and armament, forthcoming activities of British Military Intelligence, the Auxiliaries and the 'Black and Tans'.

Their meeting openly at the Bailey Restaurant, or even in a private room, would tend, one imagines, to invite suspicion by the very fact of their being seen often together. It seems inconceivable that either Collins or 'Lt. G' would deliberately draw attention to each other in so open a manner.

Just as he begins as a mystery so does 'Lt. G' end as a mystery. On the day of the Truce, July 11th, 1921, there is a last cryptic note by Collins in his diary: 'G. 5 o'clock.'[12] Presumably with the signing of a truce, the work of the Englishman—if so he was—came to an end.

What, however, may be a portrait of 'Lt. G' is given by a former inmate of Walton Jail, Liverpool. On completion of his sentence, this person—whose name is here omitted for obvious reasons—undertook to do spy work in Ireland.

'Early in 1920, after serving a prison sentence, I was contacted by certain persons who asked me if I would care to go on a visit to Dublin. Being aware of what was happening in Ireland, I was not keen. Eventually, I was persuaded into going—backed, I must admit, by the appearance of quite a few £5 notes.

In Dublin I was informed that my job would be to make acquaintance with Michael Collins, who, I was told, was the most dangerous man in Ireland. After several fruitless attempts, I made a contact with Collins. I think it would be about the night of March 14th, 1920.

My instructions were to walk slowly from the Stephen's Green end of Dawson Street down towards College Green. I was to put my left hand in my overcoat pocket, and—against any chance of coincidence—was to pull repeatedly at the brim of my trilby hat in a sort of nervous gesture. I had walked barely thirty yards down the street when someone nudged my arm and beckoned me to follow him. The resulting journey down a maze of streets and alleys must have taken at least fifteen minutes. My guide knocked at the door of a tall, narrow house. We were admitted into a room in which four or five men were standing, talking and smoking. While I was still trying to guess which one of them was Collins, I was summoned again. I followed my guide up a flight of narrow stairs.

The guide knocked once on a door, opened it, and pushed me inside a room. Two men were sitting at a table. Instinctively I knew one of them to be Collins. He began to question me, all the time eyeing me fixedly. My impression was that he was a man of some physical strength, not only because of his thick-set figure slouched across the table. His companion was half turned away from me. He had dark features and fair hair. He wore a trench coat and laced, almost knee-length, boots.

I knew now that the other man was Collins because his companion addressed him as "Mick"; and when Collins' companion spoke it was in a cultured English voice.

Our interview must have lasted about a half-hour. Then Collins got to his feet and told me to follow him. At the foot of the stairs we again met my former guide. At approximately 10.15 I was back again in Dawson Street, a baffled and not much wiser man.

I went to my lodgings, and there I was handed an envelope in which was a note. The mystery so far as I was concerned was ended, for the note stated:

"If you value your life, the first boat from Ireland is at 7.30 in the morning." '[13]

Towards the end of the year 1920 the situation, so far as the British Authorities were concerned, was of so desperate a nature that nothing was overlooked in attempting to rid themselves of the opposition.

Within the bounds of Dublin City were two significant terror groups (apart from the military and the bands of spies and informers), the 'G' Division and the Auxiliaries, the latter force a more or less hand-picked unit recruited from the civilian ranks of British ex-officers. The scope given to the 'G' Division and the Auxiliaries was wide enough to permit of raids, shootings, torture and even murder. They were almost a law unto themselves, their methods rarely, if ever, being questioned by the persons in authority. Indeed, the Secretary of State for Ireland, Sir Hamar Greenwood, in typically official replies either glossed over their offences or denied knowledge of them, whenever he was questioned in Westminster.

Over the 'G' Division there was a certain amount of official jurisdiction by the authorities in Dublin Castle. The Auxiliaries, on the other hand, were, it would seem, completely independent of any authority save their own. The ranks which they had formerly held in the British Army were those of captain and upwards and several were holders of the D.S.O. and the M.C. They were tough, seasoned fighting men, experienced in warfare at its worst in the Flanders trenches. By and large, they were men who had been unable to settle down into the rut of civilian life and their existence as members of the 'Auxies', as they were called, gave them the promised excitement and good pay, plus, of course, a very considerable lack of criticism from the authorities. As fighting men, and in their general conduct, they were superior to the 'Black and Tans', the terror groups of which functioned outside the boundary of Dublin City.*

* The Auxiliaries were regarded by the Volunteers as the fighting *élite* of the British forces. Very brave and reckless, heedless of danger, and imbued with the spirit of the offensive, they were ruthless, cruel, and lacking in chivalry as a body. Collins said, on one occasion, that the fact that Auxiliaries were sent to garrison a district was a tribute to the latter's fighting quality.

Despite the fact that in the 'G' Division there existed the best detectives in all Ireland and that there operated a chain of regular informers and that the Auxiliaries possessed the best fighting men, both groups nevertheless still failed in one of their primary objectives: the capture or killing of Collins and the breaking up of his intelligence system—the power of which became greater as week succeeded week.

Every effort was made to counteract this state of affairs. By threats and bribery the 'G' Division and the Auxiliaries sought loose-tongued men, if possible among Collins' direct contacts. Time after time they were led away on a false trail by a supposed informer, who eventually left them, richer by a fair sum of money.

In their Crossley tenders the Auxiliaries were a familiar sight in the streets of Dublin. They had a policy which usually went 'shoot first, ask questions afterwards'. But despite such well-known hall-marks, the name 'Auxiliary' did not seem to earn the hatred of the people to the same extent as that of 'Black and Tan'. Perhaps the ex-officers and, presumably, gentlemen bore up well when compared to the ex-inmates of the English jails, which was the basic character of many of the 'Black and Tans'.

Yet it is certain that, of all these groups, the British Army still remained the greatest threat. In the country the use of the 'Black and Tans' as a force designed to buffer the rapidly approaching neutralization of the Royal Irish Constabulary as a surveillance, defensive and garrison force was a grave mistake. The R.I.C. was run much on the same lines as those on which the British Army was run; and to graft onto such orderliness the undisciplined elements of the 'Black and Tans' was plainly a project doomed from the start to failure; whereas the Auxiliaries acted independently of the military and the 'G' Division.

A particularly heavy phase of raids, threats, imprisonments, and murder having failed to achieve the desired result, it was decided by those in authority to try out a new plan. As a direct result of this plan occurred the events of what afterwards became known as 'Bloody Sunday', November 21st, 1920.

In essentials, the plan was a simple one, and yet, for all its simplicity, it had links in a chain which stretched from Dublin Castle to London and from London to Cairo in Egypt. There, in Cairo, sixteen British officers were chosen for a special task. Their ultimate destination was Dublin, Ireland.

The Cairo group travelled under assumed names, and arrived in Dublin singly and on different dates. They were dressed in plain clothes, and were posing as commercial travellers. Some rented flats in Pembroke Street, others lived in Mount Street and in various hotels in the city. They had one object in view: to locate and destroy Collins and his organization and they very nearly accomplished what they had set out to do.

From the first it was a battle of wits with Collins in the dark regarding the identities of certain persons who were conducting a particularly vicious terror campaign. The Cairo group, likewise, were in the dark with regard to the actual identity of Collins and his lieutenants. But a remarkable piece of luck and two stupid blunders by the Cairo group began to weight the scales in Collins' favour. First, a British spy in a fit of morbid penitence blurted out the story to one of Collins' intelligence officers, in course of which several names were mentioned. Collins immediately went into action. He had the correspondence of the Cairo group tapped, the contents of their waste-paper baskets examined, and duplicate keys made to fit the locks of their rooms. He also set Frank Thornton and others to watch the movements of the men.

The leaders were two men named Aimes and Bennet; and also among their number—though not of the Cairo group—were a man named Mahon and an Irishman who went by the name of 'Peel'. There was also McLean, the Chief Intelligence Officer.

The first strike went to the Cairo group. They caught Frank Thornton and held him in custody for ten days. The blunder came when, after a series of gruelling examinations, they allowed him to go. Immediately Thornton reported back to Collins.

There followed a second blunder when the Cairo group trapped Tobin and Cullen in Vaughan's Hotel. Both were subjected to a fierce examination but were then allowed to go.

Within the space of a few days, three men of Collins' immediate circle had been trapped, examined, and allowed to go. It seemed to Collins that such a run of luck could not continue. It was further obvious to him that the Cairo group formed the greatest menace yet to his organization. Either they must be got rid of or the end was in sight.

He had several conferences called. According to other biographers, plans for the operation of 'Bloody Sunday' were made at Vaughan's Hotel on the Saturday night, November 20th. There was certainly a meeting and discussion and things may have been finalized there; but as early as the 17th Collins had written to Dick McKee, Commander of the Dublin Brigade:

> 'Dick—Have established addresses of the particular ones. Arrangements should now be made about the matter. Lt. G is aware of things. He suggests the 21st. A most suitable date and day I think. M.'[14]

The Dublin Brigade was now put to one more test. At 9 a.m. on Sunday, November 21st, 1920, eight groups of men went into action and fourteen spies were summarily executed in their various lodgings. McLean was one of the men shot. The list of those executed unfortunately—despite the most stringent precautions on the part of the planners—included an innocent man: an officer of the Royal Army Medical Corps, who was shot by mistake in the Gresham Hotel.

Mrs. Anna Kelly (then Anna Fitzsimons—Collins' secretary) was a witness to one of the executions.

> 'One of them got shot next door to me. I had got out of jail the night before, and went to a house for a good sleep. Next morning I was brought to my feet by shots, and there was one of the British being shot in his pyjamas in the back garden.'[15]

Reaction from the British came almost immediately, Lorry-loads of Auxiliaries drove up to Croke Park in the afternoon. There a large crowd were assembled to watch a Gaelic football match. The Auxiliaries opened up point blank, firing into the crowd of men, women and children, killing fourteen (including one of the players) and wounding many others.

Dick McKee, Peadar Clancy, and a young man named Conor Clune (who was an innocent visitor to Dublin) were arrested and taken to Dublin Castle. There, after being cruelly maltreated, they were shot.[16]

In England the feeling was one of immediate horror and revulsion. 'Fourteen British Officers Executed' said one newspaper headline, no reference being made to the fact that the officers were out of uniform and that they were spies. The public, naturally, assumed that as military men they were discharging their normal duties.

From time to time in the years following the incidents of 'Bloody Sunday', many false accounts have been written and published. Chiefly they are the work of journalists, writing with one eye open for a 'story'. 'Bloody Sunday' provided drama enough without any need for exaggeration.

Under date November 22nd, Field-Marshal Sir Henry Wilson referred in his diary to 'These poor murdered officers . . .'.[17] As a military leader, and also the man who coined the titles 'rats', 'gunmen', and 'murder gangs', he obviously took a different view of the incident. Unfortunately for Wilson, at least two of the members of the British Cabinet thought otherwise. One of them, Churchill, notes Wilson, 'insinuated that the murdered officers were careless fellows and ought to have taken precautions'.[18] On the 26th November Wilson further notes, of Lloyd George, Churchill and Greenwood, 'I wonder they did not hide their heads in shame,' over the murdered officers.[19]

The final act of 'callous indifference' again concerns Prime Minister Lloyd George. On the 22nd—the day following the incidents—Mr. P. Moylett, an Irish business man in London, had a meeting with the Prime Minister. Mr. Moylett had endeavoured on other occasions to arrange a truce between the warring parties, as, in much the same way, Englishmen and others in Dublin sought to do the same. But on this particular occasion Mr. Moylett was quite certain in his own mind that whatever hope there had been was now lost. Indeed, he would not have been surprised had the Prime Minister refused to see him. He was, however, admitted into the Prime Minister's presence. 'Well,' said Mr. Moylett, 'I suppose this ends all further hope.' To which Lloyd George replied: 'Not at all. They got what they deserved, beaten by counterjumpers.'[20]

The final say in the matter came from Collins himself—though the document was never published. The date of his putting down the detail contained in this document is uncertain. His former secretary, Mrs. Kelly, has no recollection of ever having typed it. It is not beyond the bounds of possibility that it was typed in London, during the Treaty discussions, perhaps for use as an answer against any chance accusation against him. It is typed on a single sheet of quarto sized paper, which bears also the crest of Dail Eireann, and the alterations to the original text are in Collins' handwriting.

> 'My one intention was the destruction of the undesirables who continued to make miserable the lives of ordinary decent citizens.
>
> I have proof enough to assure myself of the atrocities which this gang of spies and informers have committed. Perjury and torture are words too easily known to them.
>
> If I had a second motive it was no more than a feeling such as I would have for a dangerous reptile.
>
> By their destruction the very air is made sweeter. That should be the future's judgment on this particular event. For myself, my conscience is clear. There is no crime in detecting and destroying, in war-time, the spy and the informer. They have destroyed without trial. I have paid them back in their own coin.'[21]

There is no mention of himself as being the primary target of the executed men. It is a simple statement of fact and one which needs no further elaboration.

But the executions of McKee and Clancy by the British was a shock from which Collins took some considerable time to recover. And for a time it put the brake on Volunteer activities. The night before burial, when the dead lay coffined in the Pro-Cathedral, Collins and others redressed the bodies in the uniform of the Volunteers. The following day at the funeral, despite the presence of detectives on the look-out for him, Collins, dressed in a trenchcoat, stepped forward from among the mourners and pinned on the coffins the following note of farewell:

> 'In memory of two good friends—Dick and Peadar—and two of Ireland's best soldiers. Michael O Coileain. 25/11/20.'

Chapter 9

MacSwiney—Trouble—Truce

NEARLY one month before the events of 'Bloody Sunday', on October 25th, 1920, Terence MacSwiney, the Lord Mayor of Cork, died on hunger strike in Brixton Jail, England. He had been arrested on the 12th August and, at his trial by military court (he was sentenced to two years' imprisonment), he had stated:

> 'I will put a limit to any term of imprisonment you may impose. I have taken no food since Thursday, therefore I will be free in a month.'[1]

MacSwiney's determination in fasting to the death had the effect —as he intended—of drawing the notice of the world to the Irish cause, including a section of the English public—although British newspapers and British statesmen generally sought to cast ridicule on the fortitude of the Brixton prisoner. During the course of MacSwiney's fast, Winston Churchill, in a characteristic speech, said at Dundee:

> 'It was during the silly season the Lord Mayor of Cork announced his determination to starve himself to death. He did not want to die, and the Government did not want him to die; but Alderman MacSwiney had many friends in Ireland who wished him to die. After six weeks' fasting, the Lord Mayor is still alive.'

It is unfortunate that the personal heroism of MacSwiney, with the consequent sympathy which he gained for the Irish cause, was largely lost by the following events of 'Bloody Sunday' although, as previously stated, 'Bloody Sunday' was greatly misinterpreted by the mass of the British people.

From the occasion in 1917 when Cathal Brugha's opinion was that the I.R.B. had outlived its usefulness, the animosity which he showed to Collins gradually developed over the years into a bitter enmity. The enmity came chiefly from Brugha although Collins, along with his admiration for the 1916 exploits of the older man, showed a marked coolness. Now, in 1920, the sabre-rattling of Brugha began to develop into something more positive.

Meantime, Austin Stack, the Minister for Home Affairs, had joined forces with Brugha against Collins. From being a firm friend of the latter, Stack, chiefly because of Collins' baiting of him, became his bitter enemy. In August, 1920, Collins mockingly admonished Stack over his Rent Restriction Bill. After the meeting, Stack said: 'That's a nice way you treated me.' Collins, repenting already but unwilling to show it, said, 'Well.' 'All right,' said Stack, 'I'll get even with you.'[2] It was noticeable, however, how Stack's character had changed over the years from that of a friendly, courteous man to that of a man continually tormented by bitterness. It is only fair to add, as some explanation of Stack's change of character, that the reason for it may have been largely accounted for by a deterioration in health, including a stomach ulcer as a result of a hunger strike.*

Note has previously been made of Brugha snatching the opportunity to castigate Collins on the occasion of the return from America of Liam Mellowes, when the latter took over the department of Director of Purchases from Collins. Brugha stated (in the grand manner) that he would not be satisfied until he was assured that the accounts had been kept in a proper manner. Stack aligned himself on the side of Brugha—the first open rift to occur between him and Collins.

So it went on—Brugha cavilling against Collins at every opportunity, amply aided by Stack and Mellowes; Collins growing more bitter on every occasion while Richard Mulcahy, the Deputy Chief of Staff, endeavoured with one thing and another to keep the peace, outwardly at any rate. On Mulcahy's pleading, de Valera

* It is also stated, on good authority, that a remark of Collins' which galled Stack was in some such terms as: 'I hope you won't make a mess of this the same as you did of the Casement landing'—in reference to the fact that Casement had been permitted to fall into British hands in 1916, while no effort was made by the Tralee Volunteers, of whom Stack had command, to rescue him. (Told to the present writer by Sean O Luing.)

remonstrated with Brugha, but it is doubtful, in view of Brugha's apparent hold over de Valera, whether the chastising had any effect. Apart from the incident of the National Loan, no sign of mistrust or misgiving had yet appeared to split the mutual friendship of de Valera and Collins.

From the year 1920 attempts at some form of conciliation between the British Government and Dail Eireann had been made. Englishmen and other prominent persons in the British Commonwealth—General Smuts, for example—regularly made note of the Irish scene and even visited Ireland, while, in London, Irish business men were active contacts with the same purpose in mind.

In April, 1921, Lord Derby arrived in Dublin and stayed, under another name, at the Shelbourne Hotel. He succeeded in obtaining an interview with de Valera; but subsequently the latter referred to his Lordship as being merely a political scout. Having failed in that direction, Derby, through intermediaries, sought to arrange a meeting between Griffith and de Valera and Prime Minister Lloyd George at Lord Derby's home in England. But again Lord Derby was unsuccessful and he returned to England. The next attempt was made by Sir James Craig, Prime Minister of the Six County Cabinet. The Six County Cabinet had come into being as a result of the 1920 Government of Ireland Act which provided for two Parliaments: one for the Six Counties and another for the remaining twenty-six counties. The Six County Parliament was formally opened by King George V on the 22nd June, 1921. After the meeting which he had with de Valera, the following statement, by agreement with both parties, was issued: that they had 'held an informal conference at which their respective points of view were interchanged, and the future of Ireland discussed'.[3] The statement naturally created something of a sensation in the Six Counties and, in actual fact, it had certain repercussions at the London Treaty discussions (*vide* Collins' letter, Chapter 13).

At this time the state of the warring elements was of a general stalemate. The British Government had at long last awakened to the fact that the 'rebel' government was not what it had previously imagined it to be: an ill-assorted, lawless rabble. Further, the 'rats', 'gunmen' and 'murderers' of Sir Henry Wilson's estimate had instead proved themselves to be a highly organized and disciplined force, while under the threat of ostracization, carried out on the orders of Collins, the Royal Irish Constabulary was rapidly being reduced to the status of a neutral force. Intrigue and the activities of Collins' intelligence had braked considerably the activities of the 'G' Division. Little wonder, then, that in the face of such stiffening in the ranks of the fighters for independence, the British

Government decided to abandon its reprisals policy and concentrate instead on improving relations with the Irish through Dail Eireann.

If the picture, so far as the British was concerned, was not very encouraging, activity on the Irish side had also slowed down to some extent. The shock of the deaths of McKee and Clancy, following the events of 'Bloody Sunday', had had a certain detrimental effect on the morale of many of the men of the brigades. But on the 25th May occurred the biggest single operation ever carried out by the Volunteers: the burning of the Custom House. While its propaganda value as an operation of war is indisputable, it proved for the Volunteers to be a major catastrophe because of the numbers of prisoners taken.

Together with this major operation of war, the record of the activities of the Dublin Brigade for the month of May, 1921, is an imposing one, involving almost one hundred distinct operations.

A new attempt to come to terms was made by the South African Prime Minister, General Smuts. Visiting Dublin in June, he had an interview with de Valera during which Smuts made great play with, and urged, the acceptance of a settlement similar to that accepted by South Africa.

One other move, at least, was made to obtain a temporary peace —through the person of Eamonn Duggan, then a prisoner in Mountjoy Jail.

To all of these de Valera paid little or no attention. It is thought by some that de Valera was playing his ace in creating an impression among the British that it did not matter in the least to the Dail whether the war dragged on endlessly, that the Irish could well stand the pace of it. The fact is, de Valera was far too astute a politician ever to be stampeded into any sort of a compromise. He would come to terms in his own time, at the proper moment, and when he had thoroughly convinced himself that no tricks of statecraft were attached to any offer which the British might care to make. And for all his astuteness, Lloyd George soon realized that, in dealing with de Valera, he was opposed to no second-rater at the game of statesmanship.

So far as Collins was concerned—in the background, but, at the same time, in the picture—it was to be either a truce to keep, or no truce at all. 'Why?' asked a particular crony. 'Because,' replied Collins, 'once a truce is agreed and we come out into the open, it is extermination for us if the truce should fail. Don't you see,' he snapped angrily, 'that we shall be, in the event of a truce, like rabbits coming out from their holes; and pot-shots for the "farmers" should the truce ever fail.'[4]

However slowly events moved, nothing could ease the tension on the Irish side, much as it was carefully hidden from the British. 'A nervous wariness among the leaders,' was how a witness described it'.[5] The fact is, the forces of independence were in a corner; willing enough, it is true, to carry on the fight but any amount of willingness and courage could not make up for lack of numbers and an appalling shortage of armament and ammunition. This fact Sir Henry Wilson realized, as he also realized another fact: that the Irish must be crushed during the summer, or Ireland and maybe the Empire also was lost.

Collins, apart from the truce question, was concentrating on trying to secure the release from the death penalty of Commandant Sean MacEoin,* the 'Blacksmith of Ballinalee', and famed commander of the Longford Brigade. The death sentence had been passed on MacEoin for a singlehanded combat which he had had with an Inspector and ten men of the R.I.C. who had been sent to arrest him. In the course of the fight, the Inspector had been killed. Shortly afterwards, Commandant MacEoin, following an action in which he was severely wounded, was captured. All attempts at rescuing him seemed doomed to failure, ill-luck seeming the deciding factor in every attempt. In vain Collins raged as each new attempt failed and it seemed that Commandant MacEoin was doomed.

Then, quite suddenly, it happened. Lloyd George came out into the open with a letter to de Valera. In return for a truce, Lloyd George offered the release of all prisoners with the exception of Commandant MacEoin. At this point Collins intervened, stating that, for him, there would be 'no discussions without MacEoin'.[6] He won his point. De Valera sent his reply· And on Monday, July 11th, 1921, the strife ended.

For the citizens of Dublin and for the populace generally, it was a day of gladness. It gives point to this unique situation when it is recorded that as General Macready, the British Military Commander in Ireland, arrived at the Mansion House, he was cheered by an enormous crowd.

For Collins working on in his office at Harcourt Terrace, it was a relief tinged with the sharpness of vinegar. He had sensed a change, slight it is true, in de Valera's attitude towards him and it worried him a great deal. The Brugha-Stack-Mellowes faction did not unduly worry him but this was different. He could not sense the purpose behind the change, for it had none of the obviousness of Brugha's barely concealed enmity. With de Valera the purpose,

* Now Lieutenant-General Sean MacEoin, T.D., Minister for Justice, 1948-51, and Minister for Defence, 1954-7.

if any, was concealed beneath a mask of dourness and the occasional wintry smile.

Somewhere along the line of this hidden distrust lurked the 'echoes' of Frongoch and Lewes. The hard-earned reputation achieved by de Valera at Lewes naturally gave great weight to any future utterance of his while the reputation earned by Collins at Frongoch—although in no way as revealing as de Valera's at Lewes—had since gathered great weight, chiefly as a result of his achievements from 1917 onwards.

Collins put the situation as clearly as he could in what for him was a time of uncertainty.

> 'Agreement is a trifling word or so I have come to look on it as such. At this moment there is more ill-will within a victorious assembly than ever could be anywhere else except in the devil's assembly. It cannot be fought against. The issue, and persons, are mixed to such extent as to make discernibility an utter impossibility except for a few.
>
> It is a trust which is rapidly breaking, for the rank and file of men and the citizens theirs is a misplaced trust. For the trusted ones, far from being in accord, are disunited. This is a time when jealousy and personal gain count for more than country. . . .'[7]

Collins was not alone in condemning the unworthiness of some of his colleagues. In England Sir Henry Wilson was saying much the same about the British Cabinet. In his diary, under date June 30th, he recorded that he and Macready 'are coming somewhere near the limit of patience'.[8] He complained bitterly that the Government were hiding the true state of things from the populace; that the more powerful of the British newspapers were on the side of Lloyd George; that events in Ireland were causing grave unrest among the troops there. On July 6th he recorded that Macready had been to a Cabinet meeting, and

> 'He gathered that they were going to come to a "gentlemanly undertaking" (as they called it) with Valera for a month's truce. Valera has done well; a month's delay makes it impossible to take on murder-gang seriously this summer, as weather breaks in September-October. Valera knows this well enough.'[9]

On both sides of the Irish Sea the soldiers were having trouble with the politicians.

Chapter 10

Truce continued—Pre-Treaty Discussions—The Irish Delegation—Leaving Ireland

FOR Collins the signing of the Truce represented a half-way stage in his career. Later, when he looked back on the pre-Truce days, the days of the 'Terror', it was to view them not as such, but as days of moderation, in comparison to the events of the days which were to come.

Shortly before Harry Boland's return from America—though his stay in Dublin was only for a short time—Collins had written a word of warning to him, not realizing at the time how profound de Valera's influence had been over Boland.

> 'I don't intend to dwell overmuch on what to me are issues more vital than truces. But I think it right that you should be warned of the changes here. There's something about which I don't like, and I have the impression that the whole thing is pressing on me. I find myself looking at friends as if they were enemies—looking at them twice just to make sure that they really are friends after all. I mention no names. After all it may be a wrong impression that's got into me. Frankly, though, I don't care for things as they are now.'[1]

Meantime, the British Army men were taking another look at the Truce, just in case. Sir Henry Wilson noted: 'We shall want 100,000 to 200,000 men, and one or two years, to stamp out the murder gang and re-establish law and order.'[2] So they prepared. Collins, not to be outdone and, incidentally, worrying himself to the point of illness, set himself the same task to accomplish. Arms and more arms, shiploads of them, were a necessity. And all the time a deadly fear gnawed away at him: if the Truce should fail. . . . Almost his first words to Boland, when the latter arrived, were: 'If this fails we're done.'[3] He also complained bitterly to Boland about the Truce situation, saying that the British were not keeping their word. In London Sir Henry Wilson was likewise complaining that Sinn Fein was not 'loyally' observing the Truce.

The more de Valera and Lloyd George discussed, the more

worried and fretful Collins became. He, who was shortly to be pushed into the arena of political craft, distrusted the politicians with all of a soldier's marked distrust—even as Wilson, in London, distrusted the British politicians.

On September 6th the British Cabinet assembled at Inverness where Lloyd George was on holiday. On the 7th Lloyd George wrote to de Valera stating that he would be prepared to commence discussions 'to ascertain how the association of Ireland with the Community of Nations known as the British Empire can best be reconciled with Irish national aspirations'. On the 14th Joseph McGrath and Harry Boland brought de Valera's answer: 'The Irish Republic would be glad to discuss this question with the Community of Nations, known as the British Empire.'

But between the time of de Valera's answer and the 19th September—five days—the preliminary negotiations almost broke down. Lloyd George stated that the report of de Valera's reply was unauthorized and the members of the British Cabinet were told to burn their copies.[4] In answer to this, de Valera said he would publish his reply letter in the evening papers—which he did. There followed a period of extreme unease; which was finally brought to an end by Lloyd George when he issued an invitation 'to a Conference in London on October 11th . . .' (the term of Reference was as already quoted in Lloyd George's letter of September 7th). This invitation the Dail accepted.

In view of the consequences arising from what eventually became known as the Treaty discussions, it is necessary to refer to several days of personal discussion which de Valera had with Lloyd George (14th to the 21st July, 1921). What actually emerged from this series of meetings between the two leaders is not known for the veil of secrecy was too tightly drawn over the discussions. Therefore, Collins had every reason to suppose, which he did, and others also, that de Valera had pretty well sighted the land as regards what the Irishmen could get from Lloyd George in the way of independence, and that such independence did not include a Republic. From this the insinuation, chiefly by Collins, is obvious: that de Valera knew full well when he sent his delegation to London that a Republic would not be forthcoming from any agreement made there and, further, that he was now in a position where he could accept or reject at will any agreement which might be arrived at by the two delegations. By the side of this surmise—it can be nothing else because of the secrecy—is a note which Collins wrote to the Irish historian, the late P. S. O'Hegarty. In it Collins refers to the men at home, in Ireland and 'we (the Irish delegation)' having 'to do what they knew must be done but had not the moral courage to do themselves'.[5] Also, in Chapter 11 of this book there will be found further evidence to what Collins refers to as a 'trap', i.e., that he himself had been trapped into membership of the delegation with, of course, the ensuing responsibility.

From then on, so far as Collins is concerned, the rift between himself and de Valera was all but an open one, much as it was carefully disguised from the populace. At the point when the Irish delegation for the London Conference was chosen Collins assumed —and rightly to the present writer's mind—that the forces aligned against him were mighty indeed.

The delegation consisted of the following five members: Chairman, Arthur Griffith; Michael Collins; Robert Barton; Eamonn Duggan; George Gavan Duffy.

On the ground that his rightful place was in Ireland and not in London, de Valera refused to go.* Cathal Brugha likewise refused to go, though he expressed his refusal in more blunt terms than de Valera.[6]

Both Brugha and Stack disclaimed any skill in negotiating and they would take none of its responsibility on themselves. They were hostile to the chief negotiators (Griffith and Collins). They occupied the position of critics but put forward no constructive proposals. They had worked themselves into a position of absolute security as regards incurring criticism for the kind of settlement subsequently made. Together with this state of affairs there is the question of the choice of Arthur Griffith as Chairman of the party. Why, if his Republicanism was open to question, was he chosen as the leader of a party instructed to obtain a Republic? Why not make an uncompromising Republican Chairman at the beginning?

The delegation itself was of oddly assorted membership. There was the political guiding spirit, Arthur Griffith; the soldier (Collins) with a distrust of politicians and statesmen in general; the ex-British officer, and Co. Wicklow landowner (Barton); Duggan, whose profession was that of a lawyer; and, finally, Duffy (son of Sir Charles Gavan Duffy, Young Ireland leader in 1848 and later Prime Minister of Victoria), himself a lawyer. Erskine Childers was chosen as Chief Secretary to the delegation.

The selection of Collins was the worst possible, for reasons of lack of the necessary attributes which make a born politician and

* The point is hotly disputed by some of de Valera's partisans, who state that he did not refuse to go. But Kathleen (Mrs. Tom) Clarke, who was present, states that he did. '. . . I was present at the meeting of An Dail held in the Oak Room of the Mansion House when the question was under discussion. I heard Mr. de Valera refusing to go. There was general dissatisfaction at his refusal but, since at the time we all trusted him, we allowed him to talk us into agreement. . . .' (Letter to the *Sunday Independent*, 25th May, 1952.)

also for personal reasons. Indeed, Collins himself vigorously protested against the inclusion of his name. His protestations were based on a number of facts, all of which rested on secure foundation. He was, he said, a soldier and not a politician; he was ill and tired, suffering generally from the effects and the strain of four years' dangerous work; and, thirdly—though he never openly expressed the view—he was strongly pressed by some of his friends not to go, for these friends saw in the selection of Collins a deliberate move on the part of his enemies to force him into a situation from which there was no retreat. It matters little, so far as Collins' case is concerned, that in the end he signed an agreement which he thought to be the best possible in the circumstances—but one, incidentally, which was at variance with his natural political inclination, as being at heart more of a Republican than the President himself.

Regarding the powers given to the delegation, two facts are worth the noting, both of which later came into prominence at the time of the debate on the Treaty.

De Valera, from the first, was opposed to any limitation being applied to the powers of the delegates. There was, he said, the matter of the approval by the Dail to any agreement which might be reached in London—that was the greatest safeguard. He did, however, issue a set of secret instructions (quoted in Chapter 16) to the delegation—instructions, it may be added, from which it is almost impossible to draw a definite conclusion as to their exact meaning. In this way he safeguarded himself against any possible implication in the signing of a treaty and, also, left himself free either to approve or condemn any agreement which might be reached.

The second fact is of equal importance. According to the late P. S. O'Hegarty, the following incident occurred prior to the departure of the Irish delegation to London. Arthur Griffith went to see de Valera.

> 'I [Griffith] found him with Cathal and Austin at his desk, all three sitting. I was standing. He told me he wanted me to go to London. I said to him, "You are my Chief, if you tell me to go, I'll go. But I know, and you know, that I can't bring back The Republic." Then he produced this External Association idea—the first I ever heard of it—and after half-an-hour's persuasion, Cathal gave a reluctant consent to it. Stack said nothing, but sat there, sullen. I said nothing. Then the other two left, and left me alone with him. I said to him, "Look here, Dev, what's the meaning of this External Association idea? What are you getting

at with it?" He replied by getting a pencil and paper and drawing a straight line thus. [Here Griffith got pencil and paper and drew the line AB.] "That," said he, "is me, in the strait jacket of The Republic. I must get out of it." Then he drew another line,

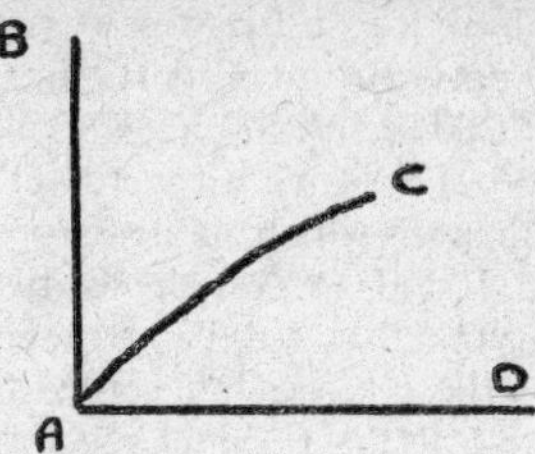

a curved line. [Here Griffith drew the curved line AC.] "That," said he, "is External Association. The purpose of it is to bring Cathal along." Then he drew another straight line. [Here Griffith drew the line AD.] "That," said he, "is where we'll eventually get to." Then I was satisfied, and said no more about it.'[7]

Meantime, the British delegation had also been selected. It consisted of Prime Minister Lloyd George; the Chancellor of the Exchequer, Sir Austen Chamberlain; the Lord Chancellor of Great Britain, Lord Birkenhead; the Chief Secretary for Ireland, Sir Hamar Greenwood; the Secretary of State for the Colonies, Winston Churchill; Sir L. Worthington-Evans; and Sir Gordon Hewart. All, with the exception of the Prime Minister, were public school and university men.

A dossier was prepared for Birkenhead which contained thumbnail 'biographies' of their Irish opposite numbers—a sort of advance warning of the type of person they were to encounter during the forthcoming discussions—but whoever prepared these 'biographies' was evidently not very well acquainted with his subjects. About Arthur Griffith—a proven negotiator if ever there was one—there is the remark 'will be ill at ease'.[8] The general assessment of the Irish delegation as a whole is wide of the mark, for all, with the exception of Duffy,

'will be very nervous and ill at ease. . . . They are leaders in Dail Eireann, which is a very nondescript assembly. They are absolutely without world experience, and considerable allowance will have to be made on this score . . . may be a bit rude and extravagant in speech. . . . They recognize their responsibilities and this, of course, adds to their nervousness.'[9]

It is these 'biographies' which provide a further point in favour of Collins, and Griffith also, for in the Dail debate on the Treaty of January 7th, 1922, Cathal Brugha said:

'. . . I asked him [Griffith] who was it that selected the two particular members—the two particular members were Mr. Griffith himself and Mr. Michael Collins—who was it that selected them? What was his answer? The British Government. I then made an answer which he insisted should be put down on the Minutes, and I said: "Yes, the British Government selected their men." In saying that I did not mean to cast any reflection on the honour of these men; but before these men were selected at all I told them—at the Cabinet meeting at which their names were suggested to be put before the Dail—I told them what I thought of their ideals of freedom from the utterances that I had heard from them; and I said at this Cabinet meeting on that fateful Saturday: "Yes, they selected their men." My meaning was this: because they knew they were the two weakest men we had on the team; and Lloyd George and his friends pretty soon discovered that; and that is how they came to select them out of the five; and they allowed the British Government to divide them up and select their own men to carry on an important Conference with them. . . .'[10]

In actual fact, neither Collins nor Griffith were considered by the British Government to be the 'two weakest men on the team' —as the following extracts from the 'biographies' prove:

'George Gavan Duffy: (Catholic) . . . son of the late Sir Gavan Duffy, Prime Minister of one of the Australian States . . . vain and self-sufficient, likes to hear himself talk.'

'Robert Barton: (Protestant) . . . cousin of Erskine Childers; held a commission during the war; . . . lost a brother in the war; educated at Rugby and Christchurch; . . . has no outstanding quality.'

'Eamonn Duggan: . . . completely under the influence of Michael Collins . . . recognises that he is not one of the strong men.'

In contrast to the above assessments—and contrary to the views expressed by Brugha—Collins is named as 'the strongest personality of the party'; and Griffith as being 'more clever than de Valera, but not so attractive, is the real power in Sinn Fein'.[11]

With the exception of Collins, who left on the next day, the delegation party sailed for England on 8th October, 1921. On their arrival in London they took up quarters at 22 Hans Place.

The following account, by a Passionist priest, Father Ignatius, C.P., covers the interval between the rest of the delegation leaving for London and Collins' later departure.

> 'The facts are these. He was staying at the "Grand Hotel", Greystones, while I was giving a Mission at the Church there. It was coming near the close of the Mission. Michael was very busy in Dublin, worked and worried almost beyond endurance. He got to Greystones one night very late and very tired. It was the eve of his departure to London re the pact. He got up next morning as early as 5.30 a.m. came to the Church and made a glorious General Confession and received Holy Communion. He said to me after Confession, "Father, say a Mass for Ireland" and "God bless you, Father". He crossed an hour or so afterwards to London.
>
> I said to the congregation that day, "You saw one of Ireland's hidden saints making no small sacrifice for the Master this morning." '[12]

Chapter 11

Arrival in London—Collins' Position—Treaty Discussions—Collins' Notes on the British Delegation—Erskine Childers—Lloyd George and Thomas Jones—Collins and O'Kane

IT WAS Monday, October 10th, when Collins reached London. The other members of the delegation, as well as the secretaries, typists and household staff, had arrived there on the Saturday evening. They were given a great reception at Euston station and afterwards made their way to 22 Hans Place.

By comparison, Collins' arrival went almost unnoticed, although in the main he was the man for whom the crowds had been looking. He went to 15 Cadogan Gardens and it was there that the reporters finally located him. He seemed in excellent spirits until he recalled that the *Daily Express* had called him a murderer.

Regarding this accusation, the following interview between Collins and the *Daily Express* representative was printed in the issue dated October 11th, 1921:

'A conference fraught with the gravest consequences for the Empire will begin at 10, Downing Street this morning when six representatives of the British Government, headed by the Prime Minister, and six Sinn Fein delegates,* will attempt to settle the Irish demand for self-government.

Mr. Michael Collins, the Sinn Fein mystery man, who will be the most striking figure at the conference, arrived in London yesterday, and was as elusive as in the days when a price was set on his head and thousands of detectives and policemen searched for him in vain.

But Mr. Collins was "captured" by a *Daily Express* representative last evening.

"How did I get to Hans Place this morning without being discovered? Why, it was the easiest thing in the world," said Mr. Collins.

"I adopted the same principle that enabled me to conceal my whereabouts so long in Ireland. I always watch the other fellow instead of letting him watch me. I make a point of keeping the other fellow on the run, instead of being on the run myself.

"That is the secret of success which I have learned during the past year or two. I travelled to Euston under an assumed name. While others were looking for me I slipped quietly and unnoticed into a taxicab with a friend, and we were away before half the other people in the sleeping-cars were awake."

Mr. Collins has the Irish sense of humour. His eyes twinkled as he told the story.

But this big, good-humoured Irishman with the rich brogue and the soft, yet decisive, voice, has another side. His face grew stern as he said, with something like emotion, "The *Daily Express* was the newspaper that called me a murderer!"

"We had neither the desire nor the intention to be unfair either to you or the Irish cause," said the *Daily Express* representative.

The cloud passed from his face.

"Well, perhaps not. I don't think that the *Daily Express* was more unfair than others, but you know, none of your English newspapers really understands us. You don't see things from our point of view."'

This was the day before the conferences commenced and if Collins appeared to be in excellent spirits his inner thoughts in no way resembled his outer cheerfulness. His personal preference was for any other place on earth except London, at least so far as the forthcoming task was concerned. The measure of Collins' mind on

* There were five: Griffith, Collins, Barton, Duggan, and Duffy.

the subject of the Conference and his selection as a delegate will be found in this short letter, written to Joe O'Reilly from Cadogan Gardens, on the day of the first Conference. For a letter only eight lines in length its contents are of tremendous import.

> 'You know the way it is. Either way it will be wrong. Wrong because of what has come to pass. You might say the trap is sprung. This could be a good thing. Enough has been said to put behind as waste the strife of other days. But that's the way it is. Neither I nor anyone else can end or mend it.'

In a footnote he added: 'I have come here to call a spade a spade. It is the only name I know it by.'[1]

This letter, so far as Collins is concerned, was the beginning and the end of the whole thing. For far too long, he felt, he had shouldered off the Brugha-Stack-Mellowes insinuations. For far too long he had pondered the question of whether de Valera was on his side or acting as a referee or on the side of those who had shown animosity to him. Now, as the letter makes plain, he sensed the true position of himself as a man lonely in the midst of intrigue.

He recognized that the Brugha-Stack-Mellowes section had one great defect: its open animosity to him. This threat he could deal with and had dealt with it in the past. The other attitude coming, as he thought, from de Valera, was something more subtle, completely in character with its instigator.

Apart from Arthur Griffith—a hero of his boyhood days—Collins had little faith in the other three members of the delegation, with the possible exception of Robert Barton whom he neither trusted nor distrusted, though one would imagine the scales of Collins' assessment as weighing slightly on the side of disfavour when he noted that Barton was Childers' cousin. Almost with a wave of his hand he banished both Duffy and Duggan: 'If Duffy spent less time admiring his voice we'd do better'; and (of Duggan): '. . . he is nervous of responsibility; tends to lean on Griffith and me; and is afraid to make a decision. . . .'[2]

So far as Duggan is concerned, let it be said now that he was out of his depth. Collins, too, a soldier and not a politician, was also out of his depth, but between them there were two great differences of character. Duggan had none of Collins' strength of personality, nor any of his keen appreciation. For his part, Collins had the wit and the shrewdness to master the intricate detail of the Conferences and to handle in a masterly manner suggestions, objections and points at issue. Duggan had none of this capability and he was overawed by the issue at stake. That he was loyal to both Griffith and Collins there can be no doubt. Collins, however, felt this loyalty to be an added encumbrance thrust on himself and, in view of what had transpired and in fairness to himself, he had every right to think in this way.

Never a man for liking a job only half completed, Collins studied carefully the characters of the members of the British delegation. It was obvious from the start that the one member of the British delegation likely to find favour in Collins' eyes was Lord Birkenhead. It may run contrary to the idea generally accepted in Ireland that Birkenhead ruthlessly exploited Collins, and other members of the Irish delegation for that matter, simply for his own ends and thereby for those of his country, but the fact remains that Birkenhead, in endeavouring to find a solution to problems confronting the delegations, favoured the Irishmen with a sense of justice the scales of which tipped the balance to some considerable extent. It is also worth recording that Birkenhead had spoken out against the use of the 'Black and Tans' in Ireland during a Parliamentary debate. The actual outcome of this fairmindedness of Birkenhead's was that he seriously jeopardized his now Parliamentary career and later was at the centre of many stormy scenes, chiefly at the hands of Sir Edward Carson, in the House of Commons. Birkenhead, like Collins, was a realist and, again like Collins, he was aggressively so: a character of strength. During the early sessions Collins watched Birkenhead and Birkenhead watched Collins. This game of watching and observing could have ended in either of two ways: they could become fiercely antagonistic towards each other or they could appreciate each other in the friendly manner often found among combatants. It is no surprise, therefore, to find that the latter course proved to be the outcome.

> 'If [Collins wrote of Birkenhead] all the British delegation had his capacity for clear thinking, capacity for work and getting ahead, things would be much easier. Lawyer, but with a great difference. Concise. Clearness of ideas a great advantage. Refuses to be drowned by the might of others. A good man.'[3]

That is clear enough. It need only be added that Birkenhead's position in the British delegation was of such standing that on no account could he be 'drowned by the might of others'.

Regarding the British Prime Minister, David Lloyd George, the position was different. It has been said that he completely outmanœuvred the Irishmen, which is only another way of saying that he fooled them. It is possible that he did indeed fool both Duggan and Duffy into thinking that his every consideration was for the Irish, but one cannot conceive of him applying the same tactics with equal success to Griffith or Barton, and still less with Collins, on account of the latter's early recognition of the Prime Minister's qualities:

'Born poor is therefore shrewd. Was lawyer therefore crafty. Nicknamed the "Welsh Wizard" and for good reason. Has a great deal of craft in his political methods, in his diplomatic approaches. Trusts that his fatherly air and benevolence will overcome all obstacles—craft again. "Now Michael . . ." he says; or "Now Mick . . ." On formal occasions it's "Now Mr. Collins . . ." Not sure how far he can go with me. Confided that Arthur G. was altogether too dour for dealings. That Barton was suspicious of him—as I am. But that Duffy and Duggan are pigeons for the plucking. Would sell his nearest and dearest for political prestige. '14-'18 war good and bad for him. Hopes this affair will gain him political prestige—which apparently he desperately needs.'[4]

On the subject of Sir Austen Chamberlain it would appear from available evidence that Collins misjudged his man. Chamberlain, in fact, took up a stand similar to that of Birkenhead, his sense of fairness predominating, whereas Collins noted:

'Don't like Chamberlain. Difficult man. Son of Joseph C. Never informal. Says one thing and apparently means another. Middle of the road man. Plays safe. Educated Rugby public school and Cambridge. Probably thinks of G. and me as heathens. Equal with Duffy, politically and otherwise.'[5]

With Sir Hamar Greenwood Collins was on common ground: that of dislike. Greenwood's consistent defence of the 'Black and Tans' and the Auxiliaries may appear in some eyes to be an act of faith and courage but in the eyes of all Irishmen—and many Englishmen—Greenwood was a person to be detested as the man responsible for many of the outrages committed by his protégés in Ireland. It will, therefore, cause no surprise to find Collins noting that Greenwood is:

'A man who earns my personal detestation. Feeling reciprocated, I would say. Canadian. Bombastic. Over-riding. Could settle this issue in one day—in favour of Britain.'[6]

Collins dealt next with Sir Gordon Hewart:

'Attorney-General. Lawyer through and through—and just as dry. Looks at one as if about to deliver sentence. Few tricks. Features rock-hard. Fastidious. A difficult man to deal with. Never relaxes.'[7]

For Sir Laming Worthington-Evans Collins could find 'no comment'.[8] But of Churchill, he said:

'Don't know quite whether he would be a crafty enemy in friendship. Outlook: political gain, nothing else. Will sacrifice all for political gain. Studies, I imagine, the detail carefully—thinks about his constituents, effect of so and so on them. Inclined to be bombastic. Full of ex-officer jingo or similar outlook. Don't actually trust him.'[9]

For a final summary Collins made quite plain in two letters his soldier's aversion for politicians.

'Whenever I think of politics I think of the false air which is a part of most politicians. However much he may blind the public, and even himself, into thinking that he is for party and country, it does not blind me into thinking the same way. To be a politician one needs to keep tongue in cheek for all of the day and most of the night; one needs to have the ability to say one thing and mean another; one needs to be abnormally successful at the "art" of twisting the truth. Can you wonder that I think and think yet never manage to achieve peace of mind? In my time I have told men and women what I thought of them, I've cursed them—and they understood me all the more for it. But what can one say to a politician? Knowing it is more than possible that one's words will be taken out of context, twisted, warped, shaped into a lie, and be flung back into my teeth. I do not in the least care for the false atmosphere of these discussions.'[10]

His observations on the new circumstances in which he found himself are refreshing in their frankness. Collins obviously would not make a diplomat of finesse, for neither in his spoken word nor his written phrase did he hesitate to come to the point.

'This is a real nest of singing birds. They chirrup mightily one to the other—and there's the falseness of it all, because not one trusts the other. Lloyd George's attitude I find to be particularly obnoxious. He is all comradely—all craft and wiliness

—all arm around shoulder—all the old friends act. Not long ago he would joyfully have had me at the rope end. He thinks that the past is all washed out now—but that's to my face. What he thinks behind my back makes me sick at thought of it.'[11]

Both delegations numbered in their parties secretarial staffs and advisers. The secretaries assigned to the Irish delegation were: Erskine Childers, John Chartres, Fionan Lynch, and Diarmuid O'Hegarty; to the British delegation: Thomas Jones and Lionel Curtis. Advisers from both countries were present for conferences on Naval and Air Defence; the Irish included Eoin O'Duffy, the British Admiral Beatty and Sir Hugh Trenchard.

The selection of Erskine Childers as Chief Secretary to the Irish delegation was the last straw. Griffith and Collins did not like him, and many of the Deputies in Dail Eireann distrusted him, recalling that he had been seconded by British Naval Intelligence to act as secretary to the abortive Irish Convention of 1917.

If ever a man had a chequered career that man was Childers. His father and mother both died when he was young and Childers had been brought up by the Barton family at Glendalough in Co. Wicklow. Educated at Cambridge, he became the first president of the 'Magpie and Stump Debating Society'. From Cambridge he went into the British Civil Service, working as a Committee clerk at the House of Commons. A veteran of both the Boer War and the 1914-18 war (he won a D.S.O. in the latter conflict) his name was a household word after the 1914 Howth gun-running exploit. A military expert, he had written treatises on tactics and he was also the author of an advance treatise on Dominion Home Rule, and a book which became a best seller, *The Riddle of the Sands*. In 1919 he finally cut the bond between himself and his British interests and went into permanent residence in Ireland, where he also became active in the fight for independence, and represented Wicklow in Dail Eireann.

There is no question of Childers being unsuited to the position of Chief Secretary, rather the reverse in fact; but it was not the abilities of the man which earned for him Griffith's animosity* and Collins' suspicion. While Griffith made plain his animosity, Collins recalled that Cathal Brugha had once borne animosity against Childers, until he learned that the latter had been selected to the Chief Secretaryship of the delegation, from which moment

* As early as 1912, Griffith, writing in *Sinn Fein*, had summed up Childers as an 'English Imperialist'. '. . . if the Irish question could be settled in England's interest without Home Rule Mr. Childers would be our opponent. Mr. Childers is a man Ireland could do business with, but he is no more her lover than the shopkeeper who is prepared to give honest value to a customer is the customer's lover.' (Sean O Luing: *Art O Griofa*, p. 381.)

Brugha's attitude changed. More, Collins regarded Childers as an informer against the delegation, regularly submitting reports to Brugha and Stack and even, Collins hazarded, to de Valera himself. These reports Collins regarded as being 'masterpieces of the half-statement, painting a picture far from the true state of things'.[12]

There could, of course, be other reasons for Collins' dislike of Childers. Collins hated fussiness and nervous habits of any kind; while Childers, for his part, worried himself into a state of distraction when he observed the difference in political experience and inexperience as typified by the British and the Irish delegations.

While he was prepared for Griffith's detestation, Collins' dislike came as rather a shock to Childers. If, however, as is recorded by Collins—and what grounds are there for doubt?—Childers was indeed supplying the Dublin faction with secret reports, then there is ample ground for Collins' suspicion and dislike. It should also be remembered that Childers exerted some influence over the person of de Valera and that, of late, de Valera's attitude to Collins had shown a marked falling off in the niceties of comradeship. At the moment it was a suspicion, even if a pretty indefinite one, on Collins' part but later it was to prove to have been a suspicion well founded.

It was not long before Lloyd George and his henchman, Thomas Jones, recognized the rift in the ranks of the Irishmen, both in London and also as between Dublin and London.

It was a game at which Lloyd George was expert, this searching for a weakness, finding it, and exploiting it, and in Thomas Jones, Assistant Secretary to the Cabinet and Chief Secretary to the British delegation, he had a very able agent. Of the two Jones was probably the more crafty because, in carrying out the schemes of Lloyd George, he was compelled to use his own ingenuity to a great extent. While it is hardly fair to say that he fooled any member of the Irish delegation, it is certain that he tricked Griffith into signing a document which was used at the crucial moment by Lloyd George as a lever against the Irish delegation.

Thus the setting was built piece by piece, the work done largely by the more experienced in political craft, and on the stage stood Griffith and Collins, hemmed in by an inescapable net of intrigue. So it was that Collins, threshing in the coils of this net, turned to one who proved in this time of frustration to be a friend indeed. The two letters of Collins' on the subject of politics and politicians and the notes on Duffy, Duggan and Childers were written to John O'Kane, an Irish businessman then living in the Hampstead district of London. There, at the home of O'Kane, Collins was made welcome, a fact which he never failed to appreciate. Mostly, whenever he found it impossible to see O'Kane personally, he sent a note or letter and it is chiefly from these documents that the real position of Collins, and the burden he bore, are to be seen.

Miss Eithne O'Kane, niece of John O'Kane, met Collins on one occasion. The visit was a well-remembered one, although, as she pointed out to the present writer, nothing regarding the 'talks' was discussed in her presence nor were politics brought into the conversation.

'My uncle lived at the time in a largish house [said Miss O'Kane to the present writer], with two bay windows on the ground floor. These two rooms were used as a dining-room and a lounge.

I met Michael Collins late in the November of 1921. It was my practice to visit my uncle on Tuesday, Thursday and Saturday of every week, going to his home direct from my employment as a secretary.

I recall the day as being a Thursday and the time of my arrival there about 6.30 in the evening. Dolly, my uncle's Co. Galway maid, opened the door, saying that my uncle was engaged in conversation with a gentleman in the lounge.

I was on the point of leaving to go to my own home, when my uncle came out of the lounge, and beckoned me to come inside. He then introduced me to Michael Collins.

My immediate impression of him—as I suppose it was to many others also—was of a man of strength. I knew his background fairly well; but for all my knowledge, meeting him in the flesh provided a rather unpleasant surprise. For all his appearance of strength, his actual bearing came as rather a shock. I could detect a man aged beyond his years, with a look, or air, of worry about him—illness perhaps.

The actual time of my meeting him was a few days before he returned to Dublin for the Cabinet meeting. On second thoughts, my impression was that he was suffering from nervous strain. He talked jerkily, seemed to be ill at ease, his mind far away from the quiet and the comfort of my uncle's home.

After greeting me warmly, he went back to his seat, a low easy-chair near the window. The only light was from a small study lamp which was heavily shaded. For the hour or so of the conversation he sat half in shadow his features quite indistinguishable.

He and my uncle (a Co. Galway man) talked about Ireland. I remember that Michael Collins asked me for my impressions of the country, with which I was fairly familiar. I replied that I knew Co. Galway very well, but Co. Cork not at all. "Then you don't know Ireland," he said. I felt bound to agree.

"You know, John," he said to my uncle, "there's nothing I'd like better than a couple of months tramping around Ireland. I'm not such a well-travelled man, you know. Travel incognito, of course. Meeting just the ordinary people. They're the earth and the history of any country." And after a moment of silence, he added: "But I doubt whether I shall ever have the opporunity."

The train of thought once started, he seemed to lose some of his reserve—or was it simply a wish for quiet after the day's work? At any rate, he now launched out on what seemed to him a favourite topic: the ordinary people of Ireland. One sensed that somewhere there was a connection between what was then happening in London and the "plain people"—as he termed them—in Ireland.

All too quickly the time for my departure came. I wished him "Goodbye and good luck!" He expressed a hope that we might meet again. But it was not to be, for I never saw him again.

The news of his death in the following year shocked me. As for my uncle, it was impossible to assist him in any way through the long period of grief which followed the dreadful news. I well remember him saying, time after time: "They have driven a knife into the heart of Ireland. God rest a great man."'

Chapter 12

Treaty Discussions continued—Collins and Dominion Status —Windsor Barracks Raid

THE Treaty discussions fall into three separate sections or meetings:

(1) The sessions of the Plenary Conference, in all seven meetings: the first two on October 11th, and the last on October 24th.

(2) Committees of the Plenary Conference, sub-divided into three sections: Naval and Air Defence, three meetings; Financial Relations, one meeting; Observation of the Truce, five meetings.

(3) After the seventh session of the Plenary Conference (October 24th), the negotiations were conducted through a series of twenty-four Sub-Conferences, of which the first was held on October 24th

and the last on December 5th-6th at which meeting the Treaty was signed.

There was also a final meeting, attended by Griffith and Duffy, at 4 p.m. on the 6th.

On the 16th November the Earl of Midleton, K.P., Sir Andrew Jameson, and Dr. Bernard, Provost of Trinity College, Dublin, had conversations with Arthur Griffith in London. The three men were the spokesmen for the Southern Irish Unionists, who were not organized in a political sense. Nevertheless, it was agreed on both sides that a Senate should be set up in Ireland.

There were nine informal meetings, the first held on November 8th, the last on December 4th, between the Irishmen and Thomas Jones. Collins attended three meetings, Duggan two, and Griffith all nine. Neither Barton nor Duffy were present at any of these meetings.

The total number of meetings of the Sub-Conferences attended by members of the Irish delegation were as follows: Arthur Griffith twenty-two attendances, Michael Collins nineteen attendances, Robert Barton three attendances, George Gavan Duffy two attendances, and Eamonn Duggan two attendances.

For the first few meetings there was an air of tension evident in the conference room. The presence of Sir Hamar Greenwood chiefly accounted for this although Lloyd George, foreseeing it, had placed himself in the position of buffer between the parties concerned. By the fifth meeting, however, much of the tension had disappeared, and had been replaced by a more cordial atmosphere.

About this time, His Holiness the Pope, in a message to the King of England, expressed a wish that a settlement would result from the conferences. King George V in his reply used the term 'Peace and happiness for my people'. By way of answer de Valera made a statement in which he expressed the perfectly legitimate point of view that the Irish owed no allegiance to the King, and, further, he pointed out that the independence of Ireland was proclaimed by elected representatives of the people, and that Britain sought to impose her will on the people of Ireland by means of brutal force.

Around the conference table de Valera's statement had a temporary bad effect on the course of the discussions. There, the statement was interpreted as being in bad taste and made at a most inopportune moment. It was described by one daily newspaper as a 'bombshell'. Collins, for his part, took a gloomy view, seeing in de Valera's statement the old bogy of a Republic as being what the latter inferred.

Collins expressed his own thoughts in the one phrase: 'You cannot create a Republic overnight.'[1] It was a state of mind based on the adequate grounds of disharmony in the country. Was Ireland sufficiently established in her own right—politically stabilized, economically sound—to warrant the drastic step of cutting herself off so completely and so suddenly from Britain? Or would there be, in the event of a Republic (and all it meant) being declared, complete chaos? Why, asked Collins, waste all that had been gained for the sake of a symbol?

It is beyond question that Collins, as early as the beginning of November, had put his mind to Dominion Status as being the best temporary settlement, though he placed particular emphasis on the fact of it being only a temporary settlement. To O'Kane he remarked that the 'achievement of Dominion Status will be to a large extent beneficial to us. I do not look on the above [Dominion Status] as being anywhere near a finalised solution. It is the first step. More than this could not be expected.'[2] The phrase 'will be to a large extent beneficial to us' means that there would in all probability be certain clauses attached to the achievement of Dominion Status, such as harbour facilities, aerodromes, etc., for the use of the British.

On the 25th November a document, 'Memorandum by M. C. (draft)', was sent to Lord Birkenhead by Sir Austen Chamberlain. It was written on Dail Eireann notepaper and the author of it was Michael Collins. The following letter from Chamberlain to Birkenhead, sent as a covering note to the document, gives point to its interest:

> '11 Downing Street, Whitehall, S.W. 25/11/21. My dear F. E., —This is extraordinarily interesting though sometimes perverse and sometimes Utopian. Who (outside our six) would guess the name of the writer? Yours sincerely, Austen Chamberlain.'[3]

The present writer is concerned mainly with the notes from which Collins sketched out the final draft of his memorandum, although the difference between the two sets of documents is negligible.* In these notes there is what at first appears to be an apparent contradiction of terms. A footnote is given at this particular section to illustrate what would appear to be the state of Collins' mind on the subject.

From these notes it will be seen how the final (draft) document foretold the Statute of Westminster (which defined the status of the

* The notes have not previously been published; but the final draft, headed 'Dail Eireann; Personal and Unofficial; Irish delegation of Plenipotentiaries Secretariat; Memorandum by M. C. (draft)', will be found in *Frederick Edwin Earl of Birkenhead: The Last Phase* (pp. 157-9), by the Earl of Birkenhead.

Dominions at the Imperial Conference of November, 1930) by at least eight years.

The notes commence by dealing with the British oppression of Ireland through the centuries. Two paragraphs are devoted to the famine of 1847, in which, Collins notes, 'Half a million or more people were murdered by the British.'

Following this and other observations, the notes proceed:

'British people do not recognise the change which has come about not only for Ireland and England but for the whole world.

So that—

(1) The business of the Irish Conference is to form some sort of alliance in which both may be associated for equal benefit.

(2) The position of Ireland is entirely different from that of Britain's Colonies.

(3) Nevertheless, both England and Ireland, by nature of their nearness to each other, have matters of common concern.

(4) The only association which will be satisfactory to Ireland to enter will be based not on the present technical legal status of the Dominions, but on the real position they claim and have secured.*

A development such as this might lead to a world League of Nations. From conflict (world conflict) to harmony.

If America were able to enter such a League, a further move would be made towards world peace. Consequently, in such an atmosphere—through improved relationship—to a condition of financial stability.

The invitation to the Irish representatives to consider how association with the nations of the British Commonwealth can best be reconciled with Irish national aspirations, makes it necessary to consider how far the members of the group have attained to independent nationality.

What steps should be taken to secure such standard of independence.'

* It may be thought that in these four headings (later to be expanded) there occurs a contradiction in terms. The present writer has therefore taken the liberty of explaining them as follows:

Para 1. The word 'alliance' presupposes something like equality of status on the part of the allies. Collins was approaching the conference on the basis that the agreement should not be an imposed one, but arrived at by mutual consent and goodwill.

Para 2. A claim to separate and distinct nationality, as opposed to Colonies—branches of England and not claiming historic separate nationality of their own.

Para 3. Self-explanatory.

Para 4. On pages 247-8 of *Peace by Ordeal* (Cape), by Frank (now Lord) Pakenham, there is a memorandum by Erskine Childers on the attractions of Canadian status being applied to the Irish question. It is evident from this particular heading that Collins had much the same idea in mind.

It was chiefly through the medium of these notes—though with the strongest possible inclination towards Dominion Status—that Collins interpreted his ideas at the conference table. He reasoned that the British would not accept a Republic and therefore he considered Dominion Status to be a not unsatisfactory alternative.

In a further document Collins noted that 'a certain state of lawlessness exists in the country', due 'to a sudden and complete reversal of affairs in the country following the Truce of July, 1921'. When he referred to 'certain elements', he meant those of the Volunteers who had lately fought the British, and who are now 'something of a disorganised force, in so much as they are the prey to any ideas, good or bad, exhibited by any leader or supposed leader'.[4] On the strength of such a statement, it can only be assumed that the people whom Collins had in mind were those whose intentions, according to Collins, were deliberately to stir up trouble, using the disorganized elements of the Volunteer Army for the purpose.

In a letter to O'Kane, dated November 4th, Collins stated:

> 'Not much achieved. Principally because P.M. [Lloyd George] recognises our over-riding difficulty—Dublin. Plays on that. On the other hand we fight every word, recognising that to betray ourselves because of the difficulty would mean disaster for us.
>
> G. [Griffith] said "What do we accept?"
>
> Indeed what do we accept? If we accept at all it will be inferred as a gross betrayal or a similar act of treachery.
>
> What have we come for? I ask myself that question a dozen times a day.
>
> Chamberlain says (on the 2nd) "Have we a meeting point, Mr. Collins?"
>
> Don't know why exactly but I don't like Chamberlain.
>
> From Dublin I don't know whether we're being instructed or confused. The latter I would say.'

Griffith complained strongly about the limitations being imposed on them from Dublin. He thought that chances of coming to any agreement were poor enough without these same chances being jeopardized by interference from Dublin. Collins was, of course, in full agreement with Griffith's point of view.

Griffith then put his views on paper and the five Irish delegates signed them.

> '. . . I have got a meeting of the delegates and secretaries. The delegates regard the first paragraph of your [de Valera's] letter

No. 7 as tying their hands in discussion and as inconsistent with the powers given them on their appointment and Nos. 1 and 2 of "Instructions to Plenipotentiaries from Cabinet" dated 7th October . . . We strongly resent, in the position in which we are placed, the interference with our powers. The responsibility, if this interference breaks the very slight possibility there is of settlement, will not and must not rest on the Plenipotentiaries. . . .'[5]

The problem of Dublin was indeed of major importance to Collins. In two further letters to O'Kane, dated 15th and 17th of November, he said:

'I do believe it is L/G's ambition to kill two birds with one stone (G. & me). If so, he didn't succeed. I looked at G. and he looked at me. We nodded and then plunged into the fray.

I prefer Birkenhead to anyone else. He understands and has real insight into our problems—the Dublin one as much as any other. Dublin is the real problem. They know what we are doing, but I don't know *exactly* the state of their activities.

No turning back now.'

And:

'G. was particularly dour today. He said to me—"You realise what we have on our hands?" I replied that I realised it long ago. He meant Dublin reaction to whatever happens here.

The thing is up and down, up and down—never steady.

G. is a good man. Only, I fear, much the worse for the strain of a life spent in toil and trouble.*

I reminded him of how when I was young I thought of him *as* Ireland. To which he replied—"We stand or fall in this together." It is the one bright hope of mine in all this welter of action and counter-action.'

Again, in a letter to O'Kane, written sometime in November, the Dublin subject was his prior thought—linked with the name of Erskine Childers (noted here by the capital letter 'C').

'Rather the years that have gone before with all their attendant risk than the atmosphere which is part of this conference. Who should one trust—even on my own side of the fence? Griffith. Beyond Griffith no one. As for C. it would be better that he

* During the conferences Griffith was in poor health.

led the delegation. He is sharp to realise how things will have due effect in Dublin—and acts accordingly.

To go for a drink is one thing. To be driven to it is another'.

Between the first and the last day of November Collins compiled a fair quantity of notes, in which he again stressed the importance of Dominion Status as being the best possible settlement.

'. . . On the level of that gained by Canada and South Africa.' He defined the status of Canada: '. . . Sir Robert Borden, in the Peace Treaty debate of September 2nd, 1919, claimed for Canada "complete sovereignty". This statement,' remarks Collins, 'has never been challenged by Britain. In fact it has been allowed by Bonar Law.'*

And, from the same debate, South Africa (statement by Smuts):

'". . . Secured a position of absolute equality and freedom, not only among the other States of the Empire, but among the other nations of the world."

Therefore [said Collins] the Dominions of the British Commonwealth are now free and secure in their freedom. This we should aim for in any treaty. We should, constitutionally, have the same equal, at least, as that of Canada. There are, of course, geographical differences. That should not make the slightest difference to security—national security.'[6]

When Collins noted that the outstanding point which concerned both Britain and Ireland was the Truce of July, 1921, he added:

'For even as we had almost reached the peak of our endeavour; world opinion regarding us was being forced on Britain. She had to recognise that fact. The terror which she created could not go on. It was never a great success, probably because it was mishandled. The idea of mixing Irish police, British ex-officers, the Military, and the "Black and Tans" would never work. It was probably the most quarrelsome force/forces ever to exist. Segregated, by us, the R.I.C. became a spent force—our pressure made it so. The Auxiliaries were little more than soldiers of fortune. The "B and T" a motley, lawless crowd. But the great danger was always the Military, probably because they chose to remain almost aloof from their mixed partners. The Military was an *organised* strength.

The British military men—Wilson for example—can never see eye to eye with the politicians. There is friction between Lloyd George and Wilson. Lloyd George calls it "the military mind".

* Bonar Law was a Canadian.

Friction and stupidity have been the main cause of the British losing foothold in Ireland. We applied the pressure in the proper places. Coupled with this is the fact that the British are in trouble in many other places apart from Ireland. But we are the chief problem child. World opinion has forced them to take the step of these conferences. They want to clear their name with the world.'[7]

Collins' worry regarding the 'Dublinites' (as he termed them) appeared to be justified by an incident which occurred during this month of November. On the 23rd a raid was carried out by Irish volunteers on the British Army barracks at Windsor. A Sergeant Roche of the Irish Guards was implicated. At once almost everyone fancied that Collins' scheming was behind the raid. This attitude is clearly typified by Field-Marshal Sir Henry Wilson. In his opinion, Collins was arranging for raids to be carried out during the period of the Truce, and while engaged in negotiations. Wilson noted that it would not have sounded well had the 'truth' leaked out, i.e., of Collins' supposed scheming. Apart from Wilson's incorrect assumption there was value in the fact that Collins was thought to be implicated—for such was the aim of the plotters in Dublin, headed by no less a person than Cathal Brugha.

Collins' reaction to it was immediate and it was also futile. He raged and he threatened. It is significant that one of the raiders, Michael Hogan, preferred to take his chance in a British court rather than face Collins' wrath.

But there was little that Collins could do for his hands were securely tied, the mesh of intrigue roped tightly about him.

Chapter 13

Treaty Discussions continued—Leadership of the Irish Delegation—The Oath and Ulster—Lloyd George Intrigues —Collins' Notes—The Collins-Griffith Memorandum

IT IS evident that the majority of the responsibility was on the shoulders of Griffith and Collins as being the main negotiators. It is further evident that from an unknown date Collins took on himself some of the decisions which would normally have fallen to Griffith as the Chairman of the delegation. In an undated letter to O'Kane, Collins said:

'G. and I had a lonely meeting—a house almost empty of customers—and talked and talked.

He confessed that he was far from well and asked me to assume leadership of our party, even if unofficial. He and I recognise that if such a thing were official it would provide bullets for the unmentionables.

I agreed. G. is in poor health and further burdens will do no more than grossly exaggerate his condition.'

If such a fact had been known by, for example, Cathal Brugha it would have been seized on by him as further 'evidence' against Collins, and the 'bullets' would have come thick and fast. As it was, Brugha looked on both Griffith and Collins as being, because of their opinions regarding what was best for Ireland in the way of an agreement, poor men for the job. So much is evident from Brugha's speech in the Dail on January 7th, 1922.*

But if the fact of Collins' unofficial leadership of the delegation was unknown in Dublin, it was guessed at by more than one member of the Irish party in London. Without the prior evidence of Collins' letter on the subject, the present writer was told by Mr. Sean MacBride, S.C., who was a minor official in the delegation party (and later Minister for External Affairs 1948-51), that in his opinion Collins was the real leader of the delegation. Equally, though, it is evident that Griffith was certainly the main influence on Collins and that many of the decisions made by Collins—unofficially, of course—were made after prior consultation with Griffith.

In this same letter to O'Kane Collins also said:

'We came to the topic for the thousandth time of the Dublinites. I have often said that Brugha commanded respect and I still say the same. I respect a fighter and B. is one. Only he is misguided. Yet even in enmity he is capable of sincerity—which is more than I can say of others.

I was warned more times than I can recall about the ONE. And when I was caught for this delegation my immediate thought was of how easily I had walked into the preparations. But having walked in I had to stay.

Read Tom Moore.'

Against George Gavan Duffy, Collins levelled a great deal of his wrath. He mentioned Duffy's 'smooth diplomacy' in such a way as to leave no one in doubt as to what he thought of 'smooth

* *See* p. 118.

diplomacy' and the person to whom the remark was addressed. In a letter to O'Kane, dated 24th November, 1921, he castigated Duffy in no uncertain terms.

> 'We had Duffy with us today. Birkenhead and Hewart opposite. It went fair, no more than that. If Duffy spent less time admiring his own voice we'd do better. Proof of it is when G. and I are together. You would appreciate the difference. . . .'

Two other incidents, one of which concerns Duffy, occurred about this time.

One afternoon Duffy and others were engaged in a game of bridge at Hans Place. To them came Collins in a towering rage. He burst into the room occupied by the bridge players, and proceeded to upbraid Duffy. What had happened was that Charlie McGuinness, captain of the arms-carrying ship the *Santa Maria*, had been arrested in the German port of Hamburg, on a charge of drunkenness. Collins attacked Duffy for sitting in Hans Place playing bridge while the *Santa Maria* was lying in Hamburg with a cargo of arms aboard her and in imminent danger of immediate discovery. In the end, Sean MacBride was sent, on Collins' instructions, to Hamburg. When he arrived there it was to find a watch being kept on the ship, but with the help of any amount of good luck the arms were transferred to another ship.[1]

The second incident was vouched for by Collins himself. He told the story to other members of the delegation party. He had, he said, just returned from a meeting with Lloyd George. He was with Lloyd George in a room on one wall of which there was a large map of the British Empire. 'He put his arm around my shoulder,' remarked Collins, 'at the same time pointing to the map, and said, "You're a capable man, Mick, supposing you help us." '[2]

From the moment of Collins telling this story a suspicion was formed in the minds of many of the delegation party that all was not well with the negotiations from the Irish point of view; but as Collins was so obviously aware of the character, personality and craft of the British Prime Minister it is not likely that he even considered for a second time the meaning behind the Prime Minister's approach.

There were two main obstacles to the furtherance of the discussions: (1) The Oath to the King, the form it should take; and (2) The question of the Six Counties (Northern Ireland). Of the two the latter was of paramount importance, involving the question of either a united or a divided Ireland.

It will be recalled that de Valera's aim in sending the delegation to London was to obtain from the British Government what he termed External Association. Collins, as will have been seen, was thinking along the lines of Dominion Status. Griffith, fully aware that neither a Republic nor de Valera's External Association idea could be got from the British, took the same line as Collins; indeed, it may be said that Collins took from Griffith's lead the line of Dominion Status. There was also a fourth element to be reckoned with: a 'rebel' movement within the Irish delegation party itself, headed by Robert Barton and seconded by Gavan Duffy. There is no doubt that the 'rebel' movement had no ulterior purpose in mind, no treachery that is, towards Collins and Griffith. The integrity and honesty of Robert Barton accounted for the split, for Barton was determined to keep in view the idea of a Republic for Ireland.

With this state of affairs there were bound to be weaknesses, and one, a particularly glaring example, became evident when the Irish delegation allowed itself to be fobbed off the important question of the Six Counties and a possibly united Ireland and, instead, to set itself in deep thought over the minor issue, by comparison, of the Oath to the King. Many writers of this period place the onus for this slip squarely on Griffith's shoulders, saying that he fell an easy victim to the wiles of Lloyd George and Thomas Jones; but, without doubt, others besides Griffith contributed, consciously or unconsciously, to this disastrous misunderstanding of a fundamental national ideal.

On the question of the Six Counties Collins wrote:

> '. . . Craig [Sir James Craig, Prime Minister of the Six County Cabinet] is the man of the moment. A wily bird—obviously. Said too much in the past. Afraid, I think, that Dev [de Valera] will out with it. Ireland is Ireland. Borderland is trouble and always will be.'[3]

The phrase which concerns de Valera is in connection with a former meeting between de Valera and Craig, at which Craig is supposed to have asked de Valera to become President of a United Ireland.*

A further note by Collins states:

* Quote from *Michael Collins and the Making of a New Ireland* (p. 225, Vol. II), by Major-General Piaras Beaslai: '. . . I was informed subsequently by the Dublin Brigadier that Sir James stated to him in conversation that he did not desire the partition of Ireland, and had come to Dublin to ask Mr. de Valera to become Prime Minister of a United Ireland. I repeat the statement for what it is worth.' (Quote by kind permission of Messrs. George G. Harrap, publishers of *Michael Collins and the Making of a New Ireland*.

'The Six Counties are held in sway not by any patriotic alliance towards England. Scottish element in population and money interests account to a large extent for the supposed allegiance.

Craig will have it otherwise.

The religious question has a great bearing on events and decisions. Protestant element is in force. Catholic population subdued.'[4]

It may be remarked here that even today (1958) there is a great deal of factual substance in what Collins wrote in 1921. It is yet another fact that in certain counties a minority Tory control is exercised over a Nationalist majority. The manipulation of the constituency boundaries ensures this, the city of Derry being a particularly appropriate example.

It was at this point, on the question of the Six Counties and a United Ireland, that Lloyd George in collaboration with the ever-faithful Thomas Jones, conceived a political manœuvre of far-reaching consequence. Jones told Griffith that Lloyd George was about to propose to the Six Counties Government that they should accept the Six Counties area under an All-Ireland Parliament and, if they refused, that he, Lloyd George, would announce his resignation, along with, Jones supposed, Chamberlain and Birkenhead. The outcome of this would be that Bonar Law would form a militarist government against Ireland. But why not, said Lloyd George, instead of the resignations and the militarist government, think over a plan which he had worked out, to the effect that the new powers under discussion would be given to the Irish, and that the Six Counties should be subjected to a Boundary Commission to delimit her area. It would thus give back to the South 'most of Tyrone and Fermanagh and part of Armagh, Derry, Down, etc.'.* The immediate effect of this manœuvre was that Griffith turned his antagonism of Britain onto the Six Counties Government and in particular onto Sir James Craig.[5] But the manœuvre had also more serious and far-reaching effects on the status of the South.

Speaking in condemnation of the Partition Act of 1920, the British ex-Premier Asquith said:

'With six you have a majority which will enable you to defeat union . . . with the result the hon. and gallant member [Captain Craig] gloats over that they will always have a majority and be able to defeat permanently a union between the two Parliaments and the demand for a single Parliament for Ireland.'[6]

* Griffith's quote.

As early as 1916 (29th May) Lloyd George had been engaged in a particularly obnoxious piece of double-crossing regarding the Six Counties and the South. In a letter to Sir Edward Carson, he stated: 'We must make it clear that at the end of the provisional period Ulster does not, whether she wills it or not, merge in the rest of Ireland.' He added a footnote: 'Will you show it [a draft proposition by Greer] to Craig?'[7]

Yet in this same week, Lloyd George handed his proposals to John Redmond, leader of the Irish Parliamentary Party, and at the same time gave him a pledge that there would be no permanent partition of Ireland.[8]

From Cadogan Gardens, Collins wrote to O'Kane on November 29th, 1921:

> 'More and more the responsibility rests with me. What responsibility it is.
>
> I find the strain of looking into Chamberlain's false eye [he wore a monocle] the most nervy of all my experiences. Birkenhead sees this—smiles and shrugs his shoulders.'

And on the 30th:

> 'The only names worth considering after this will be the names of those who have kept away from London.
>
> Integrity of purpose is defeated at all times by those whose star rests elsewhere. The advice and inspiration of C. [Childers] is like farmland under water—dead. With a purpose, I think—with a definite purpose. Soon he will howl his triumph—for what it is worth.
>
> I think also that Birkenhead's integrity of purpose is foiled in other quarters. I can almost see the gloating that is so obvious among some of our opposites—whichever way it means trouble at home, an enjoyable spectacle for more people than one imagines.'

The great difficulty in regard to the notes—as distinct from the letters—is in attempting to date them. As none bear any date, it is only possible to give approximately the dates when they were written, using as a rough guide the matter contained in them. Thus it is possible, because of a footnote to the following note, '9 30 a.m. L/G', to date this as being written on or about the 4th December. It contains matter relating to Dominion Status, the Oath, and the granting of facilities to the British.

'(1) Achievement of Dominion Status will be to a large extent beneficial to us.

(1a) I do not look on the above as being anywhere near a finalised solution. It is the first step. More than this could not be expected. [This note is heavily underlined throughout.]

(2) The Oath is the greatest difficulty. In achieving Dominion Status there is bound to be an oath of some description towards the so-called Mother Country.

(3) The same must apply to such things as harbour facilities, aerodromes, and so on. It is only a mere temporary penalty for so much gained.

The Oath is the worrying point. Adjustment of wording—text reviewed. Otherwise . . .'[9]

Next come two notes so closely allied in content as to be identified almost as one. They were evidently written towards the end of the negotiations, when a possible treaty was in sight, hence Collins' observations as to possible repercussions in Ireland.

'(I) The Treaty will not be accepted in Dublin—not by those who have in mind personal ambitions under pretence of patriotism.

(II) Am confident of achieving a victory by election. Pro-Treaty element could be 55-60% of all concerned. (G. questions this because of what may have happened during our absence.)

(III) Anti-Treaty element will possibly enlist aid of Volunteers disgruntled by present state of affairs—quiet after storm.

(IV) Believe that majority of people will welcome Treaty. There will be some suspicion, however, regarding oath.'[10]

The second note reads:

'I am never of the opinion that the majority of the Irish people will be against such a Treaty as we have in mind.

It is a question of the greater influence—de Valera will command, I think, a large part of what was formerly the Volunteer Organisation.

Dail E. will, I think, back a Treaty—to a large extent. Women danger in Dail E.'[11]

There follows a list of those whom Collins considered would vote in favour of the Treaty which 'we have in mind'. In this list Collins made two wrong assessments: those of Con Collins and

Harry Boland, both of whom subsequently voted against acceptance of the Treaty.

On a sheet of blue paper there are four headings, but no observations.

> 'Repayment of Loan.
> Stabilised army.
> Education problem.
> Industry.'[12]

Next, on a separate sheet of paper, are several observations referring to the state of the country in case of 'friction' caused by the signing of a treaty. These notes were evidently made as the negotiations were nearing an end.

> 'Need for great care in dealing with any possible attempt to disrupt Government. Country forced to go one way or the other in the event of possible friction. Offenders must, as far as is possible, be allowed certain rights of speech.
>
> Too much authority in the hands of local commanders—more used to harsh dealings.
>
> Situation could be extremely dangerous.
>
> Discussed with G.'[13]

The opinions of both Collins and Griffith are plainly expressed in the following memorandum. When the discussion took place it is not possible to say. The document is in typescript and each paper is initialled by Griffith and Collins, but there is no date to the document.

> 'M.C.: "What will be the outcome if the present talks break down. (1) A declaration of war by the British. (2) Cessation of hostilities on our part. We have, mistakenly, put all our cards on the table; we have laid ourselves open to the British. (3) Perhaps a continuation of efforts by the British to find a solution. This because world opinion is with us—proving that the British dare not engage us in full-scale war."
>
> Comment by A.G.: "No declaration of war by the British. Point number three is the most likely."
>
> M.C.: "How best to reconcile our ideas with the fixed ideas at present held by certain members of the Cabinet? I will not agree to anything which threatens to plunge the people of Ireland into a war—not without their authority. Still less do I agree to being dictated to by those not embroiled in these negotiations. If they are not in agreement with the steps which we are taking, and

hope to take, why then did they themselves not consider their own presence here in London? Example: Brugha refused to be a member of this delegation."

Comment by Griffith: "It is not so much a question of whom dictating to whom. It is a question of the powers invested in us as representatives of our country. Sooner or later a decision will have to be made."

Comment by Collins: "Exactly. What are our powers? Are we to commit our country one way or the other, yet without authority to do so?"

M.C.: "The advantages of Dominion Status, to us, as a stepping stone to complete independence are immeasurable."

Comment by Griffith: "Agreed. But with one question. How far can we trust the signatures of the British delegation in this matter? Once signed we are committed. But are they?"

M.C.: "No, we are not committed—not until both the Dail and Westminster ratify whatever agreement is made."

Comment by Griffith: "Ratification by the Dail means what precisely? That a certain amount of power is still in the hands of those whom we know will be against anything which treats of Empire Status."

M.C.: "I agree in part to the above. Supposing, however, we were to go back to Dublin tomorrow with a document which gave us a Republic. Would such a document find favour with everyone? I doubt it."

Comment by Griffith: "So do I. But sooner or later a decision will have to be made and we shall have to make it—whatever our position and our authority." '[14]

Griffith's comment 'sooner or later a decision will have to be made' finds an answering echo in this letter which Collins wrote to O'Kane on the 1st December, 1921.

'Things are working up to a pitch. Lloyd George was too preoccupied for my liking today. Didn't seem to take much notice of what was being said.

I'll give you a forecast—something definite before the 6th. And where shall I be? Dead and numb or half-dead already by then.

As a child I wanted things and had ambition for them. Now I have them, but not for long.

Whichever way it goes L/G won't lose. "Got my political life at stake," he confided. I didn't answer him. My life—not only political—is at stake.'

Chapter 14

Treaty Discussions continued—Cabinet Meeting of 3rd December—Return to London—Stalemate—The Final Meetings—The Treaty Signed

APART from the early hours of the 6th December when the Treaty was signed, the most important meetings took place in Dublin on the 3rd December. More than thirty-five years later the facts of these meetings have still not been properly revealed or assessed; and yet the implications arising from them were many, and the troubles which followed spread a wake of disaster.

The meetings were attended by members of the Cabinet of Dail Eireann and members of the Irish delegation. Present were: President Eamon de Valera, Arthur Griffith, Michael Collins, Cathal Brugha, Austin Stack, William Cosgrave, George Gavan Duffy, Eamonn Duggan, Robert Barton, Erskine Childers, Kevin O'Higgins, and Colm O Murchadha.[1]

So far as the delegation were concerned, the British had put down the bar on complete independence, on an Irish Republic or External Association. They would, however, concede Dominion Status, with the police, army, and the legislature in the hands of the Irish. On the point of Griffith attempting to barter External Association for a United Ireland, de Valera agreed, but went on to complain that he got neither one nor the other.[2]

The following is a record of the meetings as noted by Colm O Murchadha:

'MEETING OF CABINET AND DELEGATION

3rd December, 1921

Views of the Delegates.

(a) Mr. Griffith in favour of Treaty. Refused to break on question of Crown and thereby hand to Ulster the position from which she had been driven.

(b) Mr. Barton of opinion that England's last word had not been reached and that she could not declare war on question of Allegiance. The Treaty would not give Dominion Status nor any guarantee re Ulster. Would vote against acceptance.

(c) Mr. Gavan Duffy agreed with Mr. Barton that England was bluffing and that the Irish proposals, with small reservations of Defence, etc., could be obtained. Would like the Treaty to be rejected by An Dail and sent back amended. Said 'No' definitely to Treaty.

(d) Mr. Duggan agreed with Mr. Griffith. Believed Treaty to be England's last word and would not take responsibility of saying "No".

(e) Mr. Collins was in substantial agreement with Messrs. Griffith and Duggan. The non-acceptance of Treaty would be a gamble as England could arrange war in Ireland within a week. Sacrifice to N.E. Ulster made for the sake of essential unity and justified. With pressure further concessions could be obtained on Trade and Defence. Oath of Allegiance would not come into force for 12 months—question was, therefore, would it be worthwhile taking 12 months and seeing how it would work. Would recommend that Dail go to country on Treaty, but would recommend non-acceptance of Oath.

(f) Mr. Childers of opinion that par 6 of Treaty would give Ireland no national status. Sec 7 (b) was important also as it meant that when England went to war she would bring Ireland with her.

(g) In reply to a question by Minister of Defence [Cathal Brugha] as to who was responsible for the splitting of the Delegation so that two members (Messrs. Griffith and Collins) did most of the work and that the other members were not in possession of full information it was stated that the British Government was responsible for the arrangement but it had the approval of the whole Delegation.

The Minister of Defence here remarked that the British Government selected its men.

On the motion of Mr. Griffith this remark was withdrawn.

Meeting of Cabinet

3rd December, 1921

(a) In the course of a lengthy discussion on the Treaty the President gave it as his opinion that it could not be accepted in its then form. He personally could not subscribe to the Oath of Allegiance nor could he sign any document which would give N.E. Ulster power to vote itself out of the Irish State. With modifications, however, it might be accepted honourably, and he would like to see the plenipotentiaries go back and secure peace if possible. He believed the Delegates had done their utmost and that it now remained to them to show that if document not amended that they were prepared to face the consequences—war or no war. He would deal with present document exactly as with that of 20th July—say it cannot be accepted and put up counter proposals.

(b) Mr. Griffith did not like the document but did not think it dishonourable. It would practically recognise the Republic and the first allegiance would be to Ireland. If it were rejected the people would be entitled to know what the alternative is. The country would not fight on the question of allegiance and there would be a split. He would not recommend the Government to accept but would say that the plenipotentiaries should sign and leave it to the President and Dail to reject.

(c) The Minister for Defence was in perfect agreement with the President, the only matter upon which he could disagree would be the question of recognising the King of England as Head of the Associated States.

Meeting of Cabinet and Delegation

3rd December, 1921 (Resumed)

(a) Mr. Griffith would not take the responsibility of breaking on the Crown. When as many concessions as possible conceded, and accepted by Craig, he would go before the Dail. The Dail was the body to decide for or against war.

(b) The President took his stand upon last Irish proposals which meant external connection with the Crown. He suggested the following amendment to the Oath of Allegiance:

"I . . . do solemnly swear true faith and allegiance to the constitution of the Irish Free State, to the Treaty of Association and to recognise the King of Great Britain as head of the Associated States."

(c) Delegates to carry out their original instructions with same powers.

(d) Delegation to return and say that Cabinet won't accept Oath of Allegiance if not amended and to face the consequences, assuming that England will declare war.

(e) Decided unanimously that the present Oath of Allegiance could not be subscribed to.

(f) Mr. Griffith to inform Mr. Lloyd George that the document could not be signed, to state that it is now a matter for the Dail, and to try and put the blame on Ulster.

(g) On a majority vote it was decided that the Delegation be empowered to meet Sir James Craig if they should think necessary. The following voted for and against:

For: President, Finance, Foreign Affairs, Economics, and Local Government.

Against: Defence and Home Affairs.

Colm O Murchadha,
ar son Runai na hAireachta."[3]

So far as Collins and Griffith were concerned the meetings had achieved no definite purpose in the way of enlightening them. To Tom Cullen, who drove him to the docks, Collins complained bitterly of the way he was being treated. 'I've been there all day and I can't get them to say Yes or No, whether we should sign or not.'[4] It recalled to his mind a phrase he had used to O'Kane, 'From Dublin I don't know whether we're being instructed or confused.'*

On their arrival in London it soon became evident that the delegation as a whole was confused in regard to its instructions. Barton and Duffy were convinced that the Cabinet wanted another attempt at External Association, while Collins and Griffith were equally convinced that such was not the decision of the Cabinet. Duffy, Barton, and Childers then drafted a memorandum of counter-proposals, the leading heads of which had been placed before some of the British delegation on a previous occasion. It was stated by Duffy, Barton, and Childers that this memorandum faithfully described the impression arrived at during the Cabinet meetings.

At once Collins, Griffith, and Duggan refused to present it. It was for those who wanted a breakdown in the negotiations to present it, they said. Barton, on behalf of Duffy and himself, accepted the challenge, and they were then joined by Griffith, who, by accompanying them, hoped to be able to prevent a break with the British at this stage.

The situation for the Irishmen was little short of disaster. Not only were they embroiled in the mesh of the intrigue spread about them by Lloyd George and Thomas Jones but they were now, within one day in time of the signing of a vital treaty, a delegation openly split into two camps, arguing, wrangling, uncertain of what to take as the next step. It is little wonder that the situation between the two delegations resulted in a complete breakdown.

On Collins, the military man turned politician, the sense of responsibility weighed heavily. It was with good reason that he

* *See* p. 132.

considered, as he had done at the commencement of the negotiations, that he had been ensnared and that however much he threshed about he could not loosen the grip around him. On him rested the main weight of a terrible burden.

In a diary, under date Monday, December 5th, Collins records that Jones came to see him.

> 'Jones to see me. Subject: Enlarging of ours by inclusion of most of Fermanagh and Tyrone-Boundary Commission?'[5]

Significantly, the entry is followed by a question mark, as if to indicate Collins' doubt of the offer as being a genuine one—as well he might in view of the final decisions.

With the situation at a stalemate, Lloyd George asked for an interview with Collins. Collins, desperate for a solution to the whole unhappy business, agreed to a meeting. From the beginning he had been against External Association; now he fully realized that it was the bar against any possible agreement.

On the question of the Oath, Defence, and Fiscal Autonomy, the British would negotiate. That, at least, was so much gained.

A direct result of the meeting between Collins and Lloyd George was that it paved the way for a further meeting at 3 p.m. on December 5th.

The three things of major importance to emerge from the 3 p.m. meeting were the agreed (between Collins and Birkenhead) new formula for the Oath, a memorandum which Lloyd George produced (and on which he maintained Griffith was letting him down), and a supposed threat of immediate and terrible war delivered by Lloyd George. A brief examination of the history of the memorandum which Lloyd George produced provides some evidence of the wiliness of the British Prime Minister and Thomas Jones.

At a private meeting on November 12th at Park Lane between Thomas Jones and Griffith, the latter made a promise. Later, Jones enlarged the theme of Griffith's promise, had it typed, and on the following day presented it to Griffith. Griffith, under the impression that it was a manœuvre to corner the Ulster leaders, glanced over it and signed it.[6] And on the 5th December, much to the surprise of both Collins and Barton, Lloyd George flourished the document in front of the three men.

It is said that, faced with his own signature on the document, 'Griffith broke'—in other words, he gave up the fight. In fact, although the document held Griffith personally to a pledge, it did not concern any other individual of the Irish delegation; though even so, Griffith could well have countered Lloyd George by arguing that a pledge given in one set of circumstances did not hold good in another.

The prelude to the signing of the Anglo-Irish Treaty created then, and still goes on creating, more mistaken impressions than one could possibly imagine as coming from a room in which seven men were seated. The occupants of the room, Prime Minister Lloyd George, Sir Austen Chamberlain, Lord Birkenhead, and Winston Churchill representing Great Britain, and Arthur Griffith, Michael Collins, and Robert Barton representing Ireland, will go down in history not so much for the agreement which they made—and which brought to an end more than seven hundred years of strife—as for the legends which they created which run contrary to one another.

The most vital point of all, around which most of the argument rotates, is whether the Irish delegation was actually threatened, by Lloyd George, with 'immediate and terrible war' in the event of no agreement being reached.

Collins later stated:

> 'It has been said that the Treaty was signed under a threat of immediate and terrible war. The position never appeared to me to be that. I did not sign the Treaty under duress except in the sense that the position as between Ireland and England, historically, and because of superior forces on the part of England, has always been one of duress. The element of duress was present when we agreed to the Truce . . . but there was not and could not have been any personal duress. Again the threat of immediate and terrible war did not matter overmuch to me. The position appeared to be then exactly as it appears now [February 6th, 1922]. The British would not, I think, have declared terrible and immediate war upon us.'[7]

Barton said:

> 'Lloyd George stated that he had always taken it that Arthur Griffith spoke for the delegation, and that we were all plenipotentiaries, and that now it was a matter of peace or war, and we must each of us make up our minds. He required that every Delegate should sign the document, and recommend it, or there was no agreement. He said that they as a body had hazarded their political future, and we must do likewise and take the same risks. At one time he particularly addressed himself to me, and said very solemnly that those who were not for peace must take

the full responsibility for the war that would immediately follow refusal by any delegate to sign the Articles of Agreement.'*

Duggan said:

'On that last Monday night we in London got two hours to give a "Yes" or "No" answer. . . . If we had given the answer "No" that night, and if this country was now in the throes of war, it would be no answer for us to come back to the country and say "We had to do it because the Cabinet told us to come back and do it" . . .'[8]

Duffy said:

'Our delegates returned to inform us that four times they had all but broken and that the fate of Ireland had to be decided that night. Lloyd George had issued to them an ultimatum . . . "if it be a rupture, you shall have immediate war". . . . Again the ultimatum might have been bluff, but everyone of those who had heard the British Prime Minister believed beyond all reasonable doubt that this time he was not play acting, and that he meant what he said.'[9]

The phrase used by Duffy '. . . everyone of those who had heard the British Prime Minister believed beyond all reasonable doubt that this time he was not play acting, and that he meant what he said' is not a convincing statement because, as will have already been noted, Collins did not think so, and Collins was present at the time, while Duffy and Duggan were not.

Duffy repeated much the same opinion in a letter to Sean T. O'Kelly, written on the day on which the Treaty was signed. He speaks of 'terrible pressure' being brought to bear against them; and he ended the letter: 'All the most substantial concessions were made in the last 2 days. Then came the "coup de theatre".'[10]

It has been stated to the writer that Collins, because he signed an agreement which accepted Dominion Status, was a traitor to his country. But when Collins said that they, in his opinion, were not threatened with immediate and terrible war, there is a ring of truth about that statement, inasmuch as Collins, to alleviate the distress of mind to which he was shortly to be subjected, could so easily have agreed with those who maintained that they were threatened.

At the request of Arthur Griffith, Robert Barton took a record of the proceedings of the two conferences, at 3 p.m. and at 11.30

* Robert Barton's notes; *see* Appendix D.

p.m. Above all things Barton was, in the matter of these notes, fastidious to the point of painstakingly recording movement as well as speech. So that the document (*see* Appendix D) has about it an air of finality. The only thing remaining, then, is the individual way in which the document is interpreted and there lies the root of the whole argument.

So far as Griffith is concerned—and one may also perhaps include Collins in this—the matter was settled at the 3 p.m. meeting. Barton states: 'Arthur Griffith agreed that he personally would sign the Treaty. . . .' And Barton goes on to say:

> 'Considerable discussion took place here on the justice of our being asked to agree or disagree before Craig replied and Arthur Griffith made repeated efforts to avoid the question being put to Michael Collins and myself. Lloyd George stated that he had always taken it that Arthur Griffith spoke for the Delegation, and that we were all plenipotentiaries and that it was now a matter of peace or war and we must each make up our minds . . . he would have to have our agreement or refusal to the proposals by 10 p.m. that evening. . . .'

On that practical note, more or less, the delegation dismissed.

What had taken place at Downing Street was like the distant growling of thunder when compared to the storm which raged among the Irish delegation at Hans Place. Lloyd George had stipulated 10 p.m. as the time for a final answer, Yes or No; but it was turned 11 p.m. when the Irish delegation returned to Downing Street. The time spent in argument—quarrel would perhaps be a more suitable word—at Hans Place had proved to be a period of great anguish and stress.

There was the spectacle of Griffith and Collins prepared to sign. There was the sight of Barton and Duffy trying to discourage them. There was Eamonn Duggan overcome by the memory of the hangman at Mountjoy Jail—a broken man, prepared, one is driven to think, into signing anything so long as that memory was erased. As certainly as the crack had first appeared in the Irish camp, it widened that night into a split which was destined to yawn even wider in the country of Ireland.

Finally, Griffith, Collins, and Barton returned to Downing Street, and there in his own peculiar cold and formal manner Griffith announced their willingness to sign. As Barton put it:

> 'Lloyd George then asked whether we as a Delegation were prepared to accept these Articles of Agreement and to stand by

them in our Parliament as they as a Delegation would stand by them in theirs. Arthur Griffith replied "We do."'

It seemed, however, that when Griffith returned to Hans Place his iron nerve deserted him. Coffee had been prepared for the returning delegation; but Griffith ignored all pleas to eat or at least drink. Instead, he spent the remainder of the night walking up and down the hall-way, head in hands.[11]

On the day of the signing, December 6th, 1921, Collins wrote O'Kane the following letter:

> 'When you have sweated, toiled, had mad dreams, hopeless nightmares, you find yourself in London's streets, cold and dank in the night air.
>
> Think—what have I got for Ireland? Something which she has wanted these past seven hundred years. Will anyone be satisfied at the bargain? Will anyone? I tell you this—early this morning I signed my death warrant. I thought at the time how odd, how ridiculous—a bullet may just as well have done the job five years ago.
>
> I believe Birkenhead may have said an end to his political life. With him it has been my honour to work.
>
> These signatures are the first real step for Ireland. If people will only remember that—the first real step.
>
> M.'

It may be said here that Birkenhead, later, survived the attacks of the debaters in the Westminster Parliament. But Collins had left London for Dublin to face what was to be the stormiest period of his whole career.

Chapter 15

Terms of the Treaty—Cabinet Meeting—The Beginning of the 'Split'—The Question of Partition

IN GIVING to the country of Ireland practically the same status as that of Canada, Australia, New Zealand and South Africa, the Treaty thus ensured that the aims of the Emancipation Movement of the 1820's, the Repeal Movement of the 1840's, and the Home Rule agitation in the 1870's and after had been fully recognized and catered for.* What the people wanted, and had wanted, was to be found in the Articles of Agreement: full self-government, cessation of the rule long held by Dublin Castle, withdrawal of the 'red coats and the black police', and democratic power in their own country. The Treaty gave to them virtual independence on all matters of practical government, full control of most of the territory and its resources, an independent Parliament with an Executive responsible to it, and the new title Irish Free State.

In return, it had to accept a Governor-General, give the British certain harbour facilities at Berehaven, Queenstown (now Cobh), Belfast Lough and Lough Swilly, and in time of war to give such other harbour facilities as might be required by the British 'for the purposes of defence'. The Six Counties had a month after ratification of the agreement in which to decide whether to be incorporated as part of a United Ireland, or to remain as part of the United Kingdom. If their decision was to remain with the United Kingdom, a Boundary Commission would then be set up to decide the territory which properly belonged to them.

Such were the measures afforded by the Treaty to the people of a once oppressed land.

This was the Treaty which Eamon de Valera brushed aside when it was handed to him by Eamonn Duggan at the Mansion House, where de Valera was speaking at the Dante Centenary Celebrations.[1] And his attitude to it summed up the opinions of a great many of the Irish race. There was very little shouting at this time about the lack of a Republic and very little said about External Association. The two salient points were the Oath and the exclusion of Ulster. Later, these two points were to be excluded from de Valera's anti-Treaty repertoire, and, instead, one single phrase in the Oath was to be his point of condemnation. It was as Collins had said, whatever was brought back it would be condemned.

De Valera ordered the delegation back for a Cabinet meeting to be held on the Thursday '. . . to consider the circumstance under which the plenipotentiaries had signed the Agreement in London'.[2] The terms of the summons, Desmond Fitzgerald suggested, read as if he (de Valera) were opposed to the Treaty. To which de

* The Emancipation Movement in the 1820's was a purely Catholic movement; it may have had political undertones but its aims were not primarily political. The Treaty, in fact, conceded more than either the Repeal Movement or the Home Rule Movement sought and it would probably be more true to say that the aims of the physical force movements of the nineteenth century came nearer to realization by it —indeed, many of those (including Pearse and, indeed, the I.R.B. of the 1900's) associated with the physical force movement would have been highly satisfied (at least for a while) with the status the Treaty conferred on Ireland had that status been granted earlier.

Valera replied that it was the way he intended it to be read and it should be published as such.[3]

The Cabinet meeting achieved no more than Collins had for a long time been forecasting: that de Valera, Brugha and Stack were in league against Griffith and himself, himself principally. The vote finally proved it: For: Collins, Griffith, Cosgrave, and Barton; Against: de Valera, Brugha, and Stack. Even so, the victory of the pro-Treaty members of the Cabinet was won on the narrow majority of a reluctant voter, Robert Barton.

Immediately following the Cabinet meeting, de Valera issued a statement which was, even to the most indifferent of men, in furtherance of one point: that of expressing in the most appropriate terms his condemnation of the Treaty.*

Whereas the press generally was in favour of the Treaty, a large section of the population was definitely against it—a good many of them being brought under the 'anti' banner by de Valera's statement. Generally, the younger men among the 'anti' brigade were against the Oath, the older people condemning the exclusion of Ulster, while a group of the Volunteers, headed by Rory O'Connor, formerly Director of Engineering in G.H.Q., said they would never yield allegiance. The women—again as Collins had forecasted—were in the picture in a big way and predominantly anti-Treaty, going about questioning the Volunteers as to whether they were 'cowards' and 'traitors'.

Yet, significantly, the Council of County Clare, de Valera's own constituents, voted by seventeen to five in favour of the Treaty.

> '. . . The people of Clare consider that the Treaty gives us the substance of independence, that it will lead inevitably and within a short period, to the complete fulfilment of our national aspirations; and, therefore, believe that the Treaty should be ratified . . . de Valera to use his immense influence and political capacity for the maintenance of national unity.'[4]

But against this must be measured the fact that Collins' own constituents of West Cork were against the Treaty 'almost to a man'.

Such was the condition of the country; the explosive needing

* (Extract) 'A Chairde Gaedheal, You have seen in the public press the text of the proposed Treaty with Great Britain.
The terms of this Agreement are in violent conflict with the wishes of the majority of this nation as expressed freely in successive elections during the past three years.
I feel it my duty to inform you immediately that I cannot recommend the acceptance of this Treaty either to Dail Eireann or to the country. In this attitude I am supported by the Ministers for Home Affairs and Defence. . . .' (MacArdle: *The Irish Republic*, p. 618.)

only a match to set the whole ablaze. Probably the one element to turn a cold shoulder to the fury was the Irish Republican Brotherhood. In this time of crisis—as in all others—it issued a statement:

> 'The Supreme Council has considered the present situation, and, while it is of the opinion that it is to Ireland's interest that the Treaty should be passed, in the circumstances it makes no Order, but leaves every member free to vote and act according to his conscience.'[5]

For Collins the division was a tragedy too deep for words, and its effect upon him was instantaneous. There were friends whom he loved and who had fought alongside him prior to the Truce; and now they deserted him. It is recorded that he went to visit an old friend, Batt O'Connor, and that he stood hesitating on the doorstep, unsure of the welcome that awaited him.[6] As it turned out, O'Connor's welcome was full of the warmth of former days, but the hesitancy of Collins is proof enough that he no longer knew friend from foe. By one his friendship was rejected, by another he was greeted with outstretched hand.

For Collins, loyalty was the greatest thing in his life, and loyalty to old friends in particular. It was at once his greatest strength and his greatest weakness; and soon the latter was to lead him far from the path taken by many of those who were still his friends. But at this time he seemed incapable of coming to any definite orderly state of mind; his whole being appeared to be wrapped in a cloud of despondency, as the tragedy deepened from day to day. While various of his notes and letters of the London Treaty period indicate that he was fully aware of what would be the outcome of the agreement, the later actuality of the tragedy struck him with considerable force.

Even now, a few days after his return from London, he could foresee the way events were moving and he silently grieved that the main force behind the movement to break the agreement was the personality of de Valera. In two statements, de Valera made his position obvious. In the first, the statement made directly after the Cabinet meeting, he said:

> 'The greatest test of our people has come. Let us face it worthily, without bitterness and above all without recriminations. There is a definite constitutional way of resolving our political differences—let us not depart from it. . . .'[7]

Yet, on the 27th December—a matter of a few days later—he could write:

> 'I have been tempted several times to take drastic action, as I would be entitled legally, but then the army is divided and the people wouldn't stand for it, and nobody but the enemy would win if I took it.'[8]

It may be asked: what exactly did de Valera imply in the use of the words 'drastic action'? And in what way was he legally entitled to take it?

A factor greater than all was the influence which de Valera possessed over a large mass of the population, including a certain section of the Volunteers, whom he found so ready to carry out his every whim and wish. The fact is that, since Collins' absence in London, the Volunteers had degenerated from the finely disciplined fighting force which they formerly were. It is perhaps understandable that these same men, young lads many of them, could not settle to the dull routine of 'peace-time' soldiering, following the Truce. They were the acknowledged heroes, their deeds were legion—hence the lack of discipline when they thought such a thing was hardly necessary.

One of the points which Collins had put forward against his going to London was that the army needed a strong hand in control and it was he, obviously, who had the power to control it; and his absence, coupled with the fact that Cathal Brugha had thought of it as being an appropriate time to 'reorganize' the army, was sufficient reason for finding a large section of the Volunteers such pliable material for de Valera to mould.

One more reason which accounted for the indiscipline was that a fair number of the army men at this time were new recruits—'sunshine soldiers' Collins called them—men who had kept out of the way during the fighting, but who were willing enough now to reap the price of glory.

It was, however, mainly the section of the Volunteers whom Rory O'Connor had aroused who were, as Collins put it, 'spoiling for a fight'.

In much the same fashion it was happening all over the country; it all depended on whether the local commander was pro- or anti-Treaty. The devil controlled the discipline, if one can apply the term to the disorganization of the separate elements.

It is worth noting at this stage one peculiarity regarding the attacks on the Treaty. It concerns Partition—the possibility of it, the 'one real blot' on the Treaty, as the late P. S. O'Hegarty remarked. In all the attacks on the Treaty very little was said about Partition. The explanation is a simple one,* given by Sean O'Muirthile to O'Hegarty and in the presence of Collins. Partition, said O'Muirthile to O'Hegarty, '. . . is provided for. . . . Before they signed, Griffith and Collins got a personal undertaking from Smith [Birkenhead] and Churchill that if Ulster opted out they would get only four counties and that THEY would make a four-county government impossible.' O'Hegarty looked up at Collins, and he grinned and said: 'That's right.'[9]

As things turned out later, however, the Birkenhead-Churchill undertaking was conveniently found to be impossible, or was deliberately ignored.

Chapter 16

Dail Debates the Treaty—Document No. 2—Dail Accepts the Treaty—de Valera Resigns—Griffith Elected as President —Collins as Chairman of the Provisional Government

ON WEDNESDAY, December 14th, 1921, the Dail assembled at University College, Dublin, to discuss and arrive at a conclusion, ratification or otherwise, of the Treaty recently signed in London. In all there were twelve sittings in public, the final one being held on Tuesday, January 10th, 1922.

During this time two important measures were put to the vote and carried: (1) Ratification by the Dail of the Treaty, by sixty-four votes to fifty-seven, on January 7th, 1922; and (2) the election of Arthur Griffith to the Presidency of Dail Eireann, on January 10th, 1922, by a unanimous vote of those who remained after de Valera and his supporters had left the chamber in protest.

To attempt a composite picture of the twelve sittings is virtually an impossibility. They were particularly distinguished by the full range of human passion; by allowances on the part of the Speaker, Eoin MacNeill, which enabled the debaters to wander far from the issue under discussion and to allow two, sometimes more, points to be under discussion at the same time. On occasion the debate lowered itself to the level of personalities—which were not the issue at stake. In the main, the culprits were the women members, all of whom were against ratification of the Treaty.

* While the explanation is, to a certain extent, satisfactory, it does not explain the blindness of the anti-Treaty party in attacking the agreement on the basis of the Oath almost entirely to the exclusion of the really important matter of Northern Ireland. For the Oath was, in the final analysis, a mere quibble; whereas the Partition issue was of real importance.

One of the more extraordinary things to emerge from these twelve days of occasional drama and often stupefying boredom was that Collins the politician—a status completely divorced from his natural inclination, and one in which he was inexorably placed—emerged triumphant from the debate, and more, he proved himself the equal of any practised politician there.

From the very outset it was obvious that Collins was to become the main target of the anti-Treaty group, much as the emphasis was placed on the Treaty issue; and indeed the final vote was largely cast around the love or hatred of Collins by the various Deputies.

Throughout it all he preserved a remarkable bearing of calm perseverance yet showed on occasion the sudden flash of fire and fierce energy for the task in hand. He reminded the deputies that punctuality was a great thing when late attendances threatened to upset the day's programme. It was further typical of the man that he did not wait to be attacked, but, early on in the debate, assumed the attitude of attacker.

It was evident from the first session that the threatened split of opinion throughout the country was to become a fact before the sessions ended.

Little time elapsed before two points were being argued at the same time: the terms of reference and the matter of a secret session. De Valera's opening speech concerned the terms of reference (the credentials and authority) with which the Irish delegation proceeded to London for the discussions. 'Here,' stated de Valera, 'is the actual text of the instructions which I wrote with my own hand at the Cabinet meeting of the 7th October, 1921:

> "(1) The Plenipotentiaries have full powers as defined in their credentials.
>
> (2) It is understood before decisions are finally reached on a main question, that a despatch notifying the intention to make these decisions will be sent to members of the Cabinet in Dublin, and that a reply will be awaited by the Plenipotentiaries before final decision is made.
>
> (3) It is also understood that the complete text of the draft treaty about to be signed will be similarly submitted to Dublin, and reply awaited.
>
> (4) In case of a break, the text of the final proposals from our side will be similarly submitted.
>
> (5) It is understood that the Cabinet in Dublin will be kept regularly informed of the progress of the negotiations."'

De Valera asked the Dail to 'pay particular attention' to paragraph number three. It was the source of all the trouble. Despite the fact that Arthur Griffith denied that the plenipotentiaries had exceeded their instructions, de Valera insisted that '. . . after certain alterations had been made . . . we never saw the alterations'.

At once Collins was on his feet, protesting that 'the original terms that were served on each member of the delegation have not been read out. . . . I suggest that a vital matter for the representatives of the nation, and the nation itself, is that the final document which was agreed on by a united Cabinet should be put side by side with the final document which the Delegation of plenipotentiaries did not sign as a treaty, but did sign on the understanding that each signatory would recommend it to the Dail for acceptance.'

It was at this point that the matter of the private session cropped up: to be decided later in the day in favour of a private session for the purpose of discussing 'any explanations as regards the genesis of the proposed Treaty. . . .'

Collins reopened the issue of the terms of reference and it was evident from his attitude that he refused to be sidetracked away from it. He requested permission to read the original document as served on each member of the delegation. This request provoked a sharp exchange between de Valera and himself, the former demanding to know whether that document had ever been presented to, or accepted by, the British delegation. *Griffith:* 'We had no instructions to present it.' *De Valera:* 'I am asking a question.' *Collins:* 'The originals were presented and they read:

> "In view of the authority invested in me by Dail Eireann, I hereby appoint Arthur Griffith, T.D., Minister for Foreign Affairs, Chairman; Michael Collins, T.D., Minister for Finance; Robert C. Barton, T.D., Minister for Economic Affairs; Edmund J. Duggan, T.D., and George Gavan Duffy, T.D., as envoys plenipotentiaries from the elected Government of the Republic of Ireland to negotiate and conclude on behalf of Ireland, with the representatives of His Britannic Majesty George V a treaty or treaties of settlement, association and accommodation between Ireland and the community of nations, known as the British Commonwealth. In witness hereof I hereunder subscribe my name as President. Signed Eamon de Valera." '

Collins went on: '. . . Publicly and privately we did not prejudge the issue; we even refrained from speaking to members of the Dail. I have not said a hard word about anybody. I know I have been called a traitor.' (He was interrupted by cries of 'No. No.')

De Valera: 'By whom?'

Collins: 'If I am a traitor, let the Irish people decide it or not, and if there are men who act toward me as a traitor I am prepared to meet them anywhere, anytime, now as in the past. . . .' He went on to state that the honour of Ireland was not involved in accepting the document. 'Ireland is fully free to accept or reject,' he said.

De Valera then gave an explanation as to why he did not want to be a member of the delegation: by remaining in Dublin he was the brake against any possible hasty action by the delegation in London. Yet if this explanation satisfied many of the deputies present, it could not have made the same impression with Collins, judged in the light of the Collins-O'Kane correspondence.

It was J. J. O'Kelly* (Louth) who drew from Collins an angry protestation that 'I did not say accepted, I said presented' (the original credentials).

Several deputies then gave their opinions on the matter. Dr. MacCartan (Leix-Offaly) did not think the question arose: '. . . it is for us now to accept or reject what they have agreed to. . . .' To which opinion Sean McGarry (Dublin)—destined to be one of the more forthright speakers in the debate—added: 'I think that the question of the right of the Dail to ratify or reject the agreement has never been questioned.'

On December 19th the Dail reassembled in public session. It was a day of speechmaking, even for Collins, who had a distinct preference for more practical tasks.

Griffith spoke to move the ratification of the Treaty. It was a fine speech, delivered in the usual measured tones of the speaker, never eloquent yet never attempting to shirk in any way the issue in front of the assembly. He said that his hands were tied by the non-publication of Document No. 2†: 'Are my hands to be tied by this document being withheld after we are discussing it for two days?' And finally: 'By that Treaty I am going to stand.'

Next, Sean MacEoin spoke to second ratification of the Treaty. Nothing of the practised orator here but a full, rich voice weighty with sincerity: 'I take this course because I know I am doing it in the interests of my country, which I love. To me symbols, recognitions, shadows, have very little meaning. What I want, what the people of Ireland want, is not shadows but substances, and I hold that this Treaty between the two nations gives us not shadows but real substances, and for that reason I am ready to support

* 'Sceilg', writer of a number of polemical anti-Treaty pamphlets.

† De Valera's alternative document (*see* Appendix G).

it. . . . It may seem rather peculiar that one like me who is regarded as an extremist should take this step. Yes, to the world and to Ireland I say I am an extremist, but it means that I have an extreme love of my country. . . .'

It was now the turn of de Valera to put forward his views. The theme of his speech against ratification was that '. . . it will not bring peace with England. It will not even bring peace in Ireland'. The contrast in speech style between Griffith and de Valera is apparent and yet, for all the prowess of the latter, the same satisfaction in summing up his case is not so conclusive as with Griffith's pro-Treaty speech. And was there a hint of a threat in de Valera's words, 'Time will tell, time would tell, whether it would be a final settlement.'

Austin Stack—whose father, William Moore Stack, was a prominent I.R.B. man—spoke, grimly, uncompromisingly: 'I stand for full independence, and nothing short of it.' It seemed that Stack in those few words had put in a nutshell all of de Valera's phraseology.

After the interval for lunch, it was Collins' turn to speak in favour of ratification. His speech lay in front of him and he ignored it. He had none of Griffith's calm measured way of speaking, none of de Valera's practised political speechmaking; but there was an eagerness, a warmth, a passionate sincerity in what he said which commanded attention. Erskine Childers, who spoke immediately after Collins, called it 'a manly, eloquent, and worthy speech'. Like Griffith, Collins shirked no points of issue; he emphatically upheld the Treaty, speaking from the standpoint of a man who refused to 'take refuge behind any kind of subterfuge'. Therein lay its strength—that, and a point-blank refusal to avail himself of any excuses, such as the forces aligned against him, their meanness and pettiness towards him, the undercurrent of trouble which had been predominant during the London discussions.

He could not, he said, promise to be very brief, and indeed it was a lengthy speech. He laid emphasis on the fact that English interests had been the means of destroying the Gaelic civilization and that the Dail had in its hands a means of stopping it. He interpreted the Treaty: 'as a plain Irishman, I believe in my own interpretation against the interpretation of any Englishman. Lloyd George and Churchill have been quoted here against us. I say the quotation of those people is what marks the slave mind. There are people in this assembly who will take their words before they will take my words. That is the slave mind.'

His own interpretation of the Treaty was that it gave two things, both very necessary to the life of the country: security and freedom. 'If the Treaty gives us these or helps to get at these, then I maintain that it satisfies our national aspirations.' He laid emphasis on the fact that the history of Ireland was not, as so many thought, a military struggle of seven hundred and fifty years' standing, but a 'peaceful penetration' over the years by the English. To him it seemed obvious that 'peaceful penetration' because of its stranglehold over the country and its resources was infinitely more dangerous than military dominance by the English. And again he put it to the assembly that the Treaty was the means whereby this stranglehold by the British could be halted and rejected.

He poured scorn on those who insinuated that he had succumbed to 'the atmosphere of London' and that he had trod 'slippery slopes'; '. . . it is easy to be wise afterwards,' he said.

Not one hint of what he had undergone during the negotiations was reflected in his speech; rather there was a righteous upholding of what he thought to be the best bargain obtainable from the British. He laid careful stress on the constitutional position Ireland would achieve by accepting the Treaty. 'The status as defined is the same constitutional status in the "community of nations known as the British Empire", as Canada, Australia, New Zealand, South Africa'. He called it an independence 'real and solid'.

It seemed odd that, following Collins, Erskine Childers should choose to dissect the Treaty clause by clause: odd because he had at one time, in his memorandum on Dominion Status, more or less put his stamp of approval to Dominion Status,* But again the Collins-O'Kane correspondence brings to mind the fact that Childers was fully capable of doing a smart *volte-face* at any time.

Robert Barton's speech was short and dramatic, the latter not by intention, and it was easy to see that, although he recommended the Treaty because he had signed it, his personal wish was otherwise.

On Tuesday, 20th December, Dr. MacCartan tossed scorn on the heads of both the pro- and anti-Treaty members. The Republic had been laid to rest by both parties, he said. It was evident that he drew this conclusion in the matter of the anti-Treaty members from the fact that de Valera's Document No. 2 was of a non-Republican character. None the less, he had 'more respect for Michael Collins and Arthur Griffith than for the quibblers here . . .'.

It had been suggested to the journalists present that George Gavan Duffy was about to provide a sensation by rejecting the Treaty. Instead, he placed himself in the same position as Robert

* *See* footnote on page 131; also Frank Pakenham's *Peace by Ordeal*, pp. 247-8.

Barton, when he said: 'My heart is with those who are against the Treaty but my head is against them. . . .'*

The fifth member of the delegation, Eamonn Duggan, laid emphasis on the fact that he had not signed under pressure, as he was not present when it was alleged to have been used, but calmly and deliberately, remote from the actual scene of the discussions.

The 22nd December provided little or no enlightenment. Professor Hayes spoke in a learned way for the Treaty; J. J. O'Kelly was a veritable windmill of criticism; Mrs. Clarke (widow of Tom Clarke) said it was a matter of sorrow that it should have come to this.

Yet it was on this very day, towards the end of the session, that the sniping against Collins took on a more active form. It concerned—or at least that was the pretext—a motion as to whether the House should continue to sit day and night if practicable and over the Christmas season.

Collins: 'I suggest we come to a decision on this. I am prepared to stay here to continue these debates throughout the Christmas until we finish them. We can go on all night through Christmas, like last Christmas, and let us come to a decision. However, instead of doing that, I would move the adjournment of the House to some date after Christmas.'

De Valera: 'Go ahead.'

Countess Markievicz: 'I beg to second the motion of the Minister of Finance [Collins] to adjourn to some day after Christmas. My reason for doing so is that the Minister for Finance went to London to face Lloyd George, worn out and weary——'

Collins: 'I was never worn out or weary.'

Countess Markievicz: 'Perhaps he is a man who can do without sleep or rest, but he admitted to being somewhat befogged——'

Collins: 'I did not.'

Countess Markievicz: 'There are many of us who are not able to sit up night after night; we might be more befogged than he ever was. For the sake of our own intellects, we could not carry on Night Sessions. It would be very tiring.'

MacCarthy: 'The Minister of Finance has time after time said that if he was befogged it was by constitutional lawyers——'

Collins: 'Alleged constitutional lawyers.' (Laughter.)

MacCarthy did 'not see why seconding the motion of the Minister of Finance should be availed of to insult the Minister of Finance'.

* It is interesting to note that Gavan Duffy's father, Charles Gavan Duffy (later Sir Charles) wrote about the 1848 revolutions (he was himself a member of the Young Ireland 1848 group) in the following terms. 'It is an instructive fact that everywhere in Europe the cause of liberty was lost in this era by the violence of Ultras, who would not accept the possible and attainable.'—*Four Years of Irish History*, p. 769.

Countess Markievicz: 'If the Minister of Finance objects to my statement and feels insulted, I apologise.'

When the House reassembled on the 3rd January, 1922, it was to listen to a set programme of defending and denouncing the Treaty, the speakers hardly differing in their manner of address one from the other. The only exceptions seemed to be by speakers who chose to make their speeches short and striking, notably Sean McGarry, Brian O'Higgins, and Piaras Beaslai.

On the 5th January a break in the monotony of speechmaking was provided by two incidents. The first was that a group of the members were in private session and attempting to arrange some form of agreement between the two parties. There was a great hope that the members might succeed in doing so. At the same time, however, it was clear that a clash was threatening if those in private session did not succeed in coming to any agreement.[1]

The second incident concerned a British journalist, Arthur Brown Kay of *The Times*. Kay had been sent to cover the events in Ireland, and it was while he was on a tour of the south that he telegraphed an article from Cork which apparently gave offence to the local Volunteer leaders. One day, while reporting in Dublin, he was kidnapped by armed men and taken away to Cork. The kidnapping caused a storm among the leaders in Dublin and Kay was soon released, chiefly through the intervention of Collins.[2]

On the 6th January the real bombshell came when de Valera announced his resignation as President of Dail Eireann. 'What I do formally,' announced de Valera, 'is to lay before the House my resignation. Definitely as Chief Executive authority I resign and with it goes the Cabinet. . . . We worked together as one team. Now we are divided fundamentally, although we had kept together until we reached this Bridge. . . . This House has got my Document No. 2. It will be put before the House by the new Cabinet that will be formed if I am elected. We will put down that document. It will be submitted to the House.'

Instantly there was uproar. Griffith, MacCarthy, Collins, and others angrily protesting against interference with procedure.

Said Collins: '. . . The other side may say what they like, and they may put in any motion that they like, and they may take any action that they like, but we must not criticise them. That is the position that we have been put into. That is a position I won't accept from anybody; and no matter what happens today it won't be accepted by me. We will have no Tammany Hall* methods here. . . . A Committee was appointed by the House and the House

* Central organization of democratic party in Tammany Hall, New York—often implying political corruption. (*Concise Oxford Dictionary.*)

was prevented from receiving the report of that Committee by three or four bullies. Are you going to be held up by three or four bullies?'

De Valera: 'Is that a proper thing?'

The Speaker: 'I ask the Minister of Finance to withdraw that term.'

Collins: 'I can withdraw the term but the spoken word cannot be recalled. Is that right, sir? This motion to suspend the Standing Orders is a motion to draw a red herring across our path here. . . .' He went on to state that he would be satisfied with a straight vote. 'On the motion before the House we can take a vote on the Treaty, and then the President can have his Cabinet that will work with him and for him.'

De Valera: 'Not for me.'

Collins then complained that the motion to suspend the Standing Orders was a political dodge aimed at putting the pro-Treaty members in a false position.

Cathal Brugha then spoke, saying that Collins had possibly included him among the 'bullies'. 'In the ordinary way I would take exception and take offence at such a term being applied to me, but the amount of offence that I would take at it would be measured by the respect or esteem that I had for the character of the person who made the charge. In this particular instance I take no offence whatever.' He went on to say that on the motion for the suspension of the Standing Orders it precluded him (Collins) and his friends from discussing de Valera's statement; but when Standing Orders have been suspended they would be free to discuss any statements made by de Valera. On that point Collins expressed himself as being satisfied.

Still the argument went on. Harry Boland (who had arrived back from America on the 5th) accused Collins of aiming the remarks at him. He went on to say that if Collins had had a little training in Tammany Hall and had reserved some of his bullying for Lloyd George 'we would not be in the position we are in today'.

MacCarthy: 'Now we are getting the dope.'

After more argument, de Valera expressed himself as being '. . . sick and tired of politics—so sick that no matter what happens I would go back to private life. . . .'

It was an interesting admission which he made, especially in view of the fact that he had practically forced Collins into the political arena at the time of the Treaty discussions. Moreover, one cannot think that de Valera's project was accepted by many of those present at the time.

On Saturday, January 7th, the Treaty was ratified by the Dail.

An important day in every respect yet, in another way, merely a prelude for the storm which was to follow.

The debate that day opened with a crossfire of talk between Boland and Collins. There was a certain amount of reasoning in Boland's speech against the Treaty; equally, though, there was just as much in the pro-Treaty speech of Joe McGrath, who followed him.

It was not until five minutes past five that the real onslaught commenced: the speech by Cathal Brugha against the Treaty, and during which he aimed a particularly pointed attack at Collins. The attack was cloaked by the request of a Deputy from Tipperary and Waterford, who asked: (a) To define the real position Collins held in the army, and (b) what fights Collins had taken an active part in; 'or can it be authoritatively stated that he ever fired a shot at any enemy of Ireland?'

Milroy: 'Is that in order?'

Collins: 'Carry on.'

Brugha: 'That is a matter which I approach with great reluctance; and I may tell you I would never have dealt with it, and this question would never have been asked, but for the statement made by the Chairman of the Delegation [Griffith] when he was speaking here; he referred to Mr. Michael Collins as the man who won the war.'

Griffith: 'Hear, hear.'

Fionan Lynch: 'So he did.'

Brugha: 'And the war is won and we are talking here. Very well, I will explain to you how that is done.'

Collins: 'I would like to rise to a point of order. Are we discussing the Treaty or are we discussing the Minister of Finance? I think we are discussing the Treaty.'

Brugha: 'The Minister of Finance does not like what I have got to say.'

Collins: 'Anything that can be said about me, say it.'

Brugha: 'Ta go maith.' ('Very well.')

Despite two interruptions, Brugha proceeded to define the position of Collins in the army as being head of one of the sub-sections of the Head Quarters Staff. He added that none sought notoriety except one, and, 'whether he is responsible or not for the notoriety I am not going to say. . . .'

He was interrupted constantly, but still he pressed mercilessly on, piling up the 'indictment' against Collins. 'One member was specially selected by the Press and the people to put him into a position which he never held; he was made a romantic figure, a mystical character such as this person certainly is not; the gentleman I refer to is Mr. Michael Collins——'

Duggan: 'The Irish people will judge that.'

Milroy: 'Now we know things.'

MacCarthy: 'Now we know the reason for the opposition to the Treaty.'

Brugha continued despite many interruptions. Sean McGarry expressing his loathing for the way in which Brugha was 'indicting' Collins by saying, 'I think we have had enough.' But MacCarthy complained that he 'must protest against the Minister of Defence being interrupted. He is making a good speech for the Treaty.'

It was evident from Brugha's attack that this was to be the highlight of the many moves to annoy and exasperate Collins, and to belittle him in the eyes of the Dail. If so, it did not succeed. Later in the year, Collins himself was to say that it did not in any way alter his admiration and respect for Cathal Brugha.* For many Deputies, however, the attack took on a sinister aspect; others were sickened by the personal angle involved in it; others still began to look at Brugha in a different way, their estimation of his character now much less than previously. Strangely, no other Deputy on the anti-Treaty side sought to press home the attack, which leads one to suppose that it was not altogether favourably received by them. Again, it was thought by many of those present that there was less ill-will and personal animosity in the attack than at first appeared to be the case, bearing in mind that on the previous day Brugha himself had expressed great regard for the character of Collins. Certainly the attack had one great asset: it brought out into the open the undercurrent of trouble which had been steadily gaining impetus behind the scenes.

After the tea adjournment, the House reassembled at 7.15 p.m.

Harry Boland, in a short speech, explained how he had come to make two statements in America, one in favour of the Treaty and one against the Treaty. At the end of his speech, he said: 'Apart from the propriety of introducing a private conversation I find it necessary to make a personal explanation; I certainly hope we won't reproduce any more private conversations.'

Collins: 'You cannot stand them, Harry, you stood for the Treaty first.'

Boland: 'No! and you know it, Michael.'

Earlier, Brugha in a speech of remarkable point—even if a little one-sided—had given praise to the name of Arthur Griffith. Its terms were in the nature of a plea in which he suggested to Griffith that if he would only fall in with the course which he, Brugha,

* *See* p. 193.

advocated (which meant that Griffith should dishonour his signature on the Treaty document) that Griffith's name 'will live for ever in Ireland'.

Griffith's reply to the invitation to 'dishonour' his signature and 'become immortalised in Irish history' had an air of nobleness about it. It was at times impassioned, but dignified, and truly in character with the man who had scorned on more than one occasion both money and fame. In the course of it he replied to Brugha's attack on Collins: 'He [Collins] was the man whose matchless energy, whose indomitable will, carried Ireland through the terrible crisis; and though I have not now, and never had, an ambition about either political affairs or history, if my name is to go down in history I want it associated with the name of Michael Collins.' It was also a fitting answer to the poor joke—for charity's sake it should not be termed insult—put out by Countess Markievicz on January 3rd, in which she linked the names of Collins and Princess Mary of England.* . . . 'I also heard that there is a suggestion that Princess Mary's wedding is to be broken off, and that the Princess Mary is to be married to Michael Collins who will be appointed first Governor of our Saorstat na hEireann. . . .'

At 8.30 p.m. Griffith finished speaking.† De Valera protested that the Treaty document would 'rise in judgment against the men who say there is only a shadow of difference'—(one surmises he was about to say between the Treaty document and his own Document No. 2).

Collins: 'Let the Irish nation judge us now and for future years.'

The fateful vote was now taken.

'Diarmuid O'Hegarty, standing on the left of the Chair, held the roll in his hand. The assembly was hushed, awestruck, almost ceasing to breathe. Even outside the crowd seemed to have realised that the hour had come, and the voices became stilled.

The roll-call began. County Armagh was taken first.

"Michael O Coileain . . .?"

Michael Collins rose from his seat. Slowly facing the Speaker, he spoke. "Is toil" ("for"). And so O'Hegarty went through the list of one hundred and twenty members, each rising in his place and responding, "Is toil" or "Ni toil" ("against").'[3]

The second constituencies were now being called—Collins for Cork, and he claimed no second vote; nor did de Valera when his second constituency was called. But both Griffith and Sean

* Now the Princess Royal.

† Poet and economist George Russell ('A.E.'), who was present at this debate, 'thought Griffith's speech extraordinarily fine, did not think he could have spoken with such fire and on such a high level'.—*Lady Gregory's Journals*, 1916-30, p. 166.

Milroy protested against the disenfranchisement of their second constituencies.

The Speaker : '. . . I can only rule that each Deputy present shall vote once.'

The voting was now being accounted.

The Speaker : 'The result of the poll is sixty-four for approval and fifty-seven against. That is a majority of seven in favour of approval of the Treaty.'*

De Valera then said it would be his duty to resign as Chief Executive; but Collins protested against it. There was at this stage a certain warmth of understanding between Collins and de Valera; and it was further obvious that Collins wished to refrain from pressing home the advantage secured by the voting. But Miss Mary MacSwiney interrupted this momentary idyll with a vehement denunciation of what she called the betrayal of this glorious nation.

Both Collins and de Valera were visibly affected by the result of the voting. In his final words, de Valera stated: 'I would like my last word here to be this: we have had a glorious record for four years; it has been four years of magnificent discipline in our nation. The world is looking at us now . . .' He was overcome and could not continue.

It was Cathal Brugha who spoke the last few words, and in view of later events they were significant words. 'So far as I am concerned,' he said, 'I will see, at any rate, that discipline is kept in the army.'

The House then adjourned.

On Monday, January 9th, the House reassembled; and the result of the day's debate was a talking deadlock. Suggestions and rejections, ideas and counter-ideas, opinions and counter-opinions flowed backward and forward, endlessly it seemed.

First, de Valera tendered his resignation as President of Dail Eireann and in tendering it he found a great deal of sympathy among the assembly, pro-Treaty members included. One can never dispute the statecraft of Eamon de Valera, nor his natural aptitude for the game of politics. He had been more than a match for Lloyd George during the days of the Truce. The influence of de Valera was profound and it had a corner in the hearts of a considerable section of the Irish people. By many he was considered to be the strong man of Ireland and, without his hand at the helm, only disaster, they thought, would lie ahead.

Yet his handling of the London Treaty discussions left much to be desired and his treatment of Collins and Griffith in particular. On the matter of External Association, it was felt by many of the

* *See* Appendix F for the lists.

men in close touch with the nation's affairs that it was nothing more than a let-out for de Valera, because a Republic could not be got from the Treaty discussions.

But at this moment, as he tendered his resignation, he was pale with sorrow.

Collins proposed a Joint Committee as a buffer against the 'split'; the suggestion was at once downed by Sean MacEntee, who would never subverse the Republic.

Mrs. Clarke proposed the re-election of de Valera, and Liam Mellowes seconded it. Padraic O Maille and Collins at once condemned the move. Collins, limbering up his powerful frame, jerking his head, wanted action. It was a touch of the Collins of old: scorn for the politician and for the endless talking. He was impatient for action such as would bring the talking to an end and a settlement in view.

The role of the speakers went on. Richard Mulcahy's theme was to get Irish hands on Irish resources. Liam de Roiste said that the present situation could mean that British forces might remain in the country. Austin Stack bluntly said that he was for a Republic and for de Valera. No one had ever doubted otherwise; but, as Dr. MacCartan had hinted, de Valera's Document No. 2 was hardly Republican in tone. Collins pleaded: No tactics; let us be honest.

Sean Etchingham made a vivid appeal to the assembly to keep the Republican Government alive. Cathal Brugha appealed for co-operation between the two sides; but later he stated, in more blunt terms, that while the anti-Treatyites would not hinder the pro-Treaty men, neither would they co-operate with them. The statement of Deputy Robbins that '. . . I would not like to see my dog shot for the difference between the two of them . . .' (the Treaty and Document No. 2) was probably the most pointed remark of the day.

In seconding Collins' amendment 'that this House ask Mr. Griffith to form a Provisional Executive', Sean MacEoin remarked that he regrettably found no man on the opposite side with courage enough to support the decision of the assembly.

The resolution to re-elect de Valera as President of the Irish Republic was defeated by two votes: For 58; Against 60. Both de Valera and Liam de Roiste refused to vote, the latter stating that he refused to plunge his country into 'fratricidal strife'.

None the less, it was a very cordial assembly, headed in cordiality by the late President, who assured the pro-Treaty party that they would want the help of his party yet, and 'we will be there with you against any outside enemy at any price'.

On Tuesday, January 10th, the threatening storm which had been hanging over the heads of the assembly for so long came to fulfilment. But, if it was a day to be regretted, it was also a day in which much good was done, for when the anger rose and the tempers flared it was plain to see that the happenings of the past few months were at last out into the open.

A great part of the time spent in debate was squandered by interruptions and efforts made, chiefly by de Valera, to pin down Arthur Griffith on the question of whether Griffith would use the office of President, if so elected, to further the aims of the Treaty. But Griffith refused to be drawn, stating his aims in a forthright manner: . . . that he would 'keep the Republic in being until such time as the establishment of the Free State is put to the people, to decide for or against'. He went on to say that he was going to put into effect the will of the Assembly with regard to the Treaty. And he ended by saying: '. . . Let nobody have the slightest misunderstanding about where I stand. I am in favour of this Treaty. I want this Treaty put into operation. I want the Provisional Government set up. I want the Republic to remain in being until the time when the people can have a Free State election, and give their vote.' The redoubtable Miss Mary MacSwiney made the impossible ridiculous by asking Griffith for an undertaking that he would not merge the office of President with that of head of the Provisional Government. It was the last word in time-wasting speech, as even de Valera signified by his hearty laughter.

As it was, Collins' motion of the previous day, to ask Griffith to form a Provisional Executive, nearly succumbed to more delaying tactics when Sean MacEntee hinted that it was past the hour for adjournment, and that the motion could easily stand over until after the adjournment. It is understandable that many of the weary Deputies greeted MacEntee's suggestion with cries of 'Poll'.

The next few minutes were hectic, and were looked on with amazement by many of the foreign press men.

De Valera: 'As a protest against the election as President of the Irish Republic of the Chairman of the Delegation, who is bound by the Treaty conditions to set up a State which is to subvert the Republic, and who, in the interim period, instead of using the office as it should be used—to support the Republic—will, of necessity, have to be taking action which will tend to its destruction, I, while this vote is being taken, as one, am going to leave the House.'

He left the House followed by the mass of his supporters.

Collins: 'Deserters all! We will now call on the Irish people to rally to us. Deserters all!'

Ceannt: 'Up the Republic!'

Collins: 'Deserters all to the Irish nation in her hour of trial. We will stand by her.'

Countess Markievicz: 'Oath breakers and cowards.'

Collins: 'Foreigners—Americans—English.'

Countess Markievicz: 'Lloyd Georgeites.'

And then the voice of probably one of the steadiest of all the Assembly, that of W. T. Cosgrave, asking: 'Now, Sir, will you put the question . . .?'

Then and there Arthur Griffith was elected President of Dail Eireann.

The roll was then taken and sixty-one members answered their names.

Almost immediately Griffith appointed his Dail Cabinet: Collins for Finance, Duffy for Foreign Affairs, Duggan for Home Affairs, Cosgrave for Local Government, Kevin O'Higgins for Economic Affairs, and Richard Mulcahy for Defence.

It will be seen from the appointments that four members of the London Treaty delegation had been elected to office while the fifth member, Robert Barton, had left the House along with de Valera.

There was in existence now Dail Eireann (2nd Dail) of which Griffith had just been elected President and for which he had selected his Cabinet.

On January 14th the Treaty was formally ratified. Arthur Griffith, as President of Dail Eireann, sent out circulars on January 11th to the elected Deputies of the twenty-six counties, requiring them to convene on January 14th to formally ratify the Treaty and select a Provisional Government. None of the anti-Treaty Deputies attended this meeting. The pro-Treaty Deputies attended and having formally ratified the Treaty, they selected a Provisional Government. Griffith had no post in this Provisional Government; Michael Collins was the Chairman.

The position was now rather anomalous. There were in co-existence Dail Eireann, its President (Griffith) and Cabinet; and the Provisional Government of which Collins was Chairman. Some Ministers held posts both in the Dail Cabinet and the Provisional Government.

The task now facing the Provisional Government was: to receive certain powers and functions from the British Parliament to formulate a constitution; to set a general election on foot to determine the wishes of the people regarding the Treaty; and to expire automatically at the end of a year, making way for the Government of the Irish Free State. The inference is that the

Second Dail Eireann would also automatically cease to exist then, or that its authority would be assumed by the Dail of the Irish Free State. This explains the questions put to Griffith on January 10th.

Chapter 17

The Position of de Valera—Collins and His Loyalties—He Takes over Dublin Castle—The Craig-Collins Pact—The Question of the Oath—Position of the Army—Four 'Governments'—de Valera's Speeches—The Collins-de Valera Pact—Collins Explains the Pact—Opposition to the Pact—Collins at Cork—Anti-Collins Leaflets

THE debate on the Treaty, the subsequent resignation of de Valera, and the election of Griffith, had further displayed the inexperience of Collins as a politician. He admitted his lack in this respect; and yet again poured scorn on the politicians. 'They will have me for what I am not,' he wrote to O'Kane on the 21st January, 1922. 'The more the rigmarole of my life continues to encompass politics the more uneasy I feel. I am a soldier. . . .'

There was altogether too much honesty and bluntness about Collins for a politician. He was desperately sincere and, as well, utterly naïve—points which readily betray the unpractised politician. He had none of Cosgrave's masterly handling of the debating chamber, nor even a touch of Griffith's cold formality. Collins is one more case in proof that never, or very rarely, does the successful soldier make a good politician.

Despite the fact that at the Ard-Comhairle of Sinn Fein (held on the 12th) the atmosphere had been one of complete cordiality, the 'split' and now the drift towards civil war was coming home to Collins with increasing force. Contemporary observers of the Ard-Comhairle noted, when Collins arrived around midday, that he looked 'tired, worried and preoccupied'.[1] Griffith, too, bore on his features the strain and worry of months of anxiety. These were instances in sharp contrast to the buoyant ease of de Valera. The thought occurred to more than one of the gathering there that whereas de Valera had thrown off responsibility, both Collins and Griffith had taken on more, and that at a time of great stress. From the point of view of the indifferent outsider, it was further apparent that de Valera had, for the second time, successfully cast himself in the role of critic. He had taken up a position which was now free of any administrative responsibility or onus and was not the target of the criticism such a position entails, as were Collins and Griffith and the men charged with operating the Treaty. This, no doubt, accounted to some extent for the cheerfulness of de Valera at the Ard-Comhairle.

The simple fact of Collins' outlook at this time is that he was impressionable, and consequently he viewed the 'split' and the drift towards civil war as a personal tragedy, feeling that he was to a great extent responsible for the whole state of affairs. He was altogether too sensitive in character to see that what was happening and what was about to happen was inevitable; and that others, seeing the course which events were about to take, had acted accordingly and were now free of the burden. The fact that the Treaty was a great achievement and, to a great extent, a personal triumph for him did not readily appeal against his sensitivity to the coming tragedy.

Collins' attitude was apparent to Griffith as early as the 14th January, when they met to elect a Provisional Government. Then Griffith said, 'Mr. Collins does not see his way to proceed with the election.' It took all of Cosgrave's powers of statesmanship and persuasion to convince Collins that what was required was a strong government. There was a fear—certainly justified by Collins' actions—among members of the Government that Collins would perhaps undo much of the good work of the Treaty, even in personal justification and for the sake of some Irish prisoners in London whom the British would not release.

To give point to the personal misery of Collins there is a story in circulation which concerns Griffith and Collins. A friend of Griffith, meeting him one day in the street, enquired how things were going; to which Griffith replied, 'Well, if it were not for Collins.'[2]

Between the two men there was a rift of opinion which yawned wider and wider each day. For his part, Griffith, certain in the knowledge that the tragedy of civil war was about to assail the country, desired to get it over as quickly as possible.* On the other hand, Collins, chiefly because of loyalty to old comrades now opposed to him, was loth to think in like terms to Griffith. Instead, Collins sought to attempt to check the drift towards civil

* Actual hostilities were only narrowly averted between the two sides in Limerick City at the beginning of March. Griffith, realizing that civil war was inevitable, wished to have it fought and over as soon as possible.

'He wished to fight it as soon as possible so that it might be over the sooner,' stated Earnan de Blaghd [Ernest Blythe] to this writer [Sean O Luing]. 'He wanted to fight it on the occasion of the trouble in Limerick. I remember his rising at a Cabinet meeting and saying, "If we let this situation through our fingers we will be looked on as the greatest pack of poltroons that ever held the fate of Ireland in their hands. . . ."' (Sean O Luing: *Art O Griofa*, p. 395.)

war—even at the risk of offending Griffith. The latter saw only too clearly where the loyalty of Collins was likely to lead, and viewed the attempts with great alarm.

It has often been said that Collins 'for two pins' would have thrown the Treaty overboard rather than risk offending those to whom he was still, in his way, loyally bound. It has also been said that Collins, at this time, was dangerously near to crossing over from the pro-Treaty side to that of the anti-Treatyites. In the writer's opinion both these points are mere supposition. Granted, Collins was proving at times to be a little less than willing in anything that looked as if it were aimed at his former comrades, but the fact that he, possibly more than Griffith, had been instrumental in the making of the Treaty is surely a convincing argument against these suppositions. Collins would never, under any circumstances (and as he later proved), have thrown away so great an achievement as that of the Treaty.

On Saturday, January 21st, and Sunday, 22nd, Collins was in London. In his private notebook he recorded the following items:

'Saturday, 21st January, 1922.
11. 8 30 John Lavery.
12 Colonial Office.
1 Churchill's room.
Borrowed £50 for London journey.
Ticket 15——
Boat 15/-
Meals 12 6
" 5 0
Train 1 10
Dugg 30
Train 10
Boat 1 10

Sunday, 22nd January, 1922.
1 11 o'clock Colonial Office.
Paid £30 to E.J.D. [Duggan]
Note re Compton-Smith and painting.'*

At two o'clock on Thursday, February 2nd, Collins had a meeting with Sir James Craig, and the following points were

* Major Compton-Smith of the Royal Welsh Fusiliers was, in June, 1921, captured, held as hostage, and finally executed by the Cork No. 1 Brigade. Collins, although receiving news of the matter when it was too late to prevent the execution, interested himself in the return of the deceased's personal effects to his widow.

discussed: Labour and Railways; Sentenced men: Transfers of Personnel; Prisoners; Procedure.[3]

On Monday, February 6th, and again on Wednesday, February 15th, he was in London. The February 6th journey is especially notable for the following items as recorded in his notebook:

'V 4 15 Colonial Office.
VI House of Lords to see Casement diary.
VII 6 30 No. 10 Down [Downing Street].
VIII Jermyn Court—Conference and Procedure.'

At the February Convention, Collins made an agreement with de Valera. It was agreed that the elections should be postponed for a period of three months; and that, when held, the pro-Treaty section would not put up candidates in opposition to any sitting anti-Treaty Deputy. It was a fatal move on the part of Collins, and one which was destined to have disastrous results.

The sense of fairness which Collins had exhibited on so many occasions was made further evident in a letter which he wrote to the *Freeman's Journal* (which had come out with unfair and irrelevant criticism of de Valera) on January 5th, 1922.

> 'Sir—With reference to your leading article of today. I should like to emphasise what I have always said in my public and private utterances, that I do not and cannot allow my name to be associated with any personal attacks on those who are opposed to me politically in this present crisis.'

Meantime, on January 6th, Dublin Castle, the symbol of British Authority in Ireland and the scene of many grim occurrences, had been handed over to Collins by the departing British. It was a moment to remember, a moment that would go down in history. How well Collins remembered that moment he recalled in a letter,[4] written in answer to one received from John O'Rourke, living in America.

> 'Yes, as you say, the Castle is now ours. It has been a place of terror in the past, symbolising, probably because of its contents—the English—all that oppression could offer. It ought to be treasured as a national memorial—to freedom.'

On March 30th an eleven-point agreement was signed by Sir James Craig, Lord Londonderry, and E. M. Archdale on behalf of the Government of Northern Ireland, and by Collins, Duggan,

Kevin O'Higgins, and Arthur Griffith on behalf of the Provisional Government, and countersigned on behalf of the British Government by Churchill and Worthington-Evans. This was known as the Craig-Collins Pact,* and its objects were threefold: to ease a situation in which Catholics and Orangemen were increasingly coming into violent conflict, particularly in the area of the Belfast docklands; to increase the hope of a Boundary Commission; and to call off the boycott of Belfast goods, then being operated in the Free State. The Pact lasted for a little over a week.

De Valera's main point against the Treaty was the Oath. Harry Boland informed P. S. O'Hegarty and Sean O'Muirthile that such was the case. O'Hegarty then stated to Boland that 'Mick Collins has been advised by his legal people that the Oath is not mandatory and that he does not intend to have an Oath in the Constitution.'

'Yes, we've heard that,' said Boland, 'but can we get confirmation of it?'

It was then agreed that O'Muirthile would see Collins about the matter of a confirmation. In O'Muirthile's own words this is what transpired. 'I am authorized by Collins to give you Boland an undertaking, for de Valera, that if he and his crowd will stop their codding and come in as a constitutional party and help us to get the best out of the Treaty, there'll be no Oath in the Constitution, and he'll stand or fall by that.'

'And I'm a witness to that undertaking,' said O'Hegarty, 'if ever you want one.'

For a brief space Boland looked as if he could not believe his ears. Then he got up, his whole face shining, his person just a mass of animation.

'Cheers, boys,' said he, 'I'm going to Dev. We'll be all together again in an hour's time.'[5]

But it was not to be. Unless it was given in writing, and was made public at once, de Valera refused the undertaking. He knew, of course, that such was impossible in the circumstances.

It is maintained by some people that the friendship between Collins and Boland was now a thing of the past, even if they still did resort to each other's company a great deal. It was a novel situation: wordy enemies in the Dail, the best of friends outside the precincts of the Mansion House. The idea of it appealed to Collins and, no doubt, to Boland also. But it is a sorrowful pointer to the times and to the tragedy that was to come that men should be friends and enemies at one and the same time, separated by a matter of only a few words. What prompted Boland to say to Dr. MacCartan that Collins once entrenched in Dublin Castle would be

* For full text *see* Appendix H.

as ruthless as any Englishman, no one will ever know.[6] Or—again from Boland—that Collins wanted to be a dictator.[7] Diarmuid O'Hegarty, friend and confidant of Collins, gave it as his considered opinion that Collins most resembled in word and action the Polish Marshal Pilsudski—'an Irish Pilsudski', to use O'Hegarty's exact words.[8]

It was a great mistake on the part of Griffith and Collins to allow Dail Eireann to continue as a Republican Government. The best course for them to have taken would have been that of adjourning the Republican Government *sine die* and summoning the Provisional Parliament in its place.

As things stood, obstructionist tactics were comparatively easy, and question time was made an opportunity for discussing the Treaty again.

It may have been these very tactics which prompted the Speaker, MacNeill, to excuse himself from further attendance on the ground that 'continuous insomnia rendered him unable to stand the strain of presiding at the Dail meetings'.[9] MacNeill was simply unfit to control the Dail in the temper in which it was. He was a mild, scholarly man, an acknowledged authority on early Irish history and law—suited to a quiet retiring occupation like University professor but entirely unsuited to keep a stormy and emotional assembly in check.

The tactics of the anti-Treaty men (Republicans as they later became known), led by de Valera, were of an obstructionist nature. It was de Valera who discovered that the voting register was invalid because the womenfolk had no vote. In vain did Collins protest that de Valera had never objected when the Republic was voted into existence on the strength of the register as it then stood.

The anti-Treaty supporters were numerous: sections which stood by de Valera for reasons of extreme patriotism, because he was considered, by them, to be the strong man of the country; and a restless army element dissatisfied with present conditions. The conditions were such as to bear inevitably towards civil war.

There are many people who consider that de Valera deliberately fostered this idea among the restless element in the army. Such an estimate is not strictly correct; for although de Valera may have fostered the idea of an upheaval among his own political section, his control over the army was the same as that exercised by, for example, Arthur Griffith—it was negligible. Neither had Collins any control to speak of, not in comparison with what he had formerly; neither had Richard Mulcahy, the newly appointed Minister of Defence; but Rory O'Connor, by personality alone, must be regarded as one of the factors which strongly influenced the Republican stand. By and large, the army was a law unto itself, whichever side, pro-Treaty or anti-Treaty, it stood for largely depending on the whim or the wish of the local commander.

One name missing from the list of responsible persons is that of Cathal Brugha, the ex-Minister for Defence. The explanation for this is obvious. Brugha, the patriot supreme, could no longer see the point of constant parleying, while his mind, as ever dwelling on the one thing—the use of force—determined this step (the use of a lawless section of the army) as the only way in which the object of his life could be attained. There was no idea of personal gain attached to Brugha's decision; he was the most selfless of men. It was natural that he should look on the army as being the one force with any usefulness left to it. Indeed, following the signing of the Treaty, he and Liam Mellowes had toured Ireland visiting the Volunteer Commands and pledging them 'to maintain the existing Republic', and thus sowing the first seeds of revolt among impressionable young men.

It is a curious fact that what de Valera could not accept in 1922, he later accepted—with the exception of Partition—namely, the Oath of Allegiance and military commitments. On balance, therefore, the resultant civil war was fought for nothing at all—though de Valera may not have had full control of his own side of the situation. If there are people who still disbelieve the fact that he was a prime mover in the drift towards civil war, his own words, written on the 27th December, 1921—a matter of a few days before the Treaty vote was taken—provide sufficient evidence of his intentions.*

The country actually had four distinct forms of 'government': the Provisional Government of Collins, which was the legal one; the Dail which governed on paper; the Republican Party formed on the 15th March, 1922, composed of the anti-Treaty members of the Dail, and headed by de Valera; and an anti-Treaty section of the Volunteer army which, on the 26th March, 1922, seceded from the army, repudiated both Dail Eireann and de Valera, and gave itself the title of the Irish Republican Army. This element was headed by Rory O'Connor.

Of these four forms of 'government' the one which proceeded to establish itself to advantage was the army of O'Connor's section. They took possession of the Four Courts in Dublin City on the 13th April, and almost at once proceeded to extend their operations outside the city limits.

The action of the Provisional Government in allowing local volunteers to take over the barracks evacuated by the British played

* Letter to McGarrity—quoted on p. 156.

into the hands of the restless elements of the army. It happened at Limerick and other places; it would have happened at Athlone but for the intervention of Sean MacEoin, who proved to be as obstinate as the I.R.A. leader there. It was, in short, a harvest time for the gun-happy warrior.

It is said that de Valera aimed four speeches, which he made in March, directly at the gun-happy warriors; and there is no mistaking the fact that the contents of these speeches, addressed directly to the Volunteers, incited the restless element of the army into action.

At Dungarvan, on the 16th March, he said that 'the Treaty . . . barred the way to independence with the blood of fellow-Irishmen. It was only by Civil War after this that they could get their independence . . .'.[10]

At Carrick-on-Suir, on St. Patrick's Day, he said: 'If the Treaty was accepted the fight for freedom would still go on; and the Irish people, instead of fighting foreign soldiers, would have to fight the Irish soldiers of an Irish Government set up by Irishmen. If the Treaty was not rejected, perhaps it was over the bodies of the young men he saw around him that day that the fight for Irish freedom must be fought. . . .'[11]

At Thurles, on the same day, he said: 'If they accepted the Treaty, and if the Volunteers of the future tried to complete the work the Volunteers of the last four years had been attempting, they would have to complete it, not over the bodies of foreign soldiers, but over the dead bodies of their own countrymen. They would have to wade through Irish blood, through the blood of the soldiers of the Irish Government, and through, perhaps, the blood of some of the members of the Government in order to get Irish freedom. . . .'[12]

At Killarney, on the 19th March, he said: 'If we continue on that movement which was begun when the Volunteers were started, and we suppose this Treaty is ratified by your votes, then these men, in order to achieve freedom, will have, as I said yesterday, to march over the dead bodies of their own brothers. They will have to wade through Irish blood. . . .'[13]

It was at this stage, with the civil war almost under way and with Collins the object of attacks from all quarters that, in a last attempt to stop what was to become a reign of terror, Collins came to an agreement with de Valera on the 20th May. Charity will say that it was an agreement; others will say (and they are justified in doing so) that Collins practically gave away all but the Treaty itself.

Briefly, the terms of the Collins-de Valera Pact were as follows:

A National Coalition panel for the Third Dail representing both Parties and the Sinn Fein Organization; the panel to be sent forward from the Sinn Fein Organization; that the candidates be nominated through each of the existing party Executives; that every and any interest is free to contest the election equally with the National-Sinn Fein panel; in constituencies where an election is not held, to continue to be represented by their present Deputies; that after the election the Executive to consist of President, elected as formerly, the Minister of Defence representing the Army, and nine other Ministers—five from the majority party and four from the minority party, each party to choose its own nominees, and the allocation to be in the hands of the President; that in the event of the Coalition Government finding it necessary to dissolve, a general election will be held as soon as possible on adult suffrage.[14]

There is no disputing the fact that it gave to de Valera a measure of the power which he had formerly held. Sir Henry Wilson, speaking in Liverpool on the 25th, went so far as to say that de Valera had Michael Collins in his pocket, and he was not alone in this opinion. It has been asked: was such a pact feasible? To which the answer is, judging from prior events, that such a pact could hardly be of lasting consequence.

So far as the Treaty is concerned, the ambitions of generations of fighters for freedom had been realized, for the great and immediate triumph which the Treaty gave was the evacuation of British troops.

The Irish Labour Party, too, had tried to bring about an agreement which would fuse the two parties. They put forward a ten-point plan at a Mansion House Conference held in April.

1. That all the legislative, executive, and judicial authority is and shall be derived solely from the Irish people.

2. That Dail Eireann is the supreme governing authority in Ireland.

3. That the Dail shall call into Council representatives of local authorities and economic organizations from all parts of the country.

4. That the joint body should act as a Constituent Assembly to prepare a Constitution for submission to the electorate.

5. The Dail to appoint a Council of State or Ministry, not all of whom need be Ministers of Departments or members of the Dail.

6. The Council of State or Ministry to act as the Government, and be responsible to the Dail.

7. Authority to be delegated by the Dail to the Provisional

Government as a Committee for the purpose of facilitating the transfer of the administrative machinery.

8. The activities of the I.R.A. to be confined to preparation for National defence. No armed parades except by authority from the Council of State.

9. The I.R.A. to be united under common command, and to be responsible to the Civil Authority or the Council of State.

10. A Civil Police Force to be established, and to be under the control of the local Civil Authorities.[15]

This action on Collins' part all but put an end to his career; only the personal prestige which he had gained in the past and the fact that he was still recognized as a figure of power saved him from being toppled from the Government. On the other hand, there is much to be said in favour of his action, even though it was destined to recoil on him.

> 'The policy of the anti-Treaty party had now become clear [wrote Collins in explanation of the pact]—to prevent the people's will from being carried out because it differed from their own, to create trouble in order to break up the only possible National Government, and to destroy the Treaty with utter recklessness as to the consequences.
>
> A section of the army, in an attempt at military despotism, seized public buildings, took possession of the Chief Courts of Law of the Nation, dislocating private and national business, reinforced the Belfast Boycott which had been discontinued by the people's government, and "commandeered" public and private funds, and the property of the people.
>
> Met by this reckless and wrecking opposition, and yet unwilling to use force against our own countrymen, we made attempt after attempt at conciliation.
>
> We appealed to the soldiers to avoid strife, to let the old feelings of brotherhood and solidarity continue.
>
> We met and made advances over and over again to the politicians, standing out alone on the one fundamental point on which we owed an unquestioned duty to the people—that we must maintain for them the position of freedom they had secured. We could get no guarantee that we would be allowed to carry out that duty.
>
> The country was face to face with disaster, economic ruin, and the imminent danger of the loss of the position we had won by the national effort. If order could not be maintained, if no National Government was to be allowed to function, a vacuum

would be created, into which the English would necessarily be drawn back. To allow that to happen would have been the greatest betrayal of the Irish people, whose one wish was to take and to secure and to make use of the freedom which had been won.

Seeing the trend of events, soldiers from both sides met to try and reach an understanding, on the basis that the people were admittedly in favour of the Treaty, that the only legitimate government could be based on the people's will, and that the practicable course was to keep the peace, and to make use of the position we had secured.

Those honourable efforts were defeated by the politicians. But at the eleventh hour an agreement was reached between Mr. de Valera and myself for which I have been severely criticised.

It was said that I gave away too much, that I went too far to meet them, that I had exceeded my powers in making a pact which, to some extent, interfered with the people's right to make a free and full choice at the elections.

It was a last effort on our part to avoid strife, to prevent the use of force by Irishmen against Irishmen. . . .'[16]

The public received the news of the Collins-de Valera pact with relief. It was a natural state of thought because the public had, in reality, little or no idea of the undercurrents of conflict being waged among their leaders; but they knew of the opposition to the Treaty at the Dail debate and some of the consequences of it. Just how much Griffith was against the pact may be judged by what Ernest Blythe (a Northern Deputy) said to Sean O Luing, Griffith's biographer.

'He [Griffith] was very dissatisfied with the pact and did his utmost to prevent it. I remember the Cabinet meeting at which the pact was approved, and Griffith when asked was he in favour of acceptance, remained for three whole minutes reflecting, nervous, pulling at his tie and rubbing his spectacles, and it was quite clear that it went very hard with him to accept. We were all, for a period which seemed very long, waiting in silence for his answer. And instead of the usual friendly "Mick" by which he was accustomed to address his colleague, there was a very formal "Mr. Collins".'[17]

In his biography of Kevin O'Higgins, Terence de Vere White describes the position as follows.

'The British Government was furious at what they regarded as a betrayal by Collins; and Griffith, who was not consulted, was also annoyed. His temper had gradually worn thin. . . .'[18]

The British Government, 'furious', was also alarmed, and the evacuation of British troops was temporarily suspended. Collins and Griffith were called to London and asked for an explanation. Even if they did not give the true facts, it was sufficient explanation for Churchill to permit the evacuation to be resumed.*

It should not be presumed, however, in judging the disagreement between Griffith and Collins that the former bore the latter any personal animosity. Griffith's anger with Collins was more the anger of sorrow: sorrow at seeing Collins unable, because of personal attachments and feelings, to give all of his undisputed talents in complete faith to the Treaty. The pact disagreement apart, Griffith had a very sincere admiration for Collins. Charlie Fox, of Oldcastle, related that one night in Walter Cole's house, Griffith said to him: 'Michael Collins is the grandest character I met since Willie Rooney.' 'I shall never forget the way in which he said that,' added Fox. How much of a tribute it was may be judged from the fact that Rooney, who died in 1901, was reputed to be the only close friend Griffith ever had.

How much the strain was telling on the capabilities of Collins may be known when Collins addressed a monster meeting at Cork on the 12th March. A Mrs. Agnellis was present at that meeting, and her brief account, as given to the present writer, amply illustrates the Collins of that period.

'He was [she says] at one and the same time the youthful dashing leader we had learned to love and admire; and yet a figure on which strain, worry, and overwork had taken its toll. There came a momentary lull in his speech, and I said, not loudly enough as I thought, "God bless you, Michael Collins." He looked down from the raised platform on which he was standing, and said quite plainly, "I need it." '

Under date Wednesday, 19th April, Collins recorded in his notebook the state of the country generally. The notes are written in pencil, and provide the only occasion, to the present writer's

* It was at about this time that Collins was called to London, and when he arrived there he was informed, by Lloyd George, that the interview would have to be postponed because Lord Birkenhead had a temperature. Collins shouted with laughter. 'I never heard it called that before,' he said; and dashed off to see Birkenhead. Birkenhead's butler said that his Lordship was unwell, but Collins made his way into the hall. Birkenhead, hearing Collins' voice, came out on the landing in his dressing-gown and with a bottle in his hand. 'Come along up, Michael,' he said. (Told to the present writer by J. M. Hone.)

knowledge, when Collins used a pencil, for he had a particular hatred of pencilled notes and stamped signatures. In the following transcription of these notes it will be seen that sometimes a place name is used, and at other times the name of Collins' informant.

'Geo—Unity—Control—Shooting.
Meath—Understanding not kept.
Casey—
Westmeath—Election.
Waterford—
Kerry—Politics—Shooting.
Cork—
Leix—Brady—Question of spirit—thoughtful—Question of development—Control—Election.
Longford—Bitter feeling.
O'Duffy—Without hope of Unity.
Dick—Organisation.
H.B.—Goodwill Dail Eireann.
Tipperary—Stick to Republic.

M—
Car—
Offaly—Arm—
Rox—Leith.
Dan B—Dail allegiance. Clare.
Lck.
Situation has changed constitution.
Suggest.
Fighting each other.
Miceal—Do away with him.
Liam—Nothing further.
Propaganda.
Joe—Sit changed
Elections.'

One of the features of anti-Treaty criticism took the form of a vicious paper war, and it was at Collins that most of the abuse was hurled. In one anti-Collins leaflet (No. 46) the abuse was worded in Collins' own statements:

'Which Michael Collins are you supporting?

He says:

There was no duress.	There was of course a threat of war.
I am a Republican.	I am a Freestater.
I stand by my oath to the Republic.	I stand by my oath to the King of England.
I will keep my word to the Irish people.	I will keep my word to Lloyd George.'[19]

This leaflet is, in fact, a complete vindication of Collins' pro-Treaty policy because as a signatory to the Treaty he was morally bound to stand by it.

In another leaflet (No. 32), dated March 10th, 1922, it was stated that 'Four I.R.A. (Free State) officers, 8 "Black and Tans", fresh from active service, 4 resigned R.I.C. form a commission to provide the Provisional Government with a political armed force.'[20]

In the same leaflet it was asserted, apparently in connection with the '4 resigned R.I.C.', that 'Constable Kearney (of Tralee) arrested me in 1916—Austin Stack'; and that Kearney 'also had charge of the prosecutions of Con Collins and self (Austin Stack) when sentenced to penal servitude'. Still on the same leaflet, a charge was made: 'Will Michael Collins deny this? Every Unionist in Ireland is voting for the Treaty.'

Against the abuse, the scorn, the ridicule, the issue of scurrilous leaflets, the suspicion, the warlike actions of others, may be measured Collins' own words:

> 'Believe me, the Treaty gives us the one opportunity we may ever get in our history for going forward to our ideal of a free and independent Ireland. This cannot be gained without very much work yet—very hard work and perhaps more than hard work. And it is not by dissipation of the national energy that we can gain this. It is not by acts of suppression and it is not by denial of liberty that we can reach liberty.'[21]

It is the appropriate answer to those who hold that Collins would willingly have forsaken the Treaty and all it stood for.

Chapter 18

General Election—Trouble in Ulster—Free State Constitution Rejected by the British—Collins Accuses Lloyd George and Churchill—Wilson Assassinated—Civil War—Deaths of Brugha, Boland, and Griffith—Collins Journeys to the South

ON THE 16th June the delayed general election took place. Out of a total of 128 seats, the pro-Treaty party won 58, while other parties, Labour, Farmers, Independents (all of them pro-Treaty politically), secured a further 35, making a pro-Treaty grand total of 93 compared to the anti-Treaty total of 35.

But if this victory at the polls went a long way towards proving that the majority of the people were in sympathy with the Treaty, it had little or no effect on the general situation.

Troubles between Orangemen and Catholics continued in Ulster with ever-increasing violence. It was hinted that Collins had forsaken the men in the Six Counties who had fought for him. Here again loyalty played havoc with his natural sensibilities, for he bargained with Rory O'Connor, encouraging him to send armed bands of men into Ulster in an effort to counter the action against the Catholics there.[1] One particularly gruesome incident, the murder of the MacMahon family, in the night of March 23rd, brought even Churchill to tears. The MacMahons were a Catholic family of six, living in Austin Road, Belfast, and only the youngest child survived the murderous attack. That incident will suffice to illustrate the full horror of the bitterness and anger which raged in and around Belfast. Essentially it was a clash between different loyalties and it took the most cruel and deplorable forms.

It was plain to see the fanatical purpose behind it all: by destroying the Treaty, it was hoped to lure Collins into declaring war on Ulster, and therefore to pave the way for a re-entry of British troops.*

Of first-hand importance was the fact that a great deal of the resources of the Provisional Government were being used to counteract the Ulster vengeance policy, leaving very little to spare for what should have been an all-out offensive against the rebels in the home country. Griffith pleaded with Collins to take action, and he continued to plead until he knew that in doing so it was a waste of time and effort. Not until towards the end of June did Collins take major action against the rebels.

It seemed that everyone with anything like a bone to pick was after Collins. He was nagged into a state of near hysteria by people coming to him with petty complaints. The National Army (which had been set up under the Treaty) itself was not outside the scope of this persistent idea of complain, complain, complain—all, or most, of the complaints being of a petty nature.

A day book kept by Collins for the month of June records no fewer than five hundred and four cases of persons wishing to see

* In July, 1922, the streets of Belfast were patrolled by 'A' and 'B' Special Constables. Unauthorized persons found with arms or ammunition were being sentenced to flogging and penal servitude. Meanwhile, the city was placarded with an 'Appeal for Peace', by the Lord Mayor.

Maurice Wilkins, M.A., was at that time Assistant Lecturer in Latin at Queen's University, Belfast; and the writer is indebted to him for the use of a few lines from 'Pogrom or The Orangeman Soliloquizes', which he wrote during this period of trouble.

'Our curious peace-lovin' Lord Mayor of Belfast!
Sure, it isn't much sense that he's come to at last!
Sure, the way to get credit an' peace in our town
Is "Up Specials!" "Up Carson!" and "Papishes down!"
An' paintin' King Willie in scarlet an' blue—
White horse an' green meadow—all lovely an' new,
So handsome and glorious, so pious an' free,
On every pub-gable for Shinners to see. . . .'

him—an average of above sixteen per day. With a man of lesser patience than Collins at least half of these audiences would never have been tolerated, many of them arising because of jealousy among men in the National Army.

On June 6th a draft Free State Constitution was rejected by the British. On the 13th Collins had an interview with Churchill in London. From London he proceeded to Cork, and there he delivered a speech with something of his old vigour and resourcefulness.

It was while he was in London that he visited his friend O'Kane. What he said then was later passed to O'Kane's niece, and from her to the present writer.

> 'Collins [said Miss O'Kane] spared neither himself nor other people. If his intention was to invite criticism of himself, it was given, and with great force, by my uncle. In the main Collins had two complaints: the political web in which he was tangled; and the present attitude of the British, in particular that of Churchill, who, Collins maintained, seemed anxious to cut the ground from under his feet. Were the British, asked Collins, unsure of the position of Griffith and himself in Irish affairs? Were they, he again asked O'Kane, "after changing horses"—as he put it?'

In view of later events the phrase took on more than mere suspicion on Collins' part and it becomes quite obvious as to how Collins meant O'Kane to take the phrase. Formerly, in the eyes of the British, Collins had been regarded as the strong man of Ireland. Now, it seemed, their gaze was fixed more on de Valera as a man who, in defying the Provisional Government, was showing more strength than either Collins or Griffith. Could this be the true reason, Collins supposed, for Churchill refusing him badly needed arms?*

If Lloyd George and Churchill had not actually commenced to change horses, they had started to mark time. It was at this time that Eamonn Duggan told Sean McGarry that Birkenhead had informed him of Craig's intention not to see Collins until he definitely knew who could 'deliver the goods'.[2] It seems apparent, therefore, that Lloyd George and Churchill were of the same mind.

* *Wilson: Life and Diaries*. Entry of May 15th (pp. 339-40, Vol. II). 'Philip told me that Cope had come over from Collins with a request for rifles, for trench mortars, for armoured cars, etc., which even Winston thought hot stuff! Philip said to Winston that Collins had only a few men he could trust, and so the whole of these arms, etc., would be used against Ulster. Apparently Winston refused Collins's outrageous demand.'

It was chiefly as a consequence of Collins' pact election with de Valera that this state of affairs had been reached.

On the 24th June the election results were announced. In the meantime, Rory O'Connor and the Executive of the Republican Army had discussed the idea of war against the British with an army dictatorship ruling in Ireland. It is significant that both Cathal Brugha and General Liam Lynch opposed it.[3] Whereupon, O'Connor and a minority of those who wanted war proceeded to garrison the Four Courts.

Previous to this, on the 22nd, Field-Marshal Sir Henry Wilson had been assassinated in London. Despite the constancy of Wilson's hatred for the Irish leaders, there is little to commend in this particular act—only that the men responsible for the shooting, Dunne and O'Sullivan, who had acted, of course, on orders received from another source, showed great fortitude before their executions. It is said that the order to assassinate Wilson was given before the Treaty negotiations, confirmed during the negotiations, and never cancelled.

Reaction to the assassination was instantaneous. The Cabinet in Dublin were appalled. Griffith said:

> 'Whether the assassination of Sir Henry Wilson was an act of private vengeance or had a pseudo-political aspect, I do not know. But it is a fundamental principle of civilised government that the assassination of a political opponent cannot be justified or condoned. Sir Henry Wilson's political views were opposed to those of the vast majority of his countrymen; nevertheless I know that the vast majority will be unanimous in condemning and deploring this anarchic deed.'[4]

De Valera was calm and statesmanlike in his approach to the assassination; Rory O'Connor denied any conspiracy on his part; while for Collins there could be only one reaction: to save the lives of Dunne and O'Sullivan—which proved a hopeless task.

From London, Lloyd George, writing to Collins, declared that evidence found on Dunne and O'Sullivan testified to a connection with the Volunteers. He also insisted that the situation in the Four Courts be brought to an end. Collins was away in Limerick at the time of the receipt of Lloyd George's letter and the matter was handled by other persons.

On Monday, June 26th, Westminster denounced the Republicans and threw out a strong hint, or threat, that if the Provisional Government did not bring the present state of affairs to an end, the British Government would regard the Treaty as having been formallv violated, and they would 'resume full liberty of action in any direction that may seem proper'.[5]

On the same day, Henderson, a member of the Four Courts rebel garrison, made a raid in which two objectives were linked: that of operating a boycott against Belfast goods; and for the purpose of securing transport for an expedition against Ulster. The raid was on Ferguson's garage in Lower Baggot Street and took place only a stone's throw from Government Headquarters. Henderson was immediately arrested by members of the National Army.

Now the situation took on an even graver aspect, for, following the arrest of Henderson, O'Connor's men kidnapped General O'Connell (popularly known as 'Ginger' O'Connell), Deputy Chief of Staff of the National Army.

For Collins this act of wanton aggression against a member of the Government forces proved the last straw. At midnight on the 27th, and in agreement with members of the Provisional Government and the Dail Cabinet, he issued an ultimatum to the Four Courts garrison to vacate the buildings by 4 a.m. The ultimatum was ignored and, without further delay, Collins brought the National Army into action.

Because the issue of the ultimatum more or less coincided with the threatening speech made by Churchill at Westminster on the 26th June, it was put forward by the Republicans that the ultimatum was, in fact, issued at Churchill's command. In his speech he referred to the rebels in the Four Courts:

> '. . . the presence in Dublin of a band of men styling themselves the Headquarters of the Republican Executive was a gross breach and defiance of the Treaty. . . . If it does not come to an end, if through weakness, want of courage, or some other less creditable reason it is not brought to an end, and a speedy end . . . we shall regard the Treaty as having been formally violated.'*

It is said that the attitude of Lloyd George and Churchill following the signing of the Treaty had not been unfriendly towards Collins and Griffith, and this may well have been the case also in the days immediately preceding the signing. It should be obvious, however, that later, when the real trouble started, the attitude of both British politicians showed a complete lack of understanding for the position of Griffith in particular. Once they realized that there were other strong men in the country, apart from Collins,

* *See also* page 189 for short extract.

their policy seems to have been that of seeking out the strongest personality with the idea of backing him to the full, even against the legal Government. But the action of the Government in issuing the ultimatum to the Four Courts apparently put paid, temporarily at least, to that strategy. There are other factors in support of Collins' suspicion mentioned to O'Kane that the British were 'after changing horses': for example, the shipload of arms which was 'captured' by the Republicans outside Cork harbour—Cork being predominantly anti-Treaty. In any event, Collins once having set his face to the hard road was determined to keep it there. 'Let Churchill come over and do his own dirty work,' he snapped, when he learned of the speech.[6]

For the rebels in the Four Courts garrison the position was a hopeless one and the position of their own Chief of Staff, General Liam Lynch, seems to have been one of 'with the garrison,' 'not with the garrison'; and it adds little to the general picture of the situation there to know that having been shut out from the Four Courts, Lynch later returned and spent the evening there.[7]

Approximately one hundred and fifty men under the command of O'Connor garrisoned the Four Courts, while other groups—the revolt having in the meantime spread—took up various points of vantage in and around the city. Significantly enough, de Valera now chose this as an appropriate time for what he considered would be the *coup d'état*: he came out directly and openly against the Provisional Government. Again one recalls Collins' phrase, about 'changing horses', to O'Kane.

For Cathal Brugha it was another 1916. He was there—scorning the politicians—in the thick of the fighting around the Hammam Building in O'Connell Street, his presence recalling a phrase used by a former friend, 'Always a great one for fighting for lost causes.'[8]

On the 28th, 29th and 30th the garrison was heavily shelled, in particular from a big gun stationed in Bridgefoot Street. In a 'Stop Press' issue of *Poblacht na h-Eireann*, dated Friday, June 30th, it was stated that 'Yesterday a British officer, evidently an expert, was seen loading and unloading the big gun shelling the Courts from Bridgefoot Street.' It made a further accusation that R.I.C. men were 'directing Free State Troops as to whereabouts of I.R.A. sniper on roof of Craig Gardners'. Under the title of 'War News from Four Courts', it issued a list of casualties at noon, 30th June. 'John Brunswick, Thomas Keenan, serious but likely to recover. Captain MacDonald and Joseph Page, doing well. Michael Macateer, Connolly, slight.'[9]

With regard to the big gun in Bridgefoot Street, the facts are that Major-General Emmet Dalton took delivery of this gun and others from the British. Dalton was formerly a British officer; later, as a member of the Volunteers, he fought with distinction against the British up to the Truce of July, 1921. It may be that his being there, directing the gunners, led the Republicans to claim that a British officer was in charge of the operation.

In the blazing wreck of the Hammam Building Brugha fought to the last, choosing to die by gunfire rather than to suffer the ignominy of being taken prisoner. The manner of his death is recalled by Lt.-Col. Andrew J. McCarthy, who was a member of the St. John Ambulance Brigade. He states that he went into the Hammam Building and there met Cathal Brugha:

> 'I took Cathal Brugha by the arm, "Come on," I said, "I will come with you." Suddenly he snatched his arm from my grasp. Drawing a Thompson gun from inside his coat, he turned in the direction of the Lewis gunner who was covering the lane from Findlater's building, saying, "They'll never get me."
>
> I shouted at him to stop. I rushed at him and seized his left arm, at the same time shouting to my men to take cover. Cathal Brugha turned the gun on me and told me to let him go. I again indicated the Lewis gun trained on the lane and asked him what he thought he was doing.
>
> He pressed the muzzle of the gun against me and then tore himself away. He lifted the gun to his shoulder and took deliberate aim at the Lewis gunner.
>
> He fired a burst. I threw myself flat on the ground. There was a quick burst from the Lewis gunner. They were both shooting it out. But soon Brugha was on the ground, wounded, and the firing ceased.'*

The news of Brugha's death stunned Collins, and then he gave way to real grief. Always Collins had admired the spirit of the older man, admired his sincerity; and the roots went even deeper. Between the two men—enemies though they were—there existed certain links of character, a certain understanding. Both had the adventurer spirit, both were aggressive men of action, strong minded and obstinate; both loathed the world of politics. It was, perhaps, an understanding which never saw the light of day, never came out into the open. It was felt by Collins, and, no doubt, by Brugha also. The link was stronger between Collins and Brugha than between Collins and Boland—though the latter feeling was

* Article in the *Sunday Express*, May 18th, 1952. (It is said, by other observers, that Brugha was not actively armed when he fell mortally wounded.)

evident. This understanding between Collins and Brugha could only have finalized itself in either of two ways: either they would have been the best of comrades, or bitter enemies—and, to Ireland's sorrow and detriment, the relationship took the latter course.

Collins on the subject of Brugha's death provides the only occasion in which he ever criticized O'Kane. A week or two after the tragedy, O'Kane wrote Collins a congratulatory note, dismissing Brugha as a man would dismiss an annoying insect.* If Collins' reply (dated July 17th, 1922) was put in a quiet way, there was no mistaking the fact that it was a sharp rebuff.

> 'Many would not have forgiven—had they been in my place—Cathal Brugha's attack on me on January 7th. Yet I would forgive him anything. Because of his sincerity I would forgive him anything.
>
> At worst he was a fanatic—though in what has been a noble cause. At best I number him among the very few who have given their all that this country—now torn by civil war—should have its freedom.
>
> When many of us are forgotten, Cathal Brugha will be remembered.'

It is not necessary to add to that fitting epitaph except to say that Collins' tribute to Brugha is in itself a pointer to the magnanimity of Collins.

On the 1st July Collins recorded the result of an interview with the Archbishop, the Lord Mayor, and Cathal O'Shannon.

> 'Must make record of this—shows how reasonable our position is. We don't want any humiliating surrender. We want order restored. That only. Maintained for the future. Disgraceful acts must be put an end to. Archb. and L.M. agree that if arms kept by irregulars all the same things would happen again. C O'S thinks it likely that there wd. be a change of heart.'[10]

By the 5th July the fighting in Dublin was virtually ended. But in the meantime, Lynch had issued a proclamation calling on the Republicans to rally to arms. It had the effect of rousing the country, but only in a spasmodic way. Moreover, Lynch, who was by then at Cork, apparently cast the destiny of the Four Courts men to the wind and went off to Limerick. There, after some patchy action, he negotiated a truce with the National Army

* Note from O'Kane to Collins, dated July 14th, 1922.

garrison. No doubt it came as a shock to Lynch when Collins blew the truce to bits and ordered the Republicans out of the town.

The revitalized Collins was shocking more people than General Liam Lynch and it is quite clear that Collins, now the Commander-in-Chief of the army* and back on familiar ground, was endeavouring to put behind him the arena of politics and concentrate all his energies on the military aspect. Though the army now was completely changed from what it had formerly been, he bent his strength, energy and brain in a great attempt to put it on its feet. It was, indeed, a superhuman task, for the want of men had led the army chiefs into accepting what Collins called 'sunshine soldiers',[11] meaning that many of the latest recruits were men who had dodged the earlier call to arms: they were good-time soldiers only. All in all, the National Army was an odd assortment: ex-British and American officers, ex-British N.C.O.s and privates, good Irish soldiers and extremely bad Irish soldiers. It was put to the present writer that the reason for the employment of the British and Americans was that they were experienced in soldiering in the regular army. 'We had no experience of soldiering in the regular army. . . . Colonel Dunphy was perhaps the most prominent of the former British officers. He was a bit of a martinet and not popular. . . .'[12]

Soon, however, Collins was dealt another shattering blow when Harry Boland was fatally wounded by National Army soldiers in the Grand Hotel, Skerries, on the 31st July. Two incidents both connected with Boland's death are worth recording.

On the 28th July Collins wrote a note to Boland, the contents of which because of its strength of passionate sincerity can only be called a heartcry.

> 'Harry—It has come to this! Of all things it has come to this.
>
> It is in my power to arrest you and destroy you. This I cannot do. If you will think over the influence which has dominated you it should change your ideal.
>
> You are walking under false colours. If no words of mine will change your attitude then you are beyond all hope—my hope.'[13]

Some hint of Boland's reception to Collins' note may perhaps be found in a conversation which Boland had with the then Anna Fitzsimons (now Mrs. Anna Kelly) who had been Collins' secretary

* Notebook. Entry under date Wednesday, 12th July, 1922: 'At Gov. meeting this evening Council of War appointed M.C. C in C; R.J.M. M.D. & C of S; G. O'D C of S & G. C. C. South W. Command.'

for some time prior to the Treaty. On the night of July 30th, Boland dined with Mrs. Kelly at Jammet's Restaurant in Nassau Street. During the course of the dinner, Boland urged Mrs. Kelly to 'Eat well'; adding, very significantly, 'because it may be your last meal with me.'

It is not true to say that Boland was shot while attempting to escape from the National Army soldiers.

> 'They [Boland and Joe Griffin] were going to bed . . . when the place was raided in the middle of the night. Soldiers entered their bedroom to arrest the two men. . . . He [Boland] insisted in seeing the officer in charge of the raid. The soldier would not listen to him. Harry moved towards the bedroom door saying: "I want to see your officer!" But a bullet in the stomach cut short his appeal. . . . There had not been, could not have been, any attempt to escape. The stairs and hall were occupied by the raiding party. They were posted at the outer doors.
>
> He was left in Skerries for four hours, and then taken to Portobello Barracks and from that [*sic*] to the hospital, where it was thought that an operation might save his life. . . . When he was dying his sister, Kathleen, asked him, "Who murdered you, Harry?" He would not tell. All he said was to bury him beside Cathal Brugha.'[14]

It has already been recorded that Boland's services to the nation were immeasurable. What is more to the point is that his services, when the civil war was ended, would still have been of immeasurable value, for as a statesman Boland was superb. His death was one of the major tragedies of this time of great upheaval.*

Collins now concentrated on subduing the rebels in Kerry. It is strange to record that friends of his advised negotiation at this time; whereas Collins was emphatic in stating that he would not consider any form of negotiation until Cork was in the hands of the army. If the weight of personal tragedy was heavy on his shoulders, he was still the energetic Collins of the former days.

With the capture of Cork, Collins set out on a tour of inspection. He was at Limerick when yet another blow, both personal and national, was dealt him: Arthur Griffith died on August 12th. Perhaps it was the greatest of all his personal tragedies, this death of Griffith, and perhaps Collins, by his stoic attitude, as compared to open misery when Brugha and Boland died, made it so obvious. The strain of overwork, fear for the future of his country,

* Harry Boland's brother, Gerald Boland, has served with distinction as Minister for Justice in de Valera's Governments.

uncertainty—the certainty only recently re-established—regarding relations between Collins and himself, this was the tragic sequence which finally brought Griffith to the point when, while performing his morning ablutions, a blood-vessel burst in his brain and he died almost at once.

It is difficult to pin-point any particular characteristic of his, difficult to pay just homage to such a selfless man, poor when he could have been rich, lonely when he could have been adored.

The tragedy is that Griffith lived to see his own particular victory thrust back at him in the throes of civil war. He was motivated by a fear that, if public order was not restored, Ireland would lose American sympathy and that reoccupation by British troops would not cause an effective protest there—the 'split' in Ireland, of course, being duplicated in America.

And while Collins now walked as Head of the Government and the Army at Griffith's funeral, Dunne and O'Sullivan, who had shot Wilson, were awaiting the hangman in Wandsworth Prison. More than one bystander noted the set grim expression on Collins' face as he walked at the head of his Staff.

Though overcome with ill-health, Collins still persisted in going to Cork. Officially, it was for the purpose of inspecting the army garrisons; but on the night before his departure he had conversation with Mr. Moylett, and during the course of it he expressed his real intention. 'I'm going to try and bring the boys around,' said Collins; adding, 'if not, I shall have to get rough with them.'[15] The old loyalties still persisted, accentuated by his ill-health and gloomy forebodings of the future.

He said to Cosgrave: 'Do you think I shall live through this? Not likely!'[16]—'this' apparently meaning the civil war. He made a gloomy joke to his typist, and she repeated it to Joe O'Reilly.[17] So it went on. Under the weight and the personal responsibility attached to the civil war, and torn by loyalties, his great strength was breaking. He was finding it difficult to concentrate, and was in the constant grip of a restlessness such as he had never known before.

On the morning of his departure, a friend advised him that it was foolish to go, to which Collins replied that his own fellow-countrymen would not kill him.

O'Reilly awoke at six o'clock in the morning, and the last he was ever to see of the man whom he had served so faithfully was of Collins waiting for the armoured car to arrive.

'He wore a small green kitbag over his back, his head was bent in gloomy meditation, and O'Reilly thought he had never seen so tragically dejected a Collins as this man who, thinking himself unobserved, let himself fall slack in the loneliness and silence of the summer morning.'[18]

Collins went to the Curragh and there inspected the army units. 'rom the Curragh he proceeded to Limerick. From there he set out ɔr Mallow in Co. Cork. It was the beginning of the end of the ›urney of his life.

Chapter 19

The Fatal Ambush at Beal na mBlath

WHEN Collins set out on the tour of inspection to the south, one thing was uppermost in his mind: that he would be safe while ravelling among his own people, the people of County Cork. It vas not that he was afraid—simply that he wished to reassure those vho were afraid for his safety. Collins was blithely sure even hough Cork County was reputedly anti-Treaty 'to a man'. Fate, ıowever, decreed otherwise. Every mile which he travelled on the 'oad to the south brought him nearer the death which he had ıever anticipated.

It is not the purpose of this chapter to speculate, to deal in ıearsay, or to add fiction to rumour; but what the writer has earned from responsible sources undoubtedly questions the manner ›f Collins' death.*

In the differing accounts of the happenings of the fateful day vhich are accessible to us, there are significant differences of detail which may be studied in Appendices I and J and in the later ›art of this chapter) and which to the enquiring mind will raise he inevitable question: What, indeed, is the exact truth about Collins' death? It is a question which may forever remain ınanswered.

Four accounts survive to tell the story of that day and not one ingle account agrees with another. Three of these accounts are ɔy members of the Collins convoy and the other is by the late Major-General Sean Hales, officer in command of the troops at

* Michael MacDonagh in his life of William O'Brien (Benn, 1928) states, p. 248: 'That bright and ardent spirit i.e., Collins was quenched . . . not by a stray bullet n the scrimmage, but, it is said, by one aimed to find in Collins its deadly billet, and ımed, probably, by an old comrade-in-arms.'

Bandon, whose brother, Tom Hales, was in charge of the Irregular (Republican) column in the area.

The manner of Collins' death is still a subject of conversation in many parts of Ireland today. Rumour and speculation are to a great extent the aids to the conversation and the once yearly ceremony at Beal na mBlath* (the place of his death) undoubtedly reopens the topic. Speculation apart, the shot which killed Collins came at a time when the fire of ambushers and the ambushed was silent—in itself a point which favours further investigation.

A certain amount of evidence is available and it is the purpose of the early part of this chapter to put forward both this evidence and the various conflicting reports which still circulate in the country and to give, finally, a detailed account of the movements of the convoy on the days preceding, as well as on the fateful day of, Collins' death, as it was given by the members of the convoy.†

There are conflicting reports as to whether the Irregulars knew, or did not know, that Collins was in the area. 'The Republicans [Irregulars] knew Collins was coming,' say some people. 'The Republicans didn't know Collins was in the vicinity,' say the Republicans. The latter statement is borne out by Mr. Frank O'Connor, himself the author of a book on Collins.‡

'On the day of the death of Collins,' writes Mr. O'Connor, 'I was on a hillside ten miles distant from the place of ambush, and in the company of Sean Hendrick and Erskine Childers. We did not know of the death of Collins until we read of it in the papers.'

A priest, resident in the district at the time of the ambush, informed the writer that at least two ambushes were set to trap 'a large convoy'. It was in one of them, the biggest, at Beal na mBlath, that Collins died. Approximately forty men formed the ambushing party but, at the actual time of the ambush, very few of this number took part in the skirmish, the others having wearied of waiting. Further evidence, by a resident of Crookstown, states

* Beal na mBlath, literally, 'Pass of the Flowers'.

† Author's note:

In 1956 I wrote a series of seven articles on the subject of Collins for the Irish edition of the *Sunday Express*, the first article of which dealt with the ambush at Beal na mBlath. After the publication of this article, I received a letter from a man named John O'Connell who lived at Canon Sheehan's Place, Mallow, Co. Cork. He requested that I travel to Ireland and meet him at a prearranged place in order that he could convey to me certain facts regarding the ambush at Beal na mBlath.

In March of that year I met O'Connell at the Railway Hotel, Mallow; and there I learned the true facts about the Collins ambush from Mr. O'Connell who had been a member of the Collins convoy. As evidence of his worth as a witness, Mr. O'Connell produced his army papers, his birth certificate and certain proof that he had indeed been at Beal na mBlath on the day in question.

Since that meeting, I have carefully checked, as far as is possible, the evidence which Mr. O'Connell gave to me, and it is my confirmed opinion that this evidence presents a detailed factual picture of the ambush and the days prior to it. The second statement (Mr. Corry's) is a detailed and signed account; and the third statement is the published account as given by Major-General Emmet Dalton.

‡ *The Big Fellow* (Nelson).

that the ambushing party were drinking heavily in a tavern there and that they made their way to Beal na mBlath on cycles.

The story told by the ambushers is that 'the column had pulled out of position and that only a few men of a rearguard party were there when the car came in sight and that only a few shots were fired before they broke off; and that they knew that they had killed an officer of high rank with one of the last shots fired, but they had no idea who was the officer.'* But the statements of at least two members of the Collins convoy are in contradiction to this story.

The leader of the Republicans, the lately deposed President, Eamon de Valera, was himself in the area. It is said that the ambushes were laid as a means of protection for de Valera against a 'large convoy'. It is also said that the Collins' convoy was hunting de Valera. There is no truth in the latter statement; the Collins' convoy was an inspection party only.†

It has been stated that the armoured car, 'Slievenamon' (which was part of the Collins' convoy) arrived in Cork city in the morning of the 23rd 'with empty machine-gun belts draped all over it'. Rumour had it that Collins had been shot with a poisoned bullet. But, as will be seen, the armoured car did not arrive in Cork city in the morning of the 23rd: the Crossley tender did.

On the morning of the fateful day, the way of the convoy into Clonakilty town was blocked by newly felled trees. Although Collins ordered the commander of the Clonakilty garrison to have the trees removed, the order was not obeyed and, when the convoy returned by the same route in the evening, it was to find the trees still there and the way into Clonakilty still blocked. Because of this, Collins was forced to take another route, the way of Beal na mBlath.‡

Collins' death occurred during the civil war. In the course of this most tragic affair men were coerced, imprisoned, even shot, often without trial, often for little or no reason. Records were lost or deliberately destroyed. False evidence was given and readily accepted. It was a time when private hates were allowed to be settled without any interference whatsoever. It was a time of rumour, a time for speculation.

* Statement by the late Major-General Sean Hales (whose brother Tom was in charge of the Irregular Column in the area) to Sean McGarry.

† In the opinion of Liam MacGabhann, Collins' journey to the south was connected with the opening of a more intense campaign against the Irregulars. In proof of this statement, says MacGabhann, three ships loaded with troops and material came into Fenit Bay and another bay in Co. Kerry.

‡ Private O'Connell's account. According to Major-General Emmet Dalton the trees were cleared in the morning. 'About three miles from Clonakilty we found the road blocked with felled trees. We spent about half an hour clearing the road. . . .' (*Freeman's Journal*.)

Through all the hotch-potch of fact, speculation and rumour, one definite point emerges: no post-mortem was held* on the man who was the leader of his country, and this fact, curious as it is, may be the primary cause of much of the speculation and rumour.

For the purposes of narrative the account of (the then) Private John O'Connell (Army number 34093) is used in this chapter. The accounts of Mr. M. B. Corry and Major-General Emmet Dalton will be found in Appendices I and J.

On Sunday, August 20th, 1922, the inspection party headed by General Collins arrived at Mallow, a town in County Cork. Although in County Cork generally there was a certain feeling against the policy (as advocated by Collins and the late Arthur Griffith) of the Treaty, it was an antagonism tempered with some pride: pride in the fact that a man of County Cork (General Collins) had worked so hard and for so long for the freedom of his country.

The garrison at Mallow, commanded by Commandant Tom Flood—whose brother had been executed for the burning of the Custom House on May 25th, 1921—was then inspected.

While at Mallow, Collins was approached by Dr. Roche and Archdeacon Corbett with a request that the bridge spanning the River Blackwater—the virtual life-line of the town, carrying the main rail line to Cork—should be repaired as soon as possible. It had been destroyed by the Irregulars. Collins, definite as always, promised that one month from that day the bridge would be in repair.

It was at Mallow that the convoy engaged the services of Private O'Connell to act as guide through country where the system of communication had been disorganized with wrecked bridges and blocked roads.

From Mallow the convoy proceeded towards Cork, travelling a circuitous route by way of Whitechurch. *En route* they stopped at the farmhouse of Dan O'Keefe in order to replenish the car radiators with water.

They arrived in Cork at half past eight o'clock that night (August 20th). Collins and the other officers of the convoy stayed at the Imperial Hotel while the escort was billeted at the Victoria Hotel.

No active anti-Collins demonstrations were made beyond a few single rifle-shots; but chalked notices on walls and buildings announced: 'Collins marches through Cork—why not Belfast?' (a reference to the fact that, under the Treaty, the Six Counties

* Authority: Lieutenant-General Sean MacEoin, T.D.

remained a part of the United Kingdom). The city was patrolled by members of a civil body, the Cork City Police.

The morning of the 21st was spent in inspecting military posts in the city and in meetings with various prominent citizens.

In the afternoon the convoy proceeded as far as the low-lying town of Macroom. There General Collins spent some time in discussion with the garrison commander, Captain Conlon. Conlon requested extra armament for the garrison and one Lewis gun was left there.

Other small garrisons were also visited and inspected. Trouble with the armoured car, however, forced the convoy to return to Cork earlier than was anticipated. It was eight o'clock in the evening of the 21st August when they re-entered Cork city.

Before dismissal, orders for the next day were issued: the convoy to be ready for starting at four o'clock in the morning.

On the morning of the fateful day, the 22nd, the cars were brought round to the Imperial Hotel. At ten minutes past six by the clock in the entrance hall of the hotel, Collins, accompanied by his officers, appeared.

Details of the actual strength of the convoy vary. Up front was a motor-cyclist scout, Lieutenant Smith, followed by a Crossley tender with a complement of two officers, eight riflemen and two machine-gunners (Corry's account gives two Crossley tenders with ten armed men in each, ropes, picks and emergency equipment), a Leyland Thomas straight eight cylinder touring car, in which rode General Collins, Major-General Dalton and two drivers, M. B. Corry and a man named Quinn. Bringing up the rear was the Rolls-Royce Whippet armoured car 'Slievenamon'* with two drivers.

The history of 'Slievenamon' is interesting. Of a type formerly used by the British General Allenby in the Middle East during the 1914-1918 war, it was driven on this day and on subsequent days by a Scotsman named MacPeake. The reason for the inclusion of a Scotsman in the army of the Free State is that no one, except MacPeake, was familiar with the workings of the armoured car.† In the days following the tragedy of General Collins' death 'Slievenamon' was based at Bandon. MacPeake was given strict instructions to dismantle certain parts of the car every night after duty in order to prevent theft by the Irregulars. One night in November, 1922, MacPeake, after excusing himself from the

* Slievenamon. Literally, 'the mountain of women'. A place famous in Irish literature and legend. Also noted as giving its name to an Irish poem describing an engagement there in 1798.

† The co-driver of Collins' car, Corry, was an Englishman, born at Rock Ferry, Cheshire. (*See* Corry's account in Appendix I.)

company of his comrades, walked to the place where the car was kept and reassembled the dismantled parts. He then drove the car away to the Irregulars. It is said that he received five hundred pounds for it. Later, he was arrested and sentenced to five years' imprisonment. The car was eventually found, by Government forces, concealed under a pile of straw in a barn.*

The route went by way of Skibbereen, thence along bye-roads to Bandon. There Collins spent a little time in discussion with the garrison commander, Sean Hales. Leaving Bandon, the convoy proceeded through Bandon demesne, travelling in the direction of Clonakilty.

About one mile from Clonakilty, near the workhouse, occurred the first hint of trouble, the way being blocked by newly felled trees. Collins, more concerned with the fact that it would be fair-day in Clonakilty on the morrow and that people would be unable to get into the town, ordered the removal of the trees. Hatchets and saws were got from the Crossley tender and Collins himself lent a hand in the work of clearing the obstruction. Eventually he decided the work would take too long. They then retraced their route, going by another road to Clonakilty where they breakfasted. To the commander of the garrison Collins gave orders for the removal of the trees.

Proceeding from Clonakilty, they travelled the four miles over mountainous roads to Sam's Cross. There Collins pointed out the heap of grass and stones, all that remained of his former home after its destruction by the 'Black and Tans'.

At the inn kept by his cousin Jeremiah, Collins treated each member of the convoy to two pints of the 'Clonakilty Wrestler', a locally brewed stout. At this inn Collins drank his last drink. They stayed about half an hour in Sam's Cross, while Collins discussed domestic affairs with members of his family.

At six o'clock in the evening the convoy re-entered Skibbereen. After reviewing the local garrison, Collins held a short conference with his officers, and a decision was made to return to Cork.

So it was that, travelling by way of Bandon† in the direction of Clonakilty, they found their way still blocked by the trees. Meeting with a detachment of Free State soldiers who had been ordered out to clear the trees, Collins demanded to know why

* In 1954, the fate of the armoured cars was finally settled. They were stripped down and sold for an average of sixty pounds each. Some are in use today as funeral hearses. 'Slievenamon', however, was rescued from the knacker's yard, and is now at the Curragh. A 'sister ship' to 'Slievenamon', the armoured car 'Kilmichael', drove Erskine Childers to his execution at Beggar's Bush Barracks on November 24th, 1922.

† Two members of the convoy observed the time of departure from Bandon as being 8 p.m. Major-General Dalton gives the time as being about 'quarter past seven'.

the task had not been completed. He was informed that the detachment had been attacked by a force of Irregulars, from which attack the detachment had retreated. But the convoy saw no force of Irregulars, either before or after the meeting with the detachment.

Speeding along they came to the valley of Beal na mBlath, a spot north-west of Bandon, but nearer to Crookstown than to Bandon.

The road narrowed, zig-zagging into a series of blind corners. On one side of the road there was a swampy stream in which watercress grew. On the other side of the road alder and various shrubs grew, following the slope of the hill.

The touring car was now travelling ahead of the Crossley tender.* From the tender two soldiers, O'Connell and Barry (a man from Athlone), could see that Collins had lifted his rifle from its customary position at his feet to lay it across his knees. The gloomy valley seemed a likely place for an ambush.

And so it proved. Coming out of a blind corner and with a straight road in front, they saw an old four-wheel brewer's dray lying lopsided across the road with one front and one rear wheel removed. The dray was loaded with cases and bottles and immediately in front of it the road was strewn with broken bottles. Almost at once machine-gun fire commenced, coming from among the shrubs and alder. (On the other hand, Corry, differing on this point with Dalton and O'Connell, states categorically that there was no obstruction at all—*see* Appendix I.)

It would seem now as if it had been a strategic blunder to stop and return the fire of the ambushers. 'Drive like hell,' Dalton had ordered; but he states Collins forbade this. It proved in the event to be a tragic decision to allow the convoy to halt for action.

There was a haze over the road and the light was fast fading. Seeking whatever cover was possible, the ambushed soldiers returned the fire.

At the time of the commencement of the ambush, the armoured car was almost a half mile behind the rest of the convoy. After a time it arrived on the scene, but its usefulness was short-lived. In answer to shouted instructions, the guns commenced to fire but only two pans of ammunition were fired before the belts fell off.

For a time the fire of ambushers and ambushed continued with unabated intensity. Then quite suddenly there was a lull, and the ambushers were seen to be retreating in the direction of Cork.

Lieutenant Smith and Private O'Connell at once commenced a cautious survey of the road and in the course of it they found a

* Dalton states the order of the convoy as being: motor-cycle, Crossley tender, touring car, armoured car.

black oil-coat and a bag containing a quantity of black powder. At the moment of their discovery, heavy firing again broke out, this time coming from the direction of a long, low, slated, white farmhouse situated on top of the hill.

During this time General Collins had been taking a full part in the fighting. Now the moment of his death was at hand.

Again the firing died down. Collins stood up, the better to see how things were going. He was in the middle of the road, gazing around and reloading his rifle. There was a single shot and Collins went down.

At once several men leapt to his assistance, only to be beaten back by a fierce spell of firing. It was almost ten minutes later when they managed to reach the body. Collins was dead. There was a ghastly wound near the left ear.*

No more shots came. In silence, the body of the dead leader was lifted up and placed on the back seat of the touring car.

Meantime, during the last spell of firing, Lieutenant Smith had been hit, receiving a wound in the neck. His motor-cycle was abandoned.

From Beal na mBlath, the dispirited convoy proceeded to Crookstown. There, one of the officers, Commandant O'Connell, instructed a soldier to fetch the parish priest, Father O'Sullivan, so that the last respects might be paid to the dead leader.

The melancholy scene almost defies description, as the priest performed his solemn duty in the midst of a hushed group of soldiers and in the light of the car headlamps.

Lit by the headlamps through the murky night the convoy moved off, making for Cork. From now on every moment of the journey seemed dogged by ill-luck.

They came to a crossroads consisting of three branch roads and, unknowingly, they took the wrong one. Proceeding down the unfamiliar road, the headlamps of the leading car picked out the figure of a man walking towards them. At once they suspected a trap: another ambush laid to catch them at a most inopportune moment. The convoy came to a halt, every man alert for danger.

Menaced by the pointing guns carried by the nerve-strained men, the stranger told them they were on the wrong road. More, they were in deadly danger. To prove his point, he led them on a few yards to where the road plunged down into inky blackness, to the Cork-Macroom railroad forty feet below. Of the bridge which normally spanned the gulf there was no sign.

What was to be done? The only way, said the man, was to reverse a few yards, then cross over four fields and so back on to

* *See* accounts of Dalton and Corry in Appendices I and J.

the main Cork road. At gun-point, the man was made to show them the way across the fields.

Now began a battle against darkness, cold, weariness, and the skidding, churning wheels of the cars. With all this work on hand, more than one member of the convoy thought of their position as an easy target should a roving patrol of Irregulars come their way.

First they tried the Crossley tender. There was no bite in the soft earth for the wheels to grip. The engine roared, the men pushed and heaved—and the wheels spun. Another attempt; another failure. Eventually, after a desperate struggle, and on a 'carpet' of army greatcoats, blankets and petrol tins, the tender lurched out on to the road.

Worse was yet to come. The armoured car, bulky and of great weight, churned its wheels deeper and deeper amid a hail of flying turf-clods. Greatcoats, blankets and petrol tins had all been used for the tender, whose wheels had driven the 'carpet' solid into the ground. Over this the armoured car could not travel, owing to the width of the distance between the front wheels. All efforts having failed, it was decided to abandon temporarily the armoured car.

Next, the touring car refused to start. Darkness made it impossible for anyone to find the cause of the trouble. It was also abandoned.

The body of the dead leader was then shouldered across the fields. Lurching, jolting the body—it was impossible to avoid doing so—the bearers, smeared in blood and grey matter, stumbled out of the fields and on to the road. The body was then placed in the Crossley tender, with a soldier standing guard on either side.

At three o'clock in the morning of the 23rd the remnants of the convoy returned into Cork city.

Chapter 20

Mourning—Tributes—Funeral

MICHAEL COLLINS was dead. In those four words may be summed up the ending of an epoch, for, with the exception of de Valera, no one had quite succeeded in capturing the imagination of the people of Ireland, and indeed of the world, to the same extent as Collins. To many people the news of his death was like the vibratory sounding of the brass of doom. Not even General Mulcahy's clarion call to the army and the nation could sweep away the listless feeling of apathy, strong though the call was:

'Stand calmly by your posts. Bend bravely and undaunted to your work. Let no cruel act of reprisal blemish your bright honour. Every dark hour that Michael Collins met since 1916 seemed but to steel that bright strength of his and temper his gay bravery. You are left each inheritors of that strength, and of that bravery. To each of you falls his unfinished work. No darkness in the hour—no loss of comrades will daunt you at it. Ireland! The Army serves—strengthened by its sorrow.'

It is an adequate tribute to put on record the reaction to the news of his death as signified by those who were his enemies. Commandant General Tom Barry (at that time a Republican prisoner in Kilmainham Jail) says:

'I was talking with some other prisoners on the night of August 22nd, 1922, when the news came in that Michael Collins had been shot dead in West Cork. There was a heavy silence throughout the jail, and ten minutes later from the corridor outside the top tier of cells I looked down on the extraordinary spectacle of about a thousand kneeling Republican prisoners spontaneously reciting the Rosary aloud for the repose of the soul of the dead Michael Collins. . . . I have yet to learn of a better tribute to the part played by any man in the struggle with the English for Irish independence. . . .'[1]

To some the news of Collins' death was slow in arriving and when it arrived it was thought by some people to be a false alarm. How was it possible that such strength, courage, humour, and humanity should be banished from life in such a way, greatness and youth cast aside as one would throw aside a broken pipe? It was possible that Cathal Brugha, Harry Boland, even Arthur Griffith, should die; but not Michael Collins. Such was the estimation of many people when the news first spread that it was thought that Collins had been shot.

Lady Gregory, at Coole, noted in her Journals (pages 180-1):

'I read a letter from Robinson* written on Monday night, this is Wednesday August 23rd. "Collins is safe, absit omen, and

* Lennox Robinson.

dined at Kilteragh* on Saturday. He came in Lady Lavery's† train, or rather she in his, for she is his abject admirer. The Shaws were there too. G.B.S. was in great form on Sunday afternoon."

Later. John brings back from the Post Office news of Michael Collins' death—shot at Bandon. "You have bad news to bring to Coole, her ladyship will be in a great way",—and indeed it was a bad blow, my hopes had been so much in him, and he had been so good about Hugh's pictures. I was stunned. I could not stay in the house but went and sat in the garden for a long time—found at last a little comfort in Mulcahy's fine call to the army.'

(One of Collins' manifold activities was his efforts to bring about the return of Sir Hugh Lane's valuable collection of pictures from the Tate Gallery to Dublin, an effort which was deeply appreciated by Lady Gregory.)

When the rumour was finally confirmed, it was like a tidal wave of grief sweeping the land. Men and women in all walks of life felt the impact of the blow almost as a personal one, some weeping openly, some grieving in silence, all affected by a loss which they felt irreparable. All over Ireland, the Six Counties included, there was a keen sense of appreciation of the loss and in England and America it was no less felt.

Hazel Lavery said to her husband, John Lavery:

'"All day I have been seeing them carrying Michael covered with blood. Wherever I go I cannot get rid of the sight." I got her to bed and sat with her until well on into the night, and at last she went to sleep. At seven in the morning her very English maid came in with the tea. After she had put it down she said in a voice showing not the slightest trace of interest, "They have shot Mr. Collins, my Lady".'[2]

Padraic O'Maille, T.D., expressed himself forcibly when he said that Collins was 'willing to go to any extremes to reconcile the anti-Treatyites. His death will weaken the position of his opponents, who, by their tactics, are not helping Ireland, but destroying the idea of a Republic for which they professed to be fighting. . . .'[3]

The *Irish Catholic* said: '. . . When the duties of his office as head of the Irish Government were more than sufficient to bind him to his desk, he interrupted the discharge of these to take up

* Kilteragh House, residence of Sir Horace Plunkett, in Foxrock, Co. Dublin. Later burned in the Civil War.

† Wife of the portrait painter, Sir John Lavery.

the sterner tasks which he had undertaken when he became the chief military authority; for he was no ornamental figure-head. . . .'[4]

The *Midland Reporter*, in commenting on the fact that four of 'Ireland's best' were 'sleeping their last sleep in untimely graves', continued, 'Well may strong men wring their souls in the depths of black despair, and doubt if Ireland can emerge bleeding and torn from the burden and cruel Cross of calamity and red ruin laid upon her shoulders.'[5]

'We are willing,' said the *Belfast Telegraph*, 'to believe that he sincerely intended to carry out the Treaty and restore order in "Southern" Ireland. His removal is a great loss to the Government with which he was so prominently identified. It is undeniable that to him more than any other man in the Free State his countrymen looked for salvation from the ruin and destruction which threaten to overtake "Southern" Ireland.'[6]

The British Press acknowledged to the full the part played by Collins in releasing his country from the grip of foreign domination. The *Daily Telegraph* said of him: 'He was a bitter and implacable enemy of England while the British garrison remained in Ireland and Ireland was not free to govern herself in her own way. . . . The dead man, beyond all doubt, was of the stuff of which great men are made.'[7] The *Daily Chronicle* called him a 'young and brilliant leader'.[8] The *Daily Sketch* informed its readers that 'the hand that struck down Michael Collins, guided by a blinded patriotism, has aimed a blow at the unity of Ireland. . . .'[9]

The great Irish-American leader John Devoy had taken Collins' side in the Treaty question and this was, to a great extent, reflected in the way American men of distinction and the Press of America were keen in their appreciation of Collins' qualities. The *Mail* stated that it was very much mistaken in its estimate of the Irish people if the tragedy 'does not harden their wills towards ending the revolution'.[10] The *Evening Post* described his death as 'a staggering blow'.[11] A former Governor of New York, Mr. Martin H. Glynn, declared that the slayers of Collins were blackening the name of Ireland. It was obvious that the death of Collins tended to increase the sympathy of Americans with the Free State.

More than even a national mourning, the sympathy seemed world-wide in its scope. It would be true to say that because of his youth and vitality alone Collins had captured the imagination of many citizens of the world.

There were tributes from Lord Birkenhead and from Lloyd George.

'I am profoundly shocked,' said Birkenhead, 'at the death of Mr. Michael Collins. He was a complex and a very remarkable personality; daring, resourceful, volatile and merry, and differed in almost every conceivable way from the more dour and placid Mr. Arthur Griffith.' He went on to say that he had never doubted that both Collins and Griffith having once given their word 'would sacrifice life itself in order to carry out their promise'. . . .[12] It was a tribute totally in keeping with the realism and sincerity of its giver.

In a message to Cosgrave, Acting Chairman of the Provisional Government, Lloyd George expressed his admiration for the fearlessness and gallantry of Collins. '. . . His engaging personality won friendships even amongst those who first met him as foes, and to all who met him the news of his death comes as a personal sorrow. . . .'[13] Remembering Lloyd George's intrigues during the London discussions, and Collins' personal assessment of him, this tribute does not have the same impact of sincerity as that given by Birkenhead.

In a message to Cosgrave, Sir Nevil Macready, Commander of the British forces in Ireland, said:

> 'On the many occasions during the last year when we met on official business I always found him ready and willing to help in all matters that were brought to his notice in connection with the forces under my command. I deeply regret that he should not have been spared to see in a prosperous and peaceful Ireland the accomplishment of his work.'[14]

Coming from one soldier to another, Macready's tribute sounds the note of sincerity.

In a letter to Collins' sister, George Bernard Shaw wrote:

> 'My Dear Miss Collins—Don't let them make you miserable about it: how could a born soldier die better than at the victorious end of a good fight, falling to the shot of another Irishman—a damned fool, but all the same an Irishman who thought he was fighting for Ireland—"A Roman to a Roman"? I met Michael for the first and last time on Saturday last, and am very glad I did. I rejoice in his memory, and will not be so disloyal to it as to snivel over his valiant death. So tear up your mourning and hang up your brightest colours in his honour; and let us all praise God that he had not to die in a snuffy bed of a trumpery cough, weakened by age, and saddened by the

disappointments that would have attended his work had he lived. Sincerely, Bernard Shaw. August 24th, 1922.'[15]

From Cork the body was brought in the steamer *Innisfallen* to the North Wall, Dublin. Again there was a further expression of grief in the weeping crowds who gathered to await the arrival of the steamer. Even the strongest were visibly affected, no less than Joe O'Reilly and Tom Cullen when they first heard the news of his death.

The body was brought to the City Hall, where it lay in state until the funeral; and thousands paid homage to the dead leader. No Irishman before Collins' time or since has evoked such genuine grief.

Sir John Lavery states:

'I was allowed to paint him in death. Any grossness in his features, even the peculiar dent near the point of his nose, has disappeared. He might have been Napoleon in marble as he lay in his uniform, covered by the Free State flag, with a crucifix on his breast. Four soldiers stood around the bier. The stillness was broken at long intervals by someone entering the chapel on tiptoe, kissing the brow, and then slipping to the door where I could hear a burst of suppressed grief. One woman kissed the dead lips, making it hard for me to continue my work.'[16]

Then came the journey to the final rest in Glasnevin Cemetery. The guard of honour was under the command of Captain Barra O Briain,* whose command Collins had inspected at the Curragh only a few days before his death. Lack of men used to the polish of ceremonial drill necessitated the guard of honour moving at quick-march pace by back streets from the City Hall to the Pro-Cathedral and from the Pro-Cathedral to Glasnevin. One small incident put the final touch on the mourning of a nation. The cortège, passing on its way, was stopped by the flower-sellers at the Nelson Pillar in O'Connell Street and a wreath was placed on the coffin.

At the graveside the funeral oration was delivered by General Mulcahy and recorded on the back sheet of a prayer book by Patrick O'Driscoll, a brother-in-law of Collins, and at the time a reporter in Dail Eireann.

General Mulcahy dwelt at some length on the various qualities of the dead leader: his place in the hearts of the people, the fruits that would come in the determination and renewed strength

* Now Judge Barra O Briain, S.C.

resulting from his death, the light that he was in the darkness of the times. But it was in the final passages of the oration that General Mulcahy struck a note which expressed at once both the loss and the renewal of strength. Almost poetic in their feeling, the words have a remarkable beauty:

> 'Tom Ashe, Thomas MacCurtain, Traolach MacSuibhne, Dick McKee, Michael O'Coileain, and all of you who lie buried here, disciples of our great Chief, those of us you leave behind are all, too, grain from the same handful, scattered by the hand of the Great Sower over the fruitful soil of Ireland. We, too, will bring forth our own fruit.
>
> Men and women of Ireland, we are all mariners on the deep, bound for a port still seen only through storm and spray, sailing still on a sea "full of dangers and hardships, and bitter toil". But the Great Sleeper lies smiling in the stern of the boat, and we shall be filled with that spirit which will walk bravely upon the waters.'[17]

Chapter 21

Collins as Speaker and Writer

IN THE person of Collins the speaker and writer there was also something of Collins the soldier: the direct utterance, the infusion of personality, for example.

In practice, he invariably prepared a few notes in advance of making a speech. Usually, however, the notes were tossed aside soon after the commencement of the speech and from then on it followed the trend of his own thoughts. He spoke in an easy and relaxed manner, his stance erect, head thrown back, arm and hand used only to emphasize a particular point on his audience.

It is impossible to compass within the space of one chapter the full scope of his spoken and written utterances. In the interests of brevity the following extracts are given: a speech in support of the Treaty, at Cork on March 12th, 1922, a speech at Skibbereen on the 17th March, 1922, and various extracts from his writings. For those who wish further acquaintance with his speeches and writings, all sources are fully indicated in the Bibliography.

. . . . .

The Right of the People

I come here as one of the 'incompetent amateurs' who have seized the helm of the ship of the Irish State, and have driven it on to the rocks.

The captain himself was here addressing you two or three weeks ago, and he told you he went to America to speak to the people of America, and ask them to recognise the Republic that was set up in Ireland by the free will of the Irish people, but little did he dream that the day would ever come when he would have to come to the Irish people themselves asking them to affirm the Republic that itself had set up.

And while the captain was away from his ship—that time in America—the weather was very stormy. There was a regular hurricane blowing—you in Cork will remember. The helm had been left by the captain in the hands of those very same incompetent amateurs who afterwards in calm water had the ship on the rocks, and, while he was away, somehow or other we steered it safely through those troubled waters—the roughest through which the ship of the Irish nation has ever had to be navigated in all her turbulent history.

Mr. de Valera laments, he says, that it should be necessary for him to remind the Irish people to be firm for the Republic. He had to ask those who were confusing the issue whether it was or was not a fact that the Republic was established by the Irish people.

Why does Mr. de Valera not answer his question?

Well, perhaps he cannot! It is not too easy when one has been confusing issues to make them clear again. But I will help him.

What does Mr. de Valera mean by the Republic? Fortunately he has told us in a speech he made last Sunday week in Ennis. He means by a Republic, he says, the democratic right of the people of Ireland to rule themselves without interference from any outside power.

Accepting that definition, I can answer Mr. de Valera's questions. The Irish people have not disestablished their democratic right to rule themselves.

They have claimed that right and fought for it through many generations. They have now at last established that right. They have done more. They have secured recognition of that right by the Power which through all the centuries had denied it. The departure of his forces is the real recognition of that right. It was

those forces alone that prevented the Irish people fro
their right.

If Mr. de Valera's definition is right we could never h d
a Republic hitherto. It was, therefore, never established, b ause
it is only now by means of the Treaty that the interference by the outside Power has ceased. That interference has come to an end—that interference, the absence of which Mr. de Valera lays down as the condition necessary for the existence of a Republic. We took a certain amount of government out of the hands of the enemy while he was here.

We took as much as we could. But we could not grasp all of it because he used the whole of his forces to prevent us doing so, and we were unable to beat him out of the country by force of arms.

But the enemy is going—will soon be gone, if, indeed, Mr. de Valera and his friends will but allow them to depart.

There is, however, now no longer any outside power to prevent us exercising our democratic right to rule ourselves. And if Mr. de Valera's definition is right, if he really means the democratic right of the people to rule themselves, then I say the people have secured that democratic right.

And perhaps it is I who should be exhorting Mr. de Valera and his followers to stand by that democratic right, and not to destroy it or disestablish it, and to cease fomenting strife and making difficulties and delaying evacuation.

They do these things by the disunion they are causing. That disunion in itself encourages the cowardly element in Belfast to an orgy of bloodshed and ruffianism. Generally, Mr. de Valera and his friends are stepping into the shoes of the departing enemy, by preventing, or attempting to prevent, in their autocratic manner, the right of the Irish people to govern themselves.

And now let me say that I agree with Mr. de Valera's definition in that it is for their democratic right, for the power to exercise it, that Ireland has always fought.

It is for that right that we fought in the recent struggle, and it is for that right our fathers fought, and it was the desire to secure that right that inspired the Land War, and inspired the Home Rule agitation, and inspired the Repeal Agitation, and inspired the Young Ireland and the Fenian Movements. That simply is the case. It was an elementary right we fought for, not the name of a form of government.

Indeed, it would seem that Mr. de Valera himself holds the opinion that we never had a Republic. Now, if that is so, we never had one to disestablish. One of the signatories of the Treaty is now a supporter of Mr. de Valera. This man must, therefore, be a little wiser than other men, belonging to both parties as it were. When Mr. Cathal Brugha spoke here in Cork he quoted this former member of the Dail Cabinet with approval. In view of this position, the words of Mr. Barton may be of importance. Mr. Barton wrote in a paper which they call *The Republic of Ireland* that it had become plain that it was physically impossible to secure Ireland's ideal of a completely isolated Republic, otherwise than by driving the overwhelmingly superior British forces out of the country.

Obviously then we could not have had a Republic before the Truce. It was as stated, and I agree, an ideal only possible to realise by driving the overwhelmingly superior British forces out of the country.

And now let us get away from these confusions and prevarications. Let us look at the position as it really is. Let us look at it honestly for a moment—just plainly as it is, not as it should be and not as we should like it to be.

A year ago, a time Mr. de Valera and his followers wish to bring back again, we were all in a different position from what we are to-day. I need not emphasise this to you people of Cork. You know what things were twelve months ago. You know it and you can put your knowledge of the real position above any empty declarations regarding the supposed position.

We were suffering under a murderous tyranny the enemy were directing against us. We were making a very valiant effort to uphold and exercise our democratic right to rule ourselves. We were making every effort to get rid of the enemy that was preventing us from doing this. We did make it very difficult for him to govern us. He was really alarmed. He tried by violence to get his Government back. His Government rested entirely on his violence. That was his only way of governing us. He knew that if he did not succeed in retaining his hold on us by violence he would have to relax that hold.

He called it restoring law and order. You will remember he was ignoring all law and order in his attempt to prevent us having Irish law and order of our own. Our people were being hunted, tortured, imprisoned, murdered, hanged. Your houses were being burned. Women and children in many districts were spending the nights shivering in the fields. There was no peace in Ireland night or day.

But we were not broken, and the enemy flung himself in vain against the spirit of the Irish people, and by the time the summer came the British Prime Minister himself had to invite over the 'murderers' and 'head of the murder gang', to discuss with him and his Cabinet terms of peace.

If we had been able to beat the British out, and this not only from the South of Ireland and the West of Ireland, but the North-East of Ireland as well, there need have been no negotiations.

There need have been no Treaty, because we would have had our freedom as a result of a military victory. When we had achieved that result we could have expressed that freedom in whatever form we liked. We could have expressed it by a republic or by a monarchy. I am sure we could have found some descendant of the last King of Ireland modestly hidden away in one of our villages, and we could induce him to come out into the light.

We had not beaten the enemy, but neither had he beaten us. That was the plain position. And we met to see if agreement were possible, to arrange what we could get from him in return for what we wanted—namely, his departure.

What we wanted was that he should leave Ireland so that we might have our country for ourselves to live in the way we liked best.

Actually the British were prepared to go if terms could be agreed on. They had given over their claim to dominate us and to hold us in subservience to their wishes. We had made this country too uncomfortable for them. There were too many ambushed positions in our country, and there were too many gloomy street corners in Cork and Dublin.

But even so they were not militarily defeated, and we were not in the position of dictating terms of peace. The British had not surrendered. Therefore, they need not agree to what would have been to them humiliating terms, any more than we would agree to what would be to us humiliating terms.

And we did agree to a settlement. They agreed to withdraw their forces, military and administrative and economic. If we would agree to maintain an international association with them and the nations they called their 'Commonwealth', we got a guarantee that our freedom so secured would not be violated.

Now, what I want to tell you is that it is not the Treaty that is all-important in this regard. It is the fact of their withdrawal and evacuation that is all-important. The Treaty is the written endorsement of the freedom which we have obtained.

We have been told that 'if the Treaty was signed under duress, then the men who went over broke their faith with the Irish people. If they signed it without duress they were traitors to their cause. He said it was under duress it was signed'—that is a typically de Valera argument. It's a 'heads I win, tails you lose argument'.

There is always duress present on both sides during such negotiations. I made it plain to all the plenipotentiaries in London that I did not regard seriously the threat of immediate and terrible war.

Let me bring you back to realities. First, there was the 72 hours' notice of termination of the Truce—three days. Nothing immediate or terrible about that. I made it clear what my feeling was. I stated over and over again that the conflict in Ireland would be resumed not after a formal declaration of war—immediate and terrible or otherwise, but would develop simply as a result of a policeman shot here, an Irish soldier or an Irish citizen there: then again restoration of law and order in Ireland; then again the day of the Stricklands; the day of the Smyths and Prescott-Decies; the day of the lunatic murderers of Canon Magner and Father O'Callaghan. Mr. de Valera talks of signing under duress. Duress there was, and let me tell you what it was.

It was the duress that the weaker nation suffers under against the stronger. And the plenipotentiaries were not responsible for that. On the British side there was duress in that world opinion pressed upon them to conform their practice to their professions —to make an honourable peace with us, if possible. And there was on our side the duress to accept really substantial terms when we were at the pinnacle of the greatest amount of success to which we could hope to reach in this particular national effort.

And let me put another aspect of it to you. Let me recall to you that in July last 25 or 26 men lay under sentence of death. Hundreds of our people were in penal servitude, thousands were in internment, dozens of others were lying with capital charges over their heads. An offer was made by Britain. That offer to go before the people required the signatures of the plenipotentiaries. That was the reason we signed it—in order that the people would have a chance of deciding.

Will anyone tell me that we five should have refused to give the people an opportunity of deciding? Will any man stand up in this assembly and tell me that he would have refused to sign, and would, by his refusal, commit these 25 men to death, commit dozens of others to death, and commit the country generally to further bloodshed and destruction?

I know we had forced the British to the utmost limit they would go. I know what the alternative was, and every man who faces the situation in an honest and straight manner knows what the alternative was.

The suggestion underlying the criticism of the opposition is that little or nothing has been achieved. Our opponents claim that they alone are the custodians of the nation's honour. The suggestion is, in a veiled way, sometimes openly, sometimes by innuendo only, that the British Parliament still has power to legislate for Ireland. It has not, and our opponents know it has not, and you know it has not.

It is a difficult thing enough to resume normal life after a struggle such as the Irish have had. It is the duty of people, calling themselves leaders, to help the nation in that effort, not to hinder it. It is a difficult thing to change the sword for the ploughshare. The enemy has gone, or is going, and the sword will not plough the fields that are lying fallow.

Is it the doctrine of Mr. de Valera and his followers that suffering and fighting are to go on just because they are good in themselves? We hear about the hard road which the opposition is pointing out to the Irish nation, and the inducements that are put before the people towards ease, 'towards living practically the lives of beasts'.

This is the language of madness, or worse. There is no slavery under the Treaty. The chances of materialism are not greater than they would be under a Republican form of government, or any other form of government. It is undoubtedly for ourselves to decide.

We have a chance now of giving our people a better life, we have a chance of doing the things that the people require. We have a chance of securing that the people shall no longer live the life of beasts. We have a chance of ending our slums. We have a chance of ending the hovels of some of our country places. We have a chance now, not by travelling any soft road, God knows, but by a hard, united effort to make Ireland something for the next generation, which it was not for ourselves.

It is suggested that martyrdom and suffering are necessary as a refining influence. We know as well as any of our opponents their refining influence. We know what their value has been in the past, in 1916 and from 1916 onwards. But martyrdom and suffering were for an end, not for their own sakes—the end being freedom and the noble life than can be lived in freedom.

Our opponents have failed by argument to win the Irish people to support their barren and destructive policy, or rather their negation of policy. Other tactics are now necessary on their part.

Incitement to mutiny takes the place of argument in the hope of stirring up turmoil. Their only hope now lies in wrecking by arranging and exploiting incidental troubles. For factionist ends they are jeopardising the unity of Ireland. They are jeopardising its independence; they are jeopardising its progress.

'Go another round in the race,' says Mr. de Valera to you, 'and who knows that the other fellow will be able to finish it.'

Yes! Who knows? And suppose he were able to finish it—what then? Is the safety and future of the nation to be staked on such a gamble?

The captain is trying to pull the ship off the rocks, we are told.

And how is he doing it? When the former Minister for Defence has by political propaganda been inciting mutiny in the army, and when Mr. de Valera is asked to speak on the situation, 'It is too serious,' he says, 'to make a pronouncement.'

Is that the way in which he is pulling the ship off the rocks?

The former Minister for Home Affairs obstructs the formation of a police force—a police force intended by us to deal with the outbreak of violence and crime which is endangering us—he cavils as to whether the force is to be under the authority of Dail Eireann or the Provisional Government. Do Mr. de Valera and his followers acquiesce in this obstruction—in this action which is conniving at lawlessness?

Is this his way of pulling the ship off the rocks?

At this moment—and it is a serious moment in the nation's life—the only policy of our opponents has become, it seems, by hidden manœuvre, to stir up trouble.

Their desire evidently is by any trickery to delay the expression of the people's will in an election ; to prepare intimidation for the time when that election must inevitably come. Is this for the chance of being able to declare another war against the enemy who is departing? If this is so, let them tell us ; let them inform us as to what they are going to do and how they are going to do it. Let them put their policy, their constitution, their programme, before the people.

What is their object? I, for one, do not know. I know what their tactics are—they are the tactics of a discredited and defeated faction.[1]

. . . . .

DUBLIN CASTLE HAS FALLEN

On the 17th March, Mr. Collins paid his first public visit to his constituency since the Treaty was signed. Speaking to a great gathering in Skibbereen, he recalled last St. Patrick's Day, when the enemy was hammering his hardest. There was no freedom to speak the Irish language. The guns of the enemy were in action ; the firing squadron was at work ; the hangman was busy.

Very few hoped to be there all together as they were today. He certainly did not expect to be amongst them. Perhaps you did not expect to see me here, and we did not expect to see the ships sailing away to England with the Auxiliaries, the Black and Tans, the R.I.C., the British soldiery, and with the civilian occupants of Dublin Castle.

We did not expect to see the Auxiliary division walking out of Beggar's Bush Barracks and our men, who had been hunted and harried, who would have been shot like dogs if they had been caught, taking possession of these barracks in the full light of day as recognised soldiers of the Irish nation. We would almost as soon have expected to see our soldiers, by force of arms, beating the enemy out of all the strongholds, but we have beaten him out by means of the fight made in Ireland and the fight made in London.

You will remember that I was supposed to have been shot or captured many a time. If one of those reports had been true you would not have been a bit more surprised than you were when you read in the papers that Dublin Castle had been surrendered into my hands for the Irish nation.

This time last year the present P.M.G. was in penal servitude, and now he is at work at the head of his office preparing to take over the huge machine. You see already Irish letters on the stamps, which you use every day, and in a short time we will have our own Irish-designed stamps instead of stamps we have been used to from our childhood.

This is an everyday indication of what is happening.

We are forming a police force to put down those outbreaks of violence, which were not altogether unexpected and which usually follow on such conditions as prevailed in Ireland for the past three years, for in every country there is always an unlawful element ready to come in or to arise at times of change like the present, when authority is being transferred as it is today. Our opponents are not satisfied with this force.

They have many grievances. Its formation is causing them sleepless nights. It is being enrolled under the Provisional Government instead of under Dail Eireann, or is it the other way round? In any case, whatever way it is, our opponents are saying it is wrong.

They say there will be trouble—that violence and outrages are minor matters; that protection of our people and property are trifling affairs, fit work for incompetent amateurs, beneath the dignity of high-minded men of principle, who know so much more than others about freedom and 'upholding the Republic', and the 'Democratic right of the people to govern themselves'—with no right evidently to protect themselves—who know how to talk about these things, at any rate, in much finer language than you and I would be able to think of if we pressed our heads for a week.

I am not a civilian in war, and I am not a war man in peace.

We are plain people here in Co. Cork. We don't bother much about words, but we do understand facts, and we see the enemy going out of Ireland, the enemy that was here in our fathers' time, in our grandfathers', and in their grandfathers' time.

When we see the enemy marching out, we know it means something, and twenty Mr. de Valeras, no matter what their eloquence, will not persuade us that it does not.

When we see troops surrender their strongholds, the troops under whose protection the battering-ram was used all over Cork in the Land War, the troops that protected the corn which would have saved the millions that suffered from the famine, the troops that beat the Fenians and subdued the '48 men, caused burnings and horrors of '98, the troops that through all the centuries kept us crushed—when we see these going and see our troops coming into their places we know that means something and twenty Erskine Childers will not persuade us that it does not.

The leader of our opponents and his followers all wish we were back again where we were last year. Do you wish it?

I cannot say I wish it. To my eyes it is more hopeful and better to see Sean M'Keon taking over Athlone from the British than lying under sentence of death in Mountjoy Jail. It is hinted to us that under the new Irish Government the British Government will still prevail here.

The British Government had kept them in subjection by destroying their Government and replacing it by the British one. The troops were kept here to maintain the British Government, and, without these troops, there could never have been a British Government here, and when they went that Government could not be here. The British fought with tooth and claw for three years to maintain their Government and to destroy our efforts to have our own Government, and to get out of the way the men in Ireland who were preventing them from succeeding.

The British failed in the task, and they have surrendered all right to govern us, but we are, say our opponents, under the authority of Lloyd George and his Cabinet. All Government is being or has been handed over to us.

The British game is up. Dublin Castle has fallen, and with it will have gone all bureaucratic regulations and tyrannies which the people of Ireland suffered under the British regime.

The departments which the British used as the means of governing us are ended, they are handed over to the representatives of the people, and we are still under the British Government our opponents say.

The Governor-General is worrying them, and the telephone that we heard one of the deputies speaking about, the Governor-General having his mouth at this end of it, and Lloyd George his ear at the other end. How can we be free, how can we govern ourselves when such a thing exists?

We are not afraid of any telephone. We have dealt with more than a telephone. All these things are not the things that matter now. At the Ard Fheis Mr. de Valera asked, 'Are you going to keep, as in the past, trying to secure the recognition of your fundamental right to whatever form of freedom you please?'

No, we are not, we are not wasting time by forcing a door which is already open. We have already secured recognition of the right, and we mean now to exercise that right.

I ask, what function of Government is there that we cannot fulfil as we please? The future rests entirely with ourselves—a new order of things is facing us.[2]

• • • •

Advance and Use Our Liberties[3]

In my opinion the Truce of July, 1921, could have been secured in December, 1920, at the time his Grace Archbishop Clune endeavoured to mediate, but the opportunity was lost through the too precipitate action of certain of our public men and public bodies.

The actions taken indicated an over-keen desire for peace, and although terms of Truce were virtually agreed upon, they were abandoned because the British leaders thought those actions indicated weakness, and they consequently decided upon surrender of our arms. The result was the continuance of the struggle. British aggression went on unabated, and our defence was kept up to the best of our ability.

I am not aware of any negotiations that preceded the Truce of July. I do know there was much visiting by well-meaning but unauthorised persons. So far, however, as my knowledge goes, these did not have any effect on the communication from Mr.

Lloyd George to President de Valera which opened up the period of correspondence between the two Governments and the subsequent negotiations in London. If there were any official conversations prior to the Lloyd George letter, they took place entirely without my knowledge.

It has been variously stated that the Treaty was signed under duress.

I did not sign the Treaty under duress, except in the sense that the position as between Ireland and England, historically, and because of superior forces on the part of England, has always been one of duress.

The element of duress was present when we agreed to the Truce, because our simple right would have been to beat the English out of Ireland. There was an element of duress in going to London to negotiate. But there was not, and could not have been, any personal duress.

The threat of 'immediate and terrible war' did not matter overmuch to me. The position appeared to be then exactly as it appears now. The British would not, I think, have declared terrible and immediate war upon us.

They had three courses of action open to them. First, to dissolve the parliaments and put their proposals before the country; second, to resume the war by courting openly and covertly breakages of the Truce (these breakages of the Truce might easily have come from either side); thirdly, to blockade Ireland, and at the same time encourage spasmodic internal conflict.

The first course of action seemed to me to be the most likely, and, as a result of a political win on our side either No. 2 or No. 3 would have been very easily managed by the British. A political reverse would have been more damaging to us than either 2 or 3.

The threat of immediate and terrible war was probably bluff. The immediate tactics would surely have been to put the offer of July 20, which the British considered a very good offer, before the country, and, if rejected, they would have very little difficulty in carrying their own people into a war against Ireland.

Another thing I believe, is, that on resumption of hostilities the British would have been anxious to fight with us on the basis of belligerent rights. In such circumstances, I doubt if we would have been able to carry on a conflict with the success which had previously attended our efforts. I scarcely think that our resources would have been equal to bearing belligerent rights and responsibilities.

I am not impressed by the talk of duress, nor by threats of a declaration of immediate and terrible war. Britain has not made a declaration of war upon Egypt, neither has she made a declaration of war upon India. But is the conflict less terrible because of the absence of such declaration?

We must not be misled by words and phrases. Unquestionably the alternative to the Treaty, sooner or later, was war, and if the Irish Nation had accepted that, I should have gladly accepted it. The opponents of the Treaty have declared over and over again that the alternative to the Treaty was not war.

In my judgment, this was misleading the Irish Nation. The decision of the Irish Nation should not be given on a false basis. That was, and is, my own attitude, and if, indeed, it be true, as the antagonists of the Treaty say, that the alternative to the Treaty was not war, where, then, is the heroism? Where, then, is the necessity for the future sacrifices that have been talked of so freely?

To me it would have been a criminal act to refuse to allow the Irish Nation to give its opinion as to whether it would accept this settlement or resume hostilities. That, I maintain, is a democratic stand. It has always been the stand of public representatives who are alive to their responsibilities.

The Irish struggle has always been for freedom—freedom from English occupation, from English interference, from English domination—not for freedom with any particular label attached to it.

What we fought for at any particular time was the greatest measure of freedom obtainable at the time, and it depended upon our strength whether the claim was greater than at another time or lesser than at another time.

When the national situation was very bad we lay inert; when it improved a little we looked for Repeal of the Union; when it receded again we looked for Home Rule under varying trade names; when it went still worse we spoke of some form of devolution. When our strength became greater our aim became higher, and we strove for a greater measure of freedom under the name of a Republic. But it was freedom we sought for, not the name of the form of government we should adopt when we got our freedom.

When I supported the approval of the Treaty at the meeting of Dail Eireann I said it gave us freedom—not the ultimate freedom which all nations hope for and struggle for, but freedom to achieve that end. And I was, and am now, fully alive to the implications of that statement.

Under the Treaty Ireland is about to become a fully constituted nation. The whole of Ireland, as one nation, is to compose the

Irish Free State, whose parliament will have power to make laws for the peace, order and good government of Ireland, with an executive responsible to that parliament.

This is the whole basis of the Treaty. It is the bedrock from which our status springs, and any later Act of the British Parliament derives its force from the Treaty only. We have got the present position by virtue of the Treaty, and any forthcoming Act of the British Legislature will, likewise, be by virtue of the Treaty.

It is not the definition of any status which would secure to us that status, but our power to make secure, and to increase what we have gained; yet obtaining by the Treaty the constitutional status of Canada, and that status being one of freedom and equality, we are free to take advantage of that status, and we shall set up our Constitution on independent Irish lines. And no conditions mentioned afterwards in the Treaty can affect or detract from the powers which the mention of that status in the Treaty gives us, especially when it has been proved, has been made good, by the withdrawal out of Ireland of English authority of every kind.

In fact England has renounced all right to govern Ireland, and the withdrawal of her forces is the proof of this. With the evacuation secured by the Treaty has come the end of British rule in Ireland. No foreigner will be able to intervene between our Government and our people. Not a single British soldier, nor a single British official, will ever step again upon our shores, except as guests of a free people.

Our Government will have complete control of our army, our schools, and our trade. Our soldiers, our judges, our ministers will be the soldiers, judges, and ministers of the Irish Free State. We can send our own ambassadors to Washington, to Paris, to the Vatican; we can have our own representatives on the League of Nations (if we wish).

It was freedom we fought for—freedom from British interference and domination. Let us ask ourselves these few questions: Are the English going? To what extent are they going? If the Treaty is put into operation will they, for all practical purposes, be gone?

The answer to the first question is to be seen in the evacuation that is proceeding apace. We claimed that the Treaty would secure this evacuation. The claim is being fulfilled. The Auxiliaries are practically gone. The regular British military forces are rapidly following them. The answer to the second and third questions is that they remain for negligible purposes in that the extent to which they remain is negligible.

We shall have complete freedom for all our purposes. We shall be rid completely of British interference and British rule. We can establish in its place our own rule, and exactly what kind of rule we like. We can restore our Gaelic life in exactly what form we like. We can keep what we have gained, and make it secure and strong. The little we have not yet gained we can go ahead and gain.

All other questions are really questions of arrangement, in which our voice shall be the deciding voice. Any names, any formulas, any figureheads, representing England's wish to conceal the extent of her departure, to keep some pretence of her power over us, which is now gone, will be but names, formulas, figureheads. England exercised her power over us simply by the presence of her forces—military forces, police forces, legal, and social forces.

Is it seriously to be suggested that in the new order some functionary, no matter what we may call him, will serve the purpose of all these forces, or, apart from him, the particular interpretation of the words of a document?

The British Government could only be maintained by the presence of British forces. Once these are gone the British Government can no longer arrange the form our National Government and our National life will take, nor can they set any limits to either. If we wish to make our nation a free and a great and a good nation we can do so now. But we cannot do it if we are to fight among ourselves as to whether it is to be called Saorstat or Poblacht.

Whatever the name or the political phraseology, we cannot restore Ireland without a great united effort.

Any difficulty now in making a noble Irish-Ireland will lie in our people themselves and in the hundreds of years of anglicisation to which we have been subjected. The task before us, having got rid of the British, is to get rid of the British influences—to de-anglicise ourselves; for there are many among us who still cling to English ways, any thoughtlessness, any carelessness, will tend to keep things on the old lines—the inevitable danger of the proximity of the two nations.

Can any restriction or limitation in the Treaty prevent us making our nation great and potent? Can the presence of a representative of the British Crown, depending on us for his resources, prevent us from doing that? Can the words of a document as to what our status is prevent us from doing that? One thing only can prevent us—disunion among ourselves.

Can we not concentrate and unite, not on the negative, but on the positive, task of making a real Ireland distinct from Britain—a nation of our own?

The only way to get rid of British contamination and the evils of corrupt materialism is to secure a united Ireland intent on democratic ways, to make our free Ireland a fact, and not to keep it for ever in dreamland as something that will never come true, and which has no practical effect or reality except as giving rise to everlasting fighting and destruction, which seem almost to have become ends in themselves in the minds of some—some who appear to be unheeding and unmindful of what the real end is.

Ireland is one—perhaps the only—country in Europe which has now living hopes for a better civilization. We have a great opportunity. Much is within our grasp. Who can lay a finger on our liberties?

If any power menaces our liberties, we are in a stronger position than before to repel the aggressor. That position will grow stronger with each year of freedom if we will all unite for the aims we have in common.

Let us advance and use these liberties to make Ireland a shining light in a dark world, to reconstruct our ancient civilization on modern lines, to avoid the errors, the miseries, the dangers, into which other nations, with their false civilizations, have fallen.

In taking the Treaty we are not going in for the fleshpots of the British Empire—not unless we wish to. It is futile to suppose that all these tendencies would disappear under freedom by some other name, or that the government of an externally associated nation, or of a Republic, any more than of a Free State, would be able to suppress them, and to force Gaelicism upon the nation.

Whatever form of free government we had, it would be the Government of the Irish Nation. All the other elements, old Unionists, Home Rulers, Devolutionists, would have to be allowed freedom and self-expression. The only way to build the nation solid and Irish is to effect these elements in a friendly national way—by attraction, not by compulsion, making them feel themselves welcomed into the Irish Nation, in which they can join and become absorbed, as long ago the Geraldines and the de Burgos became absorbed.

The Treaty is already vindicating itself. The English Die-hards said to Mr. Lloyd George and his Cabinet: 'You have surrendered.' Our own Die-hards said to us: 'You have surrendered.' There is a simple test. Those who are left in possession of the battlefield have won.

• • • • •

Alternative to the Treaty

Ireland 'A Mother Country'

Document No. 2 Analysed[4]

The main difference between the Treaty and the alternative proposals put forward by Mr. de Valera (known as Document No. 2) is that one is signed by the Plenipotentiaries of both nations and has been approved by the representatives of both nations; the other is not signed.

In my belief it would not be signed in its present form; not, indeed, that it contains much that is not in the Treaty, nor that it contains much that England objects to, but simply that in its construction it is too loose. Undoubtedly, in the application of its details we should constantly have been faced with conflicting interpretations leading to inevitable discordance.

It was claimed for the document by its sponsors that it would be approved by the English people; that, on the other hand, England never kept a Treaty, nor would she keep the present Treaty. The inference, of course, is that England would keep a Treaty which she had not signed but would not keep a Treaty which she had signed.

The document was not drafted by Mr. de Valera. There is little difficulty in guessing the author. Dominionism tinges every line. No Irishman who understands the tradition and the history of Ireland would think or write of his country's aspirations in the terms used in this document. In the official laudation given it by the organ of its supporters the following occurs:

> 'Clause 3 and 4 must be read together. What they mean is this, that the association in matters of "common concern" shall be a free one, not binding Ireland to submit to the decisions either of the British alone or of a majority of the States of the Commonwealth of which Britain is one.
>
> It is on that footing that an Irish representative would attend meetings of the body known as the "Imperial Conference", consisting of Dominion Premiers and British Cabinet Ministers to discuss and co-operate in matters of "common concern". That is the footing on which the Commonwealth States act together now, and the words within quotation marks at the end of

> Clause 4 are taken from what is known as the Constitutional Resolution passed at the Imperial Conference of 1917.
>
> It will be seen that the Commonwealth States, including Britain, are bound to "consultation" and no more. They are free to take action "as their several Governments may determine"—a partnership based on individual freedom. Ireland would be in the same position.'

Thus Ireland is by our own free offer, under this document, represented at the Imperial Conference. Our status is taken from a Constitutional Resolution passed at an Imperial Conference. The outlook of the author of the document is bounded entirely by the horizon of the British Empire.

This is not my stand, and at a Conference in London with the British representatives I made it quite clear that Ireland was A MOTHER COUNTRY, with the duties and responsibilities and feelings and devotions of a mother country.

This simple statement had more effect on the British delegates than all the arguments about Dominion status, or all the arguments basing the claim of our historic nation on any new-found idea. Irish nationhood springs from the Irish people, not from any comparison with any other nation, not from any equality—inherent or acquired—with any other nation.

Clause 1 of the document, which states:

> 'That the legislative, executive and judicial authority of Ireland shall be derived solely from the people of Ireland'.

is a declaration of rights more suitable to form the basis of the Constitution of a free nation than to be incorporated in a Treaty of Peace between two nations that had been at war.

The opponents of the Treaty were most insistent on the argument that it was Britain (by passing the Treaty through her Parliament) who conferred on us the Rights and Powers of the Treaty. But we definitely stipulate for a like British acquiescence in Document No. 2.

That is clear from the clause asking for ratification by the British Parliament. British ratification is a legal thing. It is no worse in one case than in the other. It is no better either. But surely no one recognises any right in Britain to agree or to disagree with that fundamental principle of freedom which concerns the people of Ireland alone.

In fact, the Treaty secures this position. Under the Treaty, the

English will no longer have any legislative, executive, or judicial authority in Ireland.

All such authority will be vested in the Parliament of Ireland, which alone will have power to make laws for the peace, order, and good government of Ireland.

Clauses 2, 3 and 4 of the document are all a loose paraphrase of the Treaty, dangerous and misleading in their looseness. They read:

> (2) 'That for purposes of "common concern" Ireland shall be associated with the States of British Commonwealth, viz., the Kingdom of Great Britain, the Dominion of Canada, the Commonwealth of Australia, the Dominion of New Zealand, and the Union of South Africa.
>
> (3) 'That while voting as an associate, the rights, status, and privileges of Ireland shall be in no respect less than those enjoyed by any of the component States of the British Commonwealth.
>
> (4) 'That the matters of "common concern" shall include Defence, Peace and War, Political Treaties, and all matters now treated as of "common concern" amongst the States of the British Commonwealth, and that in these matters there shall be between Ireland and the States of the British Commonwealth such concerted action, founded on consultation, as the several Governments may determine.'

Under these clauses Ireland would be committed to an association so vague that it might afford grounds for claims by Britain which might give her an opportunity to press for control in Irish affairs as 'common concerns', and to use, or to threaten to use, force. The Irish people could not have been asked, and would not have agreed, to commit themselves to anything so vague.

Clause 4 does not mend the matter; it makes it worse, as 'common concern' may include anything else besides the things named. In fact, it is common knowledge that there are many common concerns in the inter-dealings between the various States of the Commonwealth.

This is a very vital point. We know that there are many things which the States of the British Commonwealth can afford to regard as 'common concerns' which we could not afford so to regard. This is where we must be careful to protect ourselves as best we can against the disadvantages of geographical propinquity. This is where we had to find some form of association which would safeguard us, as far as we could be safeguarded, in somewhat the same degree as the 3,000 miles of ocean safeguards Canada.

And it is obvious that the 'association with the British Commonwealth' mentioned in the British Prime Minister's invitation, which was accepted by Mr. de Valera on behalf of Dail Eireann, meant association of a different kind from that of mere alliance of isolated nations, and now to suggest otherwise is not straightforward.

The question was of an association which would be honourable to Ireland, which would give us full freedom to manage our own affairs, and prevent interference by Britain; which would give the maximum security that this freedom would be observed (and we may be trusted to see that it is so observed), and which would be acceptable to Ireland as recognising her nationhood.

We negotiated from the standpoint of an independent sovereign nation, with a view to finding means of being honourably associated with the British group of nations in a way in which we were not associated with them before the negotiations.

The link which binds that group is a link which binds free nations in a voluntary association. This is what we obtained in the Treaty—freedom within our nation, freedom of association without.

The external association mentioned in Document No. 2 has neither the honesty of complete isolation (a questionable advantage in these days of warring nationalities, when it is not too easy for a small nation to stand rigidly alone) nor the strength of free partnership satisfying the different partners. Such external association was not practical politics.

Actually in this regard the terms of the Treaty are less objectionable than the formulas of the document. Restrictions in the Treaty there unquestionably are. Restrictions in Document No. 2 equally unquestionably there are. But the Treaty will be operative, and the restrictions must gradually tend to disappear as we go on more and more strongly solidifying and establishing ourselves as a free nation.

> Clause 5. 'That in virtue of this association of Ireland with the States of the British Commonwealth citizens of Ireland in any of these States shall not be subject to any disabilities which a citizen of one of the component States of the British Commonwealth would not be subject to, and reciprocally for citizens of these States in Ireland,'

is unintelligible, and does not meet the Irish wish to have some sentimental and racial ties with all the children of our race. The expression 'common citizenship' in the Treaty is not ideal, but it is less indefinite, and it does not attempt to confine Ireland's mother claim to the States of the British Commonwealth.

> Clause 6. 'That for purposes of association, Ireland shall recognise his Britannic Majesty as head of association,'

gives the recognition of the British Crown—a recognition which is as precise as any given in the Treaty.

It was after discussion of this Clause that Mr. de Valera's alternative oath was produced. That oath, which has already been published, was incorporated in a document submitted to the British by the Irish delegation. It reads as follows:

> 'I do swear to bear true faith and allegiance to the Constitution of Ireland and to the Treaty of Association of Ireland with the British Commonwealth of Nations, and to recognise the King of Great Britain as head of the Associated States.'

It was explained at the Dail debate by one of the foremost anti-Treatyites that the King of Great Britain could be regarded as a managing director, the explanation being that in these modern days industrial concerns were amalgamating and entering into agreements, etc.

The King of Great Britain would then occupy the same relative position towards the Associated States as a managing director occupied towards associated businesses. Whereupon it was very wisely pointed out by a journalist who was listening to the debate that a managing director is one who manages and directs. After all, whatever we may say of royal prerogatives, or anything of that kind, no modern democratic nation is managed and directed by one ruler.

Plain people will not be impressed by this managing director nonsense. Plain people will see no difference between these oaths.

We must always rely upon our own strength to keep the freedom we have obtained and to make it secure. And the constitutional status of Canada, defined in the Treaty, gives us stronger assurance of our immunity from interference by Britain than the indefinite clauses in Document No. 2.

These clauses have nothing effective to back them. They have practically all the disadvantages of the Treaty. It is too uncertain to have our future relationship based on 'ifs' and 'unless' and terms like 'so far as our resources permit'. These attempts at improvement are nothing but dangerous friction spots which it is the interest of Ireland to avoid.

Much has been said by the opponents of the Treaty about 'buttressing up the British Empire'. All these defence clauses in Document No. 2 are open to exactly the same attack. Under these clauses we could not assist an Indian or Egyptian craft that happened to get into Irish waters. These countries are at war with Britain, and we should be bound by our proffered agreement to help Britain.

Under the Treaty we should have a representative on the League of Nations (if we approved of a League of Nations), and that representative would have a real power to prevent aggression against Egypt and India.

To deal with Clauses 7 and 10 together, these clauses have reference to the matter of defence, and to the ordinary observer there is little difference between them and the clauses of the Treaty covering the same subject.

The Treaty secures that the harbours at certain ports can be used only for purposes of common defence, and not for any purpose of interfering with Irish freedom (and, again, we may be trusted to ensure that this shall be so).

There is one other thing under these clauses that I should like to explain from my own knowledge of how the matter arose. The British representatives made it quite clear to us that the British people could not, or would not, for the sake of their own safety, allow any Irish Government to build submarines. Document No. 2 concedes this British claim fully. Britain does not mind if we build a dreadnought or two, a battleship or two. One submarine would be a greater menace to her than these. Document No. 2, therefore, gives way to her on the only point that really matters. Such a concession to British necessity, real or supposed, is nothing but dishonesty. Let us agree, if need be, that we shall not build submarines; but don't let us pretend that we are doing it from any motive other than the real motive.

The remaining clauses seem nothing but a repetition of the clauses of the Treaty, with only such slight verbal alterations as no one but a factionist looking for means of making mischief would have thought it worth while to have risked wrecking the Treaty for.

It is fair criticism that the Treaty contains obsolete phraseology no longer suited to the status of freedom and equality of the States of the British Commonwealth and out of touch with the realities of our freedom. But phraseology does not alter the fact of our freedom, and we have the right and will exercise the right, to use a form of words to secure an interpretation more in accordance with the facts.

As an improvement on the Treaty Document No. 2 is not honest. It may be more dictatorial in language. It does not contain in principle a 'greater reconciliation with Irish national aspirations'. It merely attaches a fresh label to the same parcel, or, rather, a label written, of purpose, illegibly in the hope of making belief that the parcel is other than it is.

. . . . .

Building up Ireland

Resources to be Developed[5]

Mr. de Valera, in a speech he made on February 19, warned the people of Ireland against a life of ease, against living practically 'the life of the beasts', which, he fears, they may be tempted to do in Ireland under the Free State.

The chance that materialism will take possession of the Irish people is no more likely in a free Ireland under the Free State than it would be in a free Ireland under a Republican or any other form of government. It is in the hands of the Irish people themselves.

In the ancient days of Gaelic civilization the people were prosperous and they were not materialists. They were one of the most spiritual and one of the most intellectual peoples in Europe. When Ireland was swept by destitution and famine the spirit of the Irish people came most nearly to extinction. It was with the improved economic conditions of the last twenty years or more that it has re-awakened. The insistent needs of the body more adequately satisfied, the people regained desire once more to reach out to the higher things in which the spirit finds its satisfaction.

What we hope for in the new Ireland is to have such material welfare as will give the Irish spirit that freedom. We want such widely diffused prosperity that the Irish people will not be crushed by destitution into living practically 'the lives of the beasts'.

They were so crushed during the British occupation that they were described as being 'without the comforts of an English sow'. Neither must they be obliged, owing to unsound economic conditions, to spend all their powers of both mind and body in an effort to satisfy the bodily needs alone. The uses of wealth are to provide good health, comfort, moderate luxury, and to give the freedom which comes from the possession of these things.

Our object in building up the country economically must not

be lost sight of. That object is not to be able to boast of enormous wealth or of a great volume of trade, for their own sake. It is not to see our country covered with smoking chimneys and factories. It is not to show a great national balance-sheet, not to point to a people producing wealth with the self-obliteration of a hive of bees.

The real riches of the Irish nation will be the men and women of the Irish nation, the extent to which they are rich in body and mind and character.

What we want is the opportunity for everyone to be able to produce sufficient wealth to ensure these advantages for themselves. That such wealth can be produced in Ireland there can be no doubt:

'For the island is so endowed with so many dowries of nature, considering the fruitfulness of the soil, the ports, the rivers, the fishings, and especially the race and generation of men, valiant, hard, and active, as it is not easy to find such a confluence of commodities.'

Such was the impression made upon a visitor who came long ago to our island. We have now the opportunities to make our land indeed fruitful, to work up our natural resources, to bring prosperity for all our people.

If our national economy is put on a sound footing from the beginning it will, in the new Ireland, be possible for our people to provide themselves with the ordinary requirements of decent living. It will be possible for each to have sufficient food, a good home in which to live in fair comfort and contentment. We shall be able to give our children bodily and mental health; and our people will be able to secure themselves against the inevitable times of sickness and old age.

That must be our object. What we must aim at is the building up of a sound economic life in which great discrepancies cannot occur. We must not have the destitution of poverty at one end, and at the other an excess of riches in the possession of a few individuals, beyond what they can spend with satisfaction and justification.

Millionaires can spend their surplus wealth bestowing libraries broadcast upon the world. But who will say that the benefits accruing could compare with those arising from a condition of things in which the people themselves everywhere, in the city, town, and village, were prosperous enough to buy their own books and to put together their own local libraries in which they could take a personal interest and acquire knowledge in proportion to that interest?

The growing wealth of Ireland will, we hope, be diffused through all our people, all sharing in the growing prosperity, each receiving according to what each contributes in the making of that prosperity, so that the weal of all is assured.

How are we to increase the wealth of Ireland and ensure that all producing it shall share in it? That is the question which will be engaging the minds of our people, and will engage the attention of the new Government.

The keynote to the economic revival must be development of Irish resources by Irish capital for the benefit of the Irish consumer in such a way that the people have steady work at just remuneration and their own share of control.

How are we to develop Irish resources? The earth is our bountiful mother. Upon free access to it depends not only agriculture, but all other trades and industries. Land must be freely available. Agriculture, our main industry, must be improved and developed. Our existing industries must be given opportunities to expand. Conditions must be created which will make it possible for new ones to arise. Means of transit must be extended and cheapened. Our harbours must be developed. Our water-power must be utilised; our mineral resources must be exploited.

Foreign trade must be stimulated by making facilities for the transport and marketing of Irish goods abroad and foreign goods in Ireland. Investors must be urged and encouraged to invest Irish capital in Irish concerns. Taxation, where it hinders, must be adjusted, and must be imposed where the burden will fall lightest and can best be borne, and where it will encourage rather than discourage industry.

We have now in Ireland, owing to the restrictions put upon emigration during the European War, a larger population of young men and women than we have had for a great many years. For their own sake and to maintain the strength of the nation room must and can be found for them.

Agriculture is, and is likely to continue to be, our chief source of wealth. If room is to be found for our growing population, land must be freely available. Land is not freely available in Ireland. Thousands of acres of the best land lie idle or are occupied as ranches or form part of extensive private estates.

Side by side with this condition there are thousands of our people who are unable to get land on which to keep a cow or even to provide themselves and their families with vegetables.

If the ranches can be broken up, if we can get the land back again into the hands of our people, there will be plenty of employment and a great increase in the national wealth.

If land could be obtained more cheaply in town and country the housing problem would not present so acute a problem. There are large areas unoccupied in towns and cities as well as in country districts. When the Convention sat in 1917 it was found that in urban areas alone 67,000 houses were urgently needed. The figure must at the present moment be considerably higher. To ease the immediate situation, the Provisional Government has announced a grant to enable a considerable number of houses to be built. This grant, although seemingly large, is simply a recognition of the existence of the problem.

For those who intend to engage in agriculture we require specialised education. Agriculture is in these days a highly technical industry. We have the experiences of countries likes Holland, Germany, Denmark to guide us. Scientific methods of farming and stock-raising must be introduced. We must have the study of specialised chemistry to aid us, as it does our foreign competitors in the countries I have named. We must establish industries arising directly out of agriculture, industries for the utilisation of the by-products of the land—bones, bristles, hides for the production of soda glue, and other valuable substances.

With plenty of land available at an economic rent or price such industries can be established throughout the country districts, opening up new opportunities for employment.

Up to the sixteenth century Ireland possessed a colonial trade equal to England's. It was destroyed by the jealousy of English shipowners and manufacturers, and, by means of the Navigation Laws, England swept Ireland's commerce off the seas. It is true that these Navigation Laws were afterwards removed. But the removal found the Irish capital which might have restored our ruined commerce drained away from the country by the absence of opportunities for utilising it, or by absentee landlordism, or in other ways.

The development of industry in the new Ireland should be on lines which exclude monopoly profits. The product of industry would thus be left sufficiently free to supply good wages to those employed in it. The system should be on co-operative lines rather than on the old commercial capitalistic lines of the huge joint stock companies. At the same time I think we shall safely avoid State Socialism, which has nothing to commend it in a country like Ireland, and, in any case, is monopoly of another kind.

Given favourable conditions, there is a successful future for dressed meat industries on the lines of the huge co-operative industry started in Wexford; while there are many opportunities for the extension of dairying and cheese-making.

The industries we possess are nearly all capable of expansion. We can improve and extend all the following:

Brewing and distilling.
Manufacture of tobacco.
Woollen and linen industry.
Manufacture of hosiery and underclothing.
Rope and twine industry.
Manufacture of boots and shoes, saddlery, and all kinds of leather articles.
Production of hardware and agricultural machinery.
Production and curing of fish.

Of manufactured articles £48,000,000 worth are imported into Ireland yearly. A large part of these could be produced more economically at home. If land were procurable abundantly and cheaply it would be necessary also that capital should be forthcoming to get suitable sites for factories, a more easily obtained supply of power, an improvement, increase, and cheapening of the means of transport.

There are facilities for producing an enormous variety of products both for the home and foreign markets, if factories could be established. These should, as far as possible, be dispersed about the country instead of being concentrated in a few areas. This disposal will not only have the effect of avoiding congestion, but will incidentally improve the status and earnings of the country population and will enlarge their horizon.

I am not advocating the establishment of an industrial system as other countries know industrialism. If we are to survive as a distinct and free nation, industrial development must be on the general lines I am following. Whatever our solution of the question may be, we all realise that the industrial *status quo* is imperfect. However we may differ in outlook, politically or socially, it is recognised that one of the most pressing needs—if not the most pressing—is the question of labour in relation to industry, and it is consequently vitally necessary for the development of our resources that the position of employers and employees should rest on the best possible foundation.

And with this question of labour and industry is interwoven the question of land. It is no less important to have our foundations secure here. In the development of Ireland the land question presents itself under four main headings:

(1) The completion of purchase of tenanted lands;

(2) The extension and increase of powers of purchase of untenanted lands;

(3) The question of congestion in rural districts;

(4) The utilisation of lands unoccupied or withheld in urban areas.

For the purpose of such development Ireland has three great natural resources. Our coal deposits are by no means inconsiderable. The bogs of Ireland are estimated as having 500,000 million tons of peat fuel. Water-power is concentrated in her 237 rivers and 180 lakes. The huge Lough Corrib system could be utilised, for instance, to work the granite in the neighbourhood of Galway. In the opinion of experts, reporting to the Committee on the Water-Power Resources of Ireland, from the Irish lakes and rivers a total of 500,000 h.p. is capable of being developed.

The magnitude of this is more readily seen if it is appreciated that to raise this power in steam would require 7,500,000 tons of coal. With the present price of coal it should be a commercial proposition to develop our water-power as against steam, even though it did not take the place of steam-power entirely.

Schemes have been worked out to utilise the water-power of the Shannon, the Erne, the Bann, and the Liffey. It is probable that the Liffey and the Bann, being closely connected with industrial centres, can be dealt with at once. With unified control and direction, various sources of water-power could be arranged in large stations for centralised industries, and the energy could be re-distributed to provide light and heat for the neighbouring towns and villages.

That the advantages of our water-power are not lost on some of the keenest minds of the day is shown by the following extract from a speech made by Lord Northcliffe on St. Patrick's Day, 1917: 'The growth of the population of Great Britain has been largely due to manufactures based on the great asset, black coal. Ireland has none of the coal which has made England rich, but she possesses in her mighty rivers white coal of which millions of horse-power are being lost to Ireland every year. . . . I can see in the future very plainly prosperous cities, old and new, fed by the greatest river in the United Kingdom—the Shannon. I should like to read recent experts' reports on the Moy, the Suir, and the Lee.'

The development of this white power will also enable the means of communication and transport by rail and road to be cheapened and extended. And there is an urgent need for cheap transit. Railway rates and shipping rates are so high that, to take one example, the cost of transit is prohibitive to the Irish fish trade.

While the Irish seas are teeming with fish, we have the Dublin market depending upon the English market for its supplies. The export of Irish fish is decreasing, and the fishing industry is neither the source of remuneration it should be to those engaged in it, nor the source of profit it could be to the country.

To facilitate the transport of agricultural produce and commodities generally, a complete system of ways of communication must be established. The extension and unifying of our railways, linking up ocean ports and fishing harbours with the interior, is essential. This system will be worked in connection with our inland waterways, and will be supplemented by a motor-lorry service on our roads—and these also must be greatly improved.

Our harbours must be developed. Ireland occupies a unique geographical position. She is the stepping-stone between the Old World and the New. She should, therefore, become a great exchange mart between Europe and America. With Galway harbour improved and developed so as to receive American liners, passengers could land in Europe one or two days earlier than by disembarking at Liverpool.

The port and docks of Dublin are already making arrangements for a great increase in the volume of trade which is expected with the establishment of an Irish Government in Dublin. They are improving the port. They have schemes for providing deep water berthage for the largest ships afloat.

Soon the port of Dublin will be fitted in every way to receive and deal with all the trade which may be expected with our growing prosperity. The Board is also reclaiming land at the mouth of the Liffey, and soon some sixty acres will be available as a building site. This land is splendidly situated for commercial purposes.

It will be important to create efficient machinery for the economic marketing of Irish goods. A first step in this direction is the establishment of a clearing house in Dublin or the most convenient centre. It would form a link between a network of channels throughout Ireland through which goods could be transmitted, connecting with another network reaching out to all our markets abroad. It would examine and take delivery of goods going out and coming in, dealing with the financial business for both sides.

Such a concern would require capital and able and experienced management. With such, its success should be assured. It would be invaluable in helping our home and foreign trade. And with improved means of transit in Ireland, and an increase in the number of direct shipping routes, facilities would be in existence to make it operate successfully. It is not difficult to see the advantages of such a house. On the one hand it would be closely associated in location and business working with a central railway station where the important trunk lines converged, and on the other conveniently situated in relation to the National Customs House.

The mineral resources of Ireland have never been properly tapped. An Irish Government will not neglect this important source of wealth. The development of mines and minerals will be on national lines, and under national direction. This will prevent the monopoly by private individuals of what are purely national resources belonging to all the people of the nation. The profits from all these national enterprises—the working of mines, development of water-power, etc.—will belong to the nation for the advantage of the whole nation.

But Irish men and women as private individuals must do their share to increase the prosperity of the country. Business cannot succeed without capital. Millions of Irish money are lying idle in banks. The deposits in Irish joint stock banks increased in the aggregate by £7,318,000 during the half-year ended December 31, 1921. At that date the total of deposits and cash balances in the Irish banks was £194,391,000, to which in addition there was a sum of almost £14,000,000 in the Post Office Savings Bank. If Irish money were invested in Irish industries, to assist existing ones, and to finance new enterprises, there would be an enormous development of Irish commerce.

The Irish people have a large amount of capital invested abroad. With scope for our energies, with restoration of confidence, the inevitable tendency will be towards return of this capital to Ireland. It will then flow in its proper channel. It will be used for opening up new and promising fields in this country. Ireland will provide splendid opportunities for the investment of Irish capital, and it is for the Irish people to take advantage of these opportunities.

If they do not, investors and exploiters from outside will come in to reap the rich profits which are to be made. And, what is worse still, they will bring with them all the evils that we want to avoid in the new Ireland.

We shall hope to see in Ireland industrial conciliation and arbitration taking the place of strikes, and the workers sharing in the ownership and management of businesses.

A prosperous Ireland will mean a united Ireland. With equitable taxation and flourishing trade our North-East countrymen will need no persuasion to come and share in the healthy economic life of the country.

Appendix A

THE 1916 PROCLAMATION[1]

Poblacht na h-Eoreann

The Provisional Government
of the
Irish Republic
To the people of Ireland

Irishmen and Irishwomen: In the name of God and of the dead generations from which she receives her old tradition of nationhood, Ireland, through us, summons her children to her flag and strikes for her freedom.

Having organised and trained her manhood through her secret revolutionary organisation, the Irish Republican Brotherhood, and through her open military organisations, the Irish Volunteers and the Irish Citizen Army, having patiently perfected her discipline, having resolutely waited for the right moment to reveal herself, she now seizes that moment and, supported by her exiled children in America and by gallant allies in Europe, but relying in the first on her own strength, she strikes in full confidence of victory.

We declare the right of the people of Ireland to the ownership of Ireland and to the unfettered control of Irish destinies, to be sovereign and undefeasible. The long usurpation of that right by a foreign people and government has not extinguished the right, nor can it ever be extinguished except by the destruction of the Irish people. In every generation the Irish people have asserted their right to national freedom and sovereignty: six times during the past three hundred years they have asserted it in arms. Standing on that fundamental right and again asserting it in arms in the face of the world, we hereby proclaim the Irish Republic as a Sovereign Independent State, and we pledge our lives and the lives of our comrades-in-arms to the cause of its freedom, of its welfare and of its exaltation among the nations.

The Irish Republic is entitled to, and hereby claims, the allegiance of every Irishman and Irishwoman. The Republic guarantees religious and civil liberty, equal rights and equal opportunities to all its citizens, and declares its resolve to pursue the happiness and prosperity of the whole nation and of all its parts, cherishing all the children of the nation equally, and oblivious of the differences, carefully fostered by an alien government, which have divided a minority from the majority in the past.

Until our arms have brought the opportune moment for the establishment of a permanent National Government, representatives of the whole of the people of Ireland, and elected by the suffrages of all her men and women, the Provisional Government, hereby constituted, will administer the civil and military affairs of the Republic in trust for the people. We place the cause of the Irish Republic under the protection of the Most High God, Whose blessing we invoke upon our arms, and we pray that no one who serves that cause will dishonour it by cowardice, inhumanity or rapine. In this supreme hour the Irish nation must, by its valour and discipline, and by the readiness of its children to sacrifice themselves for the common good, prove itself worthy of the august destiny to which it is called.

Signed on Behalf of the Provisional Government,
THOMAS J. CLARKE

SEAN MACDIARMADA	THOMAS MACDONAGH
P. H. PEARSE	EAMONN CEANNT
JAMES CONNOLLY	JOSEPH PLUNKETT.

Appendix B[2]

THE MANIFESTO OF SINN FEIN
(as prepared for circulation for the General Election of December 1918)

Manifesto to the Irish people

The coming General Election is fraught with vital possibilities for the future of our nation. Ireland is faced with the question whether this generation wills it that she is to march out into the full sunlight of freedom, or is to remain in the shadow of a base imperialism that has brought and ever will bring in its train naught but evil for our race.

Sinn Fein gives Ireland the opportunity of vindicating her honour and pursuing with renewed confidence the path of national salvation by rallying to the flag of the Irish Republic.

Sinn Fein aims at securing the establishment of that Republic.

1. By withdrawing the Irish Representation from the British Parliament and by denying the right and opposing the will of the British Government or any other foreign Government to legislate for Ireland.

2. By making use of any and every means available to render impotent the power of England to hold Ireland in subjection by military force or otherwise.

3. By the establishment of a constituent assembly comprising persons chosen by Irish constituencies as the supreme national authority to speak and act in the name of the Irish people, and to develop Ireland's social, political and industrial life, for the welfare of the whole people of Ireland.

4. By appealing to the Peace Conference for the establishment of Ireland as an Independent Nation. At that conference the future of the nations of the world will be settled on the principle of government by consent of the governed. Ireland's claim to the application of that principle in her favour is not based on any accidental situation arising from the war. It is older than many if not all of the present belligerents. It is based on our unbroken tradition of nationhood, on a unity in a national name which has never been challenged, on our possession of a distinctive national culture and social order, on the moral courage and dignity of our people in the face of alien aggression, on the fact that in nearly every generation, and five times within the past 120 years our people have challenged in arms the right of England to rule this country. On these incontrovertible facts is based the claim that our people have beyond question established the right to be accorded all the power of a free nation.

Sinn Fein stands less for a political party than for the Nation; it represents the old tradition of nationhood handed on from dead generations; it stands by the Proclamation of the Provisional Government of Easter, 1916, reasserting the inalienable right of the Irish Nation to sovereign independence, reaffirming the determination of the Irish people to achieve it, and guaranteeing within the independent Nation equal rights and equal opportunities to all its citizens.

Believing that the time has arrived when Ireland's voice for the principle of untrammelled National self-determination should be heard above every interest of party or class, Sinn Fein will oppose at the Polls every individual candidate who does not accept this principle.

The policy of our opponents stands condemned on any test whether of principle or expediency. The right of a nation to sovereign independence rests upon immutable natural law and cannot be made the subject of a compromise. Any attempt to barter away the sacred and inviolate rights of a nationhood begins in dishonour and is bound to end in disaster. The enforced exodus of millions of our people, the decay of our industrial life, the ever-increasing financial plunder of our country, the whittling down of the demand for the 'Repeal of the Union', voiced by the first Irish Leader to plead in the Hall of the Conqueror to that of Home Rule on the Statute Book, and finally the contemplated mutilation of our country by partition, are some of the ghastly results of a policy that leads to national ruin.

Those who have endeavoured to harness the people of Ireland to England's war-chariot, ignoring the fact that only a freely-elected Government in a free Ireland has power to decide for Ireland the question of peace and war, have forfeited the right to speak for the Irish people. The Green Flag turned red in the hands of the Leaders, but that shame is not to be laid at the doors of the Irish people unless they continue a policy of sending their representatives to an alien and hostile assembly, whose powerful influence has been sufficient to destroy the integrity and sap the independence of their representatives. Ireland must repudiate the men who, in a supreme crisis for the nation, attempted to sell her birthright for the vague promises of English Ministers, and who showed their incompetence by failing to have even these promises fulfilled.

The present Irish members of the English Parliament constitute an obstacle to be removed from the path that leads to the Peace Conference. By declaring their will to accept the status of a province instead of boldly taking their stand upon the right of the nation they supply England with the only subterfuge at her disposal for obscuring the issue in the eyes of the world. By their persistent endeavours to induce the young manhood of Ireland to don the uniform of our seven-century-old oppressor, and place their lives at the disposal of the military machine that holds our Nation in bondage, they endeavour to barter away and even to use against itself the one great asset still left to our Nation after the havoc of centuries.

Sinn Fein goes to the polls handicapped by all the arts and contrivances that a powerful and unscrupulous enemy can use against us. Conscious of the power of Sinn Fein to secure the freedom of Ireland the British Government would destroy it. Sinn Fein, however, goes to the polls confident that the people of this ancient nation will be true to the old cause and will vote for the men who stand by the principles of Tone, Emmet, Mitchell, Pearse and Connolly, the men who disdain to whine to the enemy for favours, the men who hold that Ireland must be as free as England or Holland, or Switzerland or France, and whose demand is that the only status befitting this ancient realm is the status of a free nation.

Issued by the Standing Committee of Sinn Fein.

Appendix C

DAIL EIREANN LOAN

Net amounts received at Head Office as on the 4th August, 1920

CONNACHT

	£	s.	d.
Galway:			
Connemara ...	1,564	13	4
East ...	4,583	0	0
North ...	4,357	5	0
South ...	3,235	0	0
Leitrim ...	4,253	17	2
Mayo:			
East ...	5,424	10	0
North ...	3,980	5	0
South ...	7,052	0	0
West ...	5,053	0	0
Roscommon:			
North ...	3,830	0	0
South ...	4,500	10	0
Sligo:			
North ...	3,565	0	0
South ...	3,356	9	6
Total:	£54,755	10	0

LEINSTER

	£	s.	d.
Carlow ...	3,383	5	0
Dublin:			
Clontarf ...	2,173	0	0
College Gn....	2,090	15	0
Harbour ...	837	10	0
Pembroke ...	2,576	10	0
Rathmines ...	1,233	0	0
St. James' ...	1,379	0	0
St. Michan's	2,764	5	0
St. Stephen's	2,234	10	0
St. Patrick's...	2,093	10	0
North Co. ...	1,346	15	0
South Co. ...	1,985	10	0
Kildare:			
North ...	2,312	10	0
South ...	3,215	10	0
Kilkenny:			
North ...	2,907	0	0
South ...	5,281	10	0
Longford ...	5,598	10	0
Louth ...	2,535	5	0
Meath:			
North ...	1,902	4	0
South ...	2,262	0	0
Offaly ...	9,198	1	6
Leix & Ossory	10,030	12	6
Westmeath ...	4,426	0	0
Wexford:			
North ...	3,146	0	0
South ...	4,378	0	0
Wicklow:			
East ...	819	4	6
West ...	3,713	0	0
Total:	£85,822	17	6

MUNSTER

	£	s.	d.
Clare:			
East ...	13,609	4	6
West ...	7,713	0	0
Cork:			
City ...	11,145	10	0
East ...	6,519	15	0
Mid ...	7,095	2	6
North ...	6,497	0	0
North E. ...	3,148	0	0
South ...	4,689	5	10
South E. ...	1,917	0	0
West ...	4,250	0	0

	£	s.	d.
Kerry:			
East ...	5,148	10	0
North ...	9,000	0	0
South ...	3,104	2	0
West ...	8,546	15	0
Limerick:			
City ...	5,684	10	0
East ...	29,897	0	0
West ...	17,385	0	0
Tipperary:			
East ...	4,170	10	0
Mid ...	2,576	6	6
North ...	4,440	0	0
South ...	4,181	0	0
Waterford:			
City ...	636	5	0
County ...	4,543	10	0
Total:	£165,897	6	4

ULSTER

	£	s.	d.
Antrim:			
Belfast ...	2,348	6	6
East & North	196	0	0
Mid ...	132	0	0
South ...	427	0	0
Armagh:			
Mid ...	437	10	0
North ...	322	10	0
South ...	1,665	0	0
Cavan:			
East ...	4,192	4	8
West ...	2,595	0	0
Derry:			
City ...	1,313	0	0
North ...	772	10	0
South ...	713	0	0
Donegal:			
East ...	556	0	0
North ...	860	0	0
South ...	965	10	0
West ...	673	0	0
Down:			
East & Mid	2,574	0	0
South ...	1,772	10	0
West ...	157	0	0
Fermanagh:			
North ...	1,768	0	0
South ...	1,458	0	0
Monaghan:			
North ...	2,457	18	0
South ...	5,661	0	0
Tyrone:			
North E. ...	2,191	10	0
North W. ...	1,164	10	0
South ...	1,701	0	0
Total:	£39,073	19	2

GRAND TOTALS

	£	s.	d.
Connacht	54,755	10	0
Leinster	85,822	17	6
Munster	165,897	6	4
Ulster	39,073	19	2
Cumann na mBan	795	0	0
Britain and France	11,457	8	0
	£357,802	1	0

Appendix D

MR. BARTON'S NOTES[4]
of
Two Sub-Conferences held
on December 5th/6th, 1921, at
10 Downing Street.
No. I . . . 3 p.m.
No. II . . . 11.30 p.m. to 2 a.m.*

Present:

British Representatives:	*Irish Representatives:*
Mr. Lloyd George	Mr. Griffith
Mr. Chamberlain	Mr. Collins
Lord Birkenhead	Mr. Barton
Mr. Churchill	

SUB-CONFERENCE NO. I
3 p.m.

The Conference opened by Lloyd George saying that he must know once and for all exactly where we stood as regards the Ulster proposals. He said that the Ulster proposals in the document now before us were exactly those to which Arthur Griffith had agreed and on which he had undertaken not to let him (Lloyd George) down.

Arthur Griffith replied that he had not let him down and did not intend to do so, but that before he gave a decision on the earlier articles in the document he must have a reply from Craig either accepting or refusing the unity of Ireland.

Chamberlain and Lloyd George argued that such a proposition was inadmissible, unreasonable and contrary to the undertaking not to let Lloyd George down.

Mr. Chamberlain stated that it was due to the confidence they had in our undertaking that they would not be let down by us that his colleagues and he had adopted the attitude they did at the Liverpool meeting and staked thereon their political future.

Michael Collins said that for us to agree to any conditions defining the future relations of Great Britain and Ireland prior to Craig's giving his assent to the unity of Ireland was impossible, that to do so would be to surrender our whole fighting position. That every document we ever sent them had stated that any proposals for the association of Ireland with the British Commonwealth of

* Times as stated on a copy of the document.

Nations was conditional upon the unity of Ireland. That, unless Craig accepted inclusion under the All-Ireland Parliament, the unity of Ireland was not assured and that if he refused inclusion we should be left in the position of having surrendered our position without having even secured the essential unity of Ireland.

Lloyd George got excited. He shook his papers in the air, declared that we were trying deliberately to bring about a break on Ulster because our people in Ireland had refused to come within the Empire and that Arthur Griffith was letting him down where he had promised not to do so. He produced a paper from an envelope, stated that he had shewn it to Arthur Griffith at ——'s house and that Arthur Griffith had agreed to its contents. Lloyd George referred to this document as a letter and thereby mystified me and appeared to mystify Michael Collins. I could not recollect the existence of any letter on this subject other than the one Arthur Griffith wrote to Lloyd George on November 2nd after consultation with the other members of the Delegation. The paper was then passed across the table. It proved to be a memorandum, not a letter, and read as follows:

> 'If Ulster did not see her way to accept immediately the principle of a Parliament of All-Ireland—coupled with the retention by the Parliament of Northern Ireland of the powers conferred upon it by the Act of 1920 and such other safeguards as have already been suggested in my letter of 10th November—we should then propose to create such Parliament for All-Ireland but to allow Ulster the right within a specified time on an address to the Throne carried in both houses of the Ulster Parliament to elect to remain subject to the Imperial Parliament for all the reserved services. In this case she would continue to exercise through her own Parliament all her present rights; she would continue to be represented in the British Parliament and she would continue subject to British taxation except in so far as already modified by the Act of 1920. In this case, however, it would be necessary to revise the boundary of Northern Ireland. This might be done by a Boundary Commission which would be directed to adjust the line both by inclusion and exclusion so as to make the Boundary conform as closely as possible to the wishes of the population.'

Arthur Griffith declared his adhesion to his undertaking but argued that it was not unreasonable for us to require that Craig should reply before we refused or accepted the proposals now before us.

Lloyd George declared his adhesion to his undertaking but argued that it was not unreasonable for us to require that Craig should reply before we refused or accepted the proposals now before us.

Lloyd George declared that to make receipt of such a reply conditional before accepting or refusing was letting him down on his proposals because the only alternative to Craig's acceptance of the unity of Ireland was the Boundary Commission and that his Government would carry the Boundary Commission proposal into effect with strict fidelity. He then said that they would have to withdraw to discuss the matter amongst themselves but first he would hear what objections or alterations we had to the proposal.

Arthur Griffith replied that he understood from Michael Collins' interview with Lloyd George that certain alterations might possibly be made in the proposals.

Lloyd George asked what were the alterations we suggested but that we must understand [*sic*] that the first three Clauses were absolutely essential. There could be no discussion about these.

Arthur Griffith replied that some alteration might be made in the Oath.

Birkenhead said that Mr. Collins had handed in to him that morning a form of oath on which he (Mr. Collins) had been working and then produced it with his (Birkenhead's) alterations. We objected to the final words being 'British Empire' and suggested 'British Commonwealth of Nations'.

Lloyd George asked for any further objections.

We objected to 'shall contribute' in Clause 5, and desired insertion of 'if any' after 'such sums' and elsewhere.

Chamberlain said that these alterations were matters of wording only. On Clause 6 we argued at great length that the word 'exclusively' precluded us from commencing to build vessels or make any preparations for taking over our own coastal defence at any time, and that the 'Conference for Review' referred to in the second paragraph might never be held if the British did not wish to reconsider the subject. There was a long argument over this in which Churchill, Michael Collins and myself went over all the arguments again.

Churchill stated that if Ireland were permitted any navy it would be impossible to get the Treaty through Parliament. That the English people would believe that we were going to build ships which in war might be used against them. That the possibility of our building submarines or mine-laying vessels to attack their food ships would be argued from every angle. The discussion lasted a long time. We demanded the removal of the word 'exclusively'; this was grudgingly accorded. We then sought to get it explicitly stated that Ireland should be required to build one or more ships for her coastal protection; this was absolutely refused, except as regards revenue and fishery protection ships, and Churchill stated that he would definitely oppose any provision that Ireland should have a navy of her own and would even oppose it five years hence if he had the opportunity.

Michael Collins then took up the Trade Clause and said that

Lloyd George had intimated that freedom on both sides might be accorded. He also dealt with the suggestion that the safeguards for Ulster should be a matter for discussion between ourselves and the Ulster representatives.

The British then withdrew and we consulted amongst ourselves and decided that if they came back to break on our refusal to accept or refuse pending Craig's answer that Arthur Griffith's last card was to demand reference to the Colonial Premiers.

Birkenhead then returned alone and took note again of the particular points we required changed.

On their return we again took up the points in dispute. First in Clause 6, to which Churchill agreed to add 'with a view to the undertaking by Ireland of a share of her own coastal defence', and to a date five years hence being fixed for the Conference to review the clause, but refused every proposition to make this apply to (b) facilities in time of war. He refused to take 'Queenstown' out of the Annex, and explained that care and maintenance parties meant gunners and trained men to take charge drawn from the R.G.A. and R.E., numbering 1,060 men and 69 officers or thereabouts. He also stated that 'Admiralty property and rights' at Berehaven did not mean that they would demand compensation if at any time the docks etc. passed to us. Birkenhead said that if they were handed over to the Crown representative in Ireland the Crown could not demand payment from the Crown.

Lloyd George said that on Trade he was prepared to agree provisionally that there should be freedom on both sides to impose any tariffs either liked subject to the Articles of Agreement being accepted by us. That he himself had been the strongest on their side on the compulsory Free State Clauses, but that he would withdraw his opposition on the conditions stated.

We then went back to Ulster.

Arthur Griffith agreed that he personally would sign the Treaty whether Craig accepted or not, but that his colleagues were in a different position from himself in that they were not party to the promise not to let Lloyd George down, and that it was not fair to demand acceptance or refusal from them before Craig replied.

Considerable discussion took place here on the justice and injustice of our being asked to agree or disagree before Craig replied and Arthur Griffith made repeated efforts to avoid the question being put to Michael Collins and myself.

Lloyd George stated that he had always taken it that Arthur Griffith spoke for the Delegation, that we were all plenipotentiaries and that it was now a matter of peace or war and we must each of us make up our minds. He required that every delegate should sign the document and recommend it, or there was no agreement. He said that they as a body had hazarded their political future and we must do likewise and take the same risks. At one time he particularly addressed himself to me and said very solemnly that those who were not for peace must take the full responsibility for the war that would immediately follow refusal by any Delegate to sign the Articles of Agreement.

He then produced two letters one of which he said he must that night sent [*sic*] to Craig. One was a covering letter to H.M. Government's proposals for the future relations of Ireland and Great Britain and stated that the Irish Delegation had agreed to recommend them for acceptance by Dail Eireann. The other stated that the Irish Delegation had failed to come to an agreement with H.M. Government and therefore he had no proposals to send to Craig.

Lloyd George stated that he would have to have our agreement or refusal to the proposals by 10 p.m. that evening. That a special train and destroyer were ready to carry either one letter or the other to Belfast and that he would give us until ten o'clock to decide.

We then argued that the twelve months' transition period was of the greatest danger to our people. Craig could say 'Yes' at any time, he could say 'No' finally before six months but he need not know whether there was to be unity or not. Meantime life might be made intolerable for our people in Ulster.

Lloyd George argued that that contingency had been apparent from the first, but if it were a serious stumbling block we could shorten the transition period at any time we chose.

Michael Collins said that the recent occurrences in Tyrone—the seizure of the County Council books, etc., and the support of the Ulster Government with English troops had shaken our confidence in their fidelity.

Lloyd George answered that they had no jurisdiction on this matter in Ulster. It was a matter over which the Northern Government had complete control under the 1920 Act. He then suggested that they should withdraw in order that we might discuss the duration of the transition period amongst ourselves. They did so.

We decided to reduce the period to one month. Rang for them to return and stated our decision.

Lloyd George said he considered the decision ill advised as a month did not give the Ulster people sufficient time to reflect. He affirmed that Craig was going to refuse the terms and that he (Lloyd George) knew this for certain. However, as we preferred one month, he was prepared to accept the alteration and redraft the Clauses. A month was the least possible that could be given Craig to make a final decision. He then proposed that we dismiss and reassemble again at 10 to give him our final decision.

There was a discussion amongst ourselves lasting from 9 to 11.15 at 22 Hans Place, at which a decision was eventually reached to recommend the Treaty to the Dail.

SUB-CONFERENCE NO. II
11.15 p.m.-2.20 a.m.*

At 11.30 we returned to Downing Street and attacked the document again. We endeavoured to get Clause 3 removed, but failed. We, however, succeeded in getting the word 'Governor-General' out, it being left to us to decide upon a term. The title 'President', Chamberlain stated, was inadmissible.

Michael Collins demanded and secured the removal of the word 'local' as a prefix to the Irish Free State's military defence force.

They agreed to the verbal changes in financial Clause 5. Chamberlain took exception to the 'if anys' going in, as he said it was too late to quibble over such small points. We pointed out that Clause 9 was still left intact and that it should have been removed under the agreement on 8. Lloyd George said that it referred to transport only. It meant ships entering harbours and that there must be provision to prevent boycotting of English shipping. Birkenhead said that the wording of the clause was ambiguous now that the compulsory Free Trade clause was gone and suggested redrafting it. This was done immediately.

Michael Collins queried the reference to summoning of the Southern-Ireland Parliament in Clauses 15 and 17, and Birkenhead immediately drafted an explanatory memorandum as follows:

'It is intended by Clauses 15 and 17 to make it plain that the functions therein referred to shall be discharged by the Provisional Government of Southern Ireland and that for that purpose a transfer shall be made by them of the necessary powers under the Government of Ireland Act, 1920, as soon as the mutual ratifications have been exchanged.

The Provisional Government will it is contemplated upon such ratification undertake the Govert. of S. Ireland immediately until the necessary Acts in both Parliaments confer upon it the statutory authority contemplated in this instrument.

B.'

Lloyd George then asked whether we as a Delegation were prepared to accept these Articles of Agreement and to stand by them in our Parliament as they as a Delegation would stand by them in theirs.

Arthur Griffith replied, 'We do.'

We then discussed the release of the prisoners and procedure for ratification and other matters whilst awaiting the final draft.

The final draft was read over, agreed to and signed; also the Annex.

THE BRITISH DELEGATION lined up to shake hands and say goodbye, and the Conference ended at 2.20 a.m. on December 6th.

* Times as stated on a copy of the document.

Appendix E

ARTICLES OF AGREEMENT AS SIGNED[5] on December 6th, 1921

1. Ireland shall have the same constitutional status in the Community of Nations known as the British Empire as the Dominion of Canada, the Commonwealth of Australia, the Dominion of New Zealand, and the Union of South Africa, with a Parliament having powers to make laws for the peace, order and good government of Ireland and an Executive responsible to that Parliament, and shall be styled and known as the Irish Free State.

2. Subject to the provisions hereinafter set out the position of the Irish Free State in relation to the Imperial Parliament and Government and otherwise shall be that of the Dominion of Canada, and the law, practice and constitutional usage governing the relationship of the Crown or the representative of the Crown and of the Imperial Parliament to the Dominion of Canada shall govern their relationship to the Irish Free State.

3. The representative of the Crown in Ireland shall be appointed in like manner as the Governor-General of Canada and in accordance with the practice observed in the making of such appointments.

4. The oath to be taken by Members of the Parliament of the Irish Free State shall be in the following form:

> I . . . do solemnly swear true faith and allegiance to the Constitution of the Irish Free State as by law established and that I will be faithful to H.M. King George V, his heirs and successors by law, in virtue of the common citizenship of Ireland with Great Britain and her adherence to and membership of the group of nations forming the British Commonwealth of Nations.

5. The Irish Free State shall assume liability for the service of the Public Debt of the United Kingdom as existing at the date hereof and towards the payment of war pensions as existing at that date in such proportion as may be fair and equitable, having regard to any just claims on the part of Ireland by way of set-off or counter-claim, the amount of such sums being determined in default of agreement by the arbitration of one or more independent persons being citizens of the British Empire.

6. Until an arrangement has been made between the British and

Irish Governments whereby the Irish Free State undertakes her own coastal defence, the defence by sea of Great Britain and Ireland shall be undertaken by His Majesty's Imperial Forces. But this shall not prevent the construction or maintenance by the Government of the Irish Free State of such vessels as are necessary for the protection of the Revenue or the Fisheries.

The foregoing provisions of this Article shall be reviewed at a Conference of Representatives of the British and Irish Governments to be held at the expiration of five years from the date hereof with a view to the undertaking by Ireland of a share in her own coastal defence.

7. The Government of the Irish Free State shall afford to His Majesty's Imperial Forces:

(*a*) In time of peace such harbour and other facilities as are indicated in the Annex hereto, or such other facilities as may from time to time be agreed between the British Government and the Government of the Irish Free State; and

(*b*) In time of war or of strained relations with a Foreign Power such harbour and other facilities as the British Government may require for the purposes of such defence as aforesaid.

8. With a view to securing the observance of the principle of international limitation of armaments, if the Government of the Irish Free State establishes and maintains a military defence force, the establishments thereof shall not exceed in size such proportion of the military establishments maintained in Great Britain as that which the population of Ireland bears to the population of Great Britain.

9. The ports of Great Britain and the Irish Free State shall be freely open to the ships of the other country on payment of the customary port and other dues.

10. The Government of the Irish Free State agrees to pay fair compensation on terms not less favourable than those accorded by the Act of 1920 to judges, officials, members of Police Forces and other Public Servants who are discharged by it or who retire in consequence of the change of Government effected in pursuance hereof.

Provided that this agreement shall not apply to members of the Auxiliary Police Force or to persons recruited in Great Britain for the Royal Irish Constabulary during the two years next preceding the date hereof. The British Government will assume responsibility for such compensation or pension as may be payable to any of these excepted persons.

11. Until the expiration of one month from the passing of the Act of Parliament for the ratification of this instrument, the powers of the Parliament and the Government of the Irish Free State shall not be exercisable as respects Northern Ireland and the provisions

of the Government of Ireland Act, 1920, shall so far as they relate to Northern Ireland remain of full force and effect, and no election shall be held for the return of members to serve in the Parliament of the Irish Free State for constituencies in Northern Ireland, unless a resolution is passed by both Houses of the Parliament of Northern Ireland in favour of the holding of such election before the end of the said month.

12. If before the expiration of the said month, an address is presented to His Majesty by both Houses of the Parliament of Northern Ireland to that effect, the powers of the Parliament and Government of the Irish Free State shall no longer extend to Northern Ireland, and the provisions of the Government of Ireland Act, 1920 (including those relating to the Council of Ireland) shall, so far as they relate to Northern Ireland, continue to be of full force and effect, and this instrument shall have effect subject to the necessary modifications.

Provided that if such an address is so presented a Commission consisting of three persons, one to be appointed by the Government of the Irish Free State, one to be appointed by the Government of Northern Ireland and one who shall be Chairman to be appointed by the British Government shall determine in accordance with the wishes of the inhabitants, so far as may be compatible with economic and geographic conditions, the boundaries between Northern Ireland and the rest of Ireland, and for the purposes of the Government of Ireland Act, 1920, and of this instrument, the boundary of Northern Ireland shall be such as may be determined by such Commission.

13. For the purpose of the last foregoing article, the powers of the Parliament of Southern Ireland under the Government of Ireland Act, 1920, to elect members of the Council of Ireland shall after the Parliament of the Irish Free State is constituted be exercised by that Parliament.

14. After the expiration of the said month, if no such address as is mentioned in Article 12 hereof is presented, the Parliament and Government of Northern Ireland shall continue to exercise as respects Northern Ireland the powers conferred on them by the Government of Ireland Act, 1920, but the Parliament and Government of the Irish Free State shall in Northern Ireland have in relation to matters in respect of which the Parliament of Northern Ireland has not power to make laws under that Act (including matters which under the said Act are within the jurisdiction of the Council of Ireland) the same powers as in the rest of Ireland, subject to such other provisions as may be agreed in manner hereinafter appearing.

15. At any time after the date hereof the Government of Northern Ireland and the Provisional Government of Southern Ireland hereinafter constituted may meet for the purpose of discussing the provisions subject to which the last foregoing article is

to operate in the event of no such address as is therein mentioned being presented and those provisions may include:

(*a*) Safeguards with regard to patronage in Northern Ireland;
(*b*) Safeguards with regard to the collection of revenue in Northern Ireland;
(*c*) Safeguards with regard to import and export duties affecting the trade or industry of Northern Ireland;
(*d*) Safeguards for minorities in Northern Ireland;
(*e*) The settlement of the financial relations between Northern Ireland and the Irish Free State;
(*f*) The establishment and powers of a local militia in Northern Ireland and the relation of the Defence Forces of the Irish Free State and of Northern Ireland respectively;

and if at any such meeting provisions are agreed to, the same shall have effect as if they were included amongst the provisions subject to which the Powers of the Parliament and Government of the Irish Free State are to be exercisable in Northern Ireland under Article 14 hereof.

16. Neither the Parliament of the Irish Free State nor the Parliament of Northern Ireland shall make any law so as either directly or indirectly to endow any religion or prohibit or restrict the free exercise thereof or give any preference or impose any disability on account of religious belief or religious status or affect prejudicially the right of any child to attend a school receiving public money without attending the religious instruction at the school or make any discrimination as respects state aid between schools under the management of different religious denominations or divert from any religious denomination or any educational institution any of its property except for public utility purposes and on payment of compensation.

17. By way of provisional arrangement for the administration of Southern Ireland during the interval which must elapse between the date hereof and the constitution of a Parliament and Government of the Irish Free State in accordance therewith, steps shall be taken forthwith for summoning a meeting of members of Parliament elected for constituencies in Southern Ireland since the passing of the Government of Ireland Act, 1920, and for constituting a provisional Government, and the British Government shall take the steps necessary to transfer to such provisional Government the powers and machinery requisite for the discharge of its duties, provided that every member of such provisional Government shall have signified in writing his or her acceptance of this instrument. But this arrangement shall not continue in force beyond the expiration of twelve months from the date hereof.

18. This instrument shall be submitted forthwith by His Majesty's Government for the approval of Parliament and by the Irish

signatories to a meeting summoned for the purpose of the members elected to sit in the House of Commons of Southern Ireland, and if approved shall be ratified by the necessary legislation.

On behalf of the British Delegation

Signed
D. LLOYD GEORGE
AUSTEN CHAMBERLAIN
BIRKENHEAD
WINSTON S. CHURCHILL
L. WORTHINGTON-EVANS
HAMAR GREENWOOD
GORDON HEWART

On behalf of the Irish Delegation

Signed
ART O GRIOBHTHA (Arthur Griffith)
MICHAEL O COILEAIN
RIOBARD BARTUN
EUDHMONN S. O DUGAIN
SEORSA GABHAIN UI DHUBHTHAIGH

December 6th, 1921

1. The following are the specific facilities required.

Dockyard Port at Berehaven

(*a*) Admiralty property and rights to be retained as at the date hereof. Harbour defences to remain in charge of British care and maintenance parties.

Queenstown

(*b*) Harbour defences to remain in charge of British care and maintenance parties. Certain mooring buoys to be retained for use of His Majesty's ships.

Belfast Lough

(*c*) Harbour defences to remain in charge of British care and maintenance parties.

Lough Swilly

(*d*) Harbour defences to remain in charge of British care and maintenance parties.

Aviation

(*e*) Facilities in the neighbourhood **of the above Ports for** coastal defence by air.

Oil Fuel Storage

(*f*)	Haulbowline Rathmullen	To be offered for sale to commercial companies under guarantee that purchasers shall maintain a certain minimum stock for Admiralty purposes.

2. A Convention shall be made between the British Government and the Government of the Irish Free State to give effect to the following conditions:

(*a*) That submarine cables shall not be landed or wireless stations for communications with places outside Ireland be established except by agreement with the British Government; that the existing cable landing rights and wireless concessions shall not be withdrawn except by agreement with the British Government; and that the British Government shall be entitled to land additional submarine cables or establish additional wireless stations for communication with places outside Ireland.

(*b*) That lighthouses, buoys, beacons, and any navigational marks or any navigational aids shall be maintained by the Government of the Irish Free State as at the date hereof and shall not be removed or added to except by agreement with the British Government.

(*c*) That war signal stations shall be closed down and left in charge of care and maintenance parties, the Government of the Irish Free State being offered the option of taking them over and working them for commercial purposes subject to Admiralty inspection, and guaranteeing the upkeep of existing telegraphic communications therewith.

3. A Convention shall be made between the same Governments for the regulations of Civil Communications by Air.

			A.G.
D.L.G.	B.	E.S.O'D.	M.C.
A.C.	W.S.C.	S.G.D.	R.B.

Appendix F

Dail Debate on the Treaty

Voting 'for' and 'against'
7th January, 1922[6]

For:

Michael O Coileain	(Michael Collins)
Art O Griobhtha	(Arthur Griffith)
Sean Mac Giolla Riogh	(Sean Milroy)
Pol O Geallagain	(Paul Galligan)
Liam T. Mac Cosgair	(Wm. T. Cosgrave)
Gearoid O Suileabhain	(Gearoid O'Sullivan)
Padraig O Braonain	(Patrick Brennan)
Sean O Lidia	(Sean Leddy)
Sean O hAodha	(Sean Hayes)
Padraig O Caoimh	(Padraig O'Keeffe)
Sean Mac Heil	(Sean Hales)
Seosamh Mac Suibhne	(Joseph Sweeney)
Peadar S. Mac an Bhaird	(Peter Ward)
Dr. S. Mac Fhionnlaoigh	(Dr. J. P. McGinley)
P. S. Mac Ualghairg	(P. J. McGoldrick)
Proinsias Laighleis	(Frank Lawless)
S. Ghabhain Ui Dhubhthaigh	(George Gavan Duffy)
Deasmhumhain Mac Gearailt	(Desmond Fitzgerald)
Seumas Mac Doirim	(James Derham)
Seaumas O Duibhir	(J. O'Dwyer)
Padraic O Maille	(Padraic O Maille)
Seoirse Mac Niocaill	(George Nicholls)
P. S. O hOgain	(P. J. Hogan)
An t-Oll. S. O Faoilleachain	(Professor J. B. Whelehan)
Piaras Beaslai	(Piaras Beaslai)
Fionan O Loingsigh	(Fionan Lynch)
S. O. Cruadhlaoich	(J. Crowley)
Riobard Bartun	(Robert Barton)
Criostoir O Broin	(C. M. Byrne)
Seumas O Dolain	(James N. Dolan)
Aindriu O Laimhin	(Andrew Lavin)
Tomas Mac Artuir	(Thomas Carter)
Dr. Padraig Mac Artain	(Dr. Patrick McCartan)
Caoimhghin O hUigin	(Kevin O'Higgins)
Seosamh O Loingsigh	(Joseph Lynch)
Proinsias Bulfin	(Frank Bulfin)

Dr. Risteard O hAodha	(Dr. Richard Hayes)
Liam O hAodha	(Wm. Hayes)
Seosamh Mac Aonghusa	(Joseph McGuinness)
Sean Mac Eoin	(Sean MacEoin)
Lorcan O Roibin	(Lorcan Robbins)
Eamon O Dugain	(Eamonn Duggan)
Peadar O hAodha	(Peter Hughes)
Seumas O Murchadha	(James Murphy)
Saerbhreathach Mac Cionaith	(Justin McKenna)
Seosamh Mac Giolla Bhrighde	(Joseph McBride)
Liam Mac Sioghuird	(William Sears)
Domhnall O Ruairc	(Daniel O'Rourke)
Earnan de Blaghd	(Ernest Blyth)
Eoin O Dubhthaigh	(Eoin O'Duffy)
Alasdar Mac Caba	(Alex. McCabe)
Tomas O Domhnaill	(Thomas O'Donnell)
Seumas de Burca	(Seumas Burke)
Dr. V. de Faoite	(Dr. Vincent White)
Risteard Mac Fheorais	(Richard Corish)
Sean Mac Gadhra	(Sean McGarry)
Micheal Mac Staim	(Michael Staines)
Risteard O Maolchatha	(Richard Mulcahy)
Seosamh Mag Craith	(Joseph McGrath)
Pilib Mac Cosgair	(Philip Cosgrave)
Domhnall Mac Carthaigh	(Daniel McCarthy)
Liam de Roiste	(Liam de Roiste)
Seumas Breathnach	(J. J. Walsh)
Micheal O hAodha	(Michael Hayes)

Against:

Seumas O Lonnain	(James Lennon)
Eamon Aidhleart	(E. Aylward)
Eamon de Valera	(Eamon de Valera)
Brian O hUigin	(Brian O'Higgins)
Sean Mac Suibhne	(Sean McSwiney)
Sean O Maolain	(Sean Moylan)
Domhnall O Corcora	(Daniel Corkery)
Sean O Nuallain	(Sean Nolan)
Tomas O Fiadhchara	(Thomas Hunter)
Seumas Mac Gearailt	(James Fitzgerald)
Daithi Ceannt	(David Kent)
Seosamh O Dochartaigh	(Joseph O'Doherty)
S. O. Flaithbheartaigh	(J. O'Flaherty)
Bean an Phiarsaigh	(Mrs. Pearse)
Sean O Mathghamhna	(John O'Mahony)
Liam O Maoiliosa	(Liam Mellowes)
Dr. Brian de Ciosog	(Dr. Brian Cusack)
Proinsias O Fathaigh	(Frank Fahy)

Aibhistin de Stac	(Austin Stack)
Conchuvhar O Coileain	(Con Collins)
Eamon de Roiste	(Eamon Roche)
P. S. O Cathael	(P. S. O'Cahill)
Tomas O Donnchu	(Thomas O'Donoghue)
Art O Conchubhair	(Art O'Connor)
Domhnall O Buachalla	(Daniel Buckley)
E. Childers	(Erskine Childers)
Seoirse Pluingceud	(George Noble Count Plunkett)
Bean Mhichil Ui Cheallachaim	(Mrs. Michael Callaghan)
M. P. Colivet	(M. P. Colivet)
Sean O Ceallaigh	(J. J. O'Kelly)
Dr. O Cruadhlaoich	(Dr. Crowley)
Tomas O Deirg	(Tomas O Deirg)
P. S. O Ruthleis	(P. J. Ruttledge)
Enri O Beolain	(Harry Boland)
Tomas Maguidhir	(Thomas Maguire)
Sean Mac an tSaoi	(Sean McEntee)
Dr. P. O. Fearain	(Dr. Fearon)
Seumas O Daimhin	(Seumas O Daimhin)
Proinsias Mac Carthaigh	(Frank Carty)
Seosamh Mac Donnchadha	(Joseph McDonagh)
P. S. O Maoldomhnaigh	(P. J. Malony)
P. S. O Broin	(P. J. Count O'Beirne)
Cathal Brugha	(Cathal Brugha)
Eamon O Deaghaidh	(Eamon Dee)
Seumas Mac Roibin	(Seumas Robinson)
Dr. Seumas O Riain	(Dr. James Ryan)
Sean Etchingham	(Sean Etchingham)
Seumas O Dubhghaill	(Seumas Doyle)
Sean T. O. Ceallaigh	(Sean T. O'Kelly)
Pilib O Seanachain	(Philip Shanahan)
Bean an Chleirigh	(Mrs. Thomas Clarke)
Constans de Markievicz	(Constance Markievicz)
Cathal O Murchadha	(Charles Murphy)
Maire Nic Shuibhne	(Mary McSwiney)
Domhnall O Ceallachain	(Daniel O'Callaghan)
Dr. Eithne Inglis	(Dr. Ada English)
An t-Oll. W. F. P. Stockley	(Professor W. P. Stockley)

Appendix G

Document No. 2[1]

This document was drafted by de Valera as an amendment to the motion for the approval of the Articles of Agreement. He intended to move the amendment on the 4th January, 1922.

That inasmuch as the 'Articles of Agreement for a treaty between Great Britain and Ireland', signed in London on December 6th, 1921, do not reconcile Irish National aspirations and the Association of Ireland with the Community of Nations known as the British Commonwealth, and cannot be the basis of an enduring peace between the Irish and the British peoples, Dail Eireann, in the name of the Sovereign Irish Nation, makes to the Government of Great Britain, to the Government of the other States of the British Commonwealth, and to the peoples of Great Britain and of these several States, the following Proposal for a Treaty of Amity and Association which, Dail Eireann is convinced, could be entered into by the Irish people with the sincerity of goodwill:

Proposed Treaty of Association Between Ireland and the British Commonwealth

In order to bring to an end the long and ruinous conflict between Great Britain and Ireland by a sure and lasting peace honourable to both nations, it is agreed

STATUS OF IRELAND

1. That the legislative, executive, and judicial authority of Ireland shall be derived solely from the people of Ireland.

TERMS OF ASSOCIATION

2. That, for purposes of common concern, Ireland shall be associated with the States of the British Commonwealth, viz: The Kingdom of Great Britain, the Dominion of Canada, the Commonwealth of Australia, the Dominion of New Zealand, and the Union of South Africa.

3. That when acting as an associate the rights, status, and privileges of Ireland shall be in no respect less than those enjoyed by any of the component States of the British Commonwealth.

4. That the matters of 'common concern' shall include Defence, Peace and War, Political Treaties, and all matters now treated as of common concern amongst the States of the British Commonwealth, and that in these matters there shall be between Ireland and the States of the British Commonwealth 'such concerted action founded on consultation as the several Governments may determine'.

5. That in virtue of this association of Ireland with the States of the British Commonwealth, citizens of Ireland in any of these States shall not be subject to any disabilities which a citizen of one of the component States of the British Commonwealth would not be subject to, and reciprocally for the citizens of these States in Ireland.

6. That, for the purposes of the Association, Ireland shall recognise His Britannic Majesty as head of the Association.

DEFENCE

7. That, so far as her resources permit, Ireland shall provide for her own defence by sea, land and air, and shall repel by force any attempt by a foreign Power to violate the integrity of her soil and territorial waters, or to use them for any purpose hostile to Great Britain and the other Associated States.

8. That for five years, pending the establishment of Irish coastal defence forces, or for such other period as the Governments of the two countries may later agree upon, facilities for the coastal defence of Ireland shall be given to the British Government as follows:

(*a*) In time of peace such harbour and other facilities as are indicated in the Annex hereto, or such other facilities as may from time to time be agreed upon between the British Government and the Government of Ireland;

(*b*) In time of war such harbour and other naval facilities as the British Government may reasonably require for the purposes of such defence as aforesaid.

9. That within five years from the date of exchange of ratifications of this Treaty a Conference between the British and Irish Governments shall be held in order to hand over the coastal defence of Ireland to the Irish Government, unless some other arrangement for naval defence be agreed by both Governments to be desirable in the common interest of Ireland, Great Britain, and the other Associated States.

10. That, in order to co-operate in furthering the principle of international limitation of armaments, the Government of Ireland shall not

(*a*) Build submarines unless by agreement with Great Britain and the other States of the Commonwealth ;

(*b*) Maintain a military defence force, the establishments whereof exceed in size such proportion of the military establishments maintained in Great Britain as that which the population of Ireland bears to the population of Great Britain.

MISCELLANEOUS

11. That the Governments of Great Britain and of Ireland shall make a convention for the regulation of civil communication by air.

12. That the ports of Great Britain and Ireland shall be freely open to the ships of each country on payment of the customary port and other dues.

13. That Ireland shall assume liability for such share of the present public debt of Great Britain and Ireland, and of payment of war pensions as existing at this date as may be fair and equitable, having regard to any just claims on the part of Ireland by way of set-off or counter-claim, the amount of such sums being determined, in default of agreement, by the arbitration of one or more independent persons, being citizens of Ireland or of the British Commonwealth.

14. That the Government of Ireland agrees to pay compensation on terms not less favourable than those proposed by the British Government of Ireland Act of 1920 to that Government's judges, officials, members of Police Forces and other Public Servants who are discharged by the Government of Ireland, or who retire in consequence of the change of government elected in pursuance hereof:

Provided that this agreement shall not apply to members of the Auxiliary Police Force, or to persons recruited in Great Britain for the Royal Irish Constabulary during the two years next preceding the date hereof. The British Government will assume responsibility for such compensations or pensions as may be payable to any of these excepted persons.

15. That neither the Parliament of Ireland nor any subordinate Legislature in Ireland shall make any law so as either directly or indirectly to endow any religion or prohibit or restrict the free exercise thereof, or give any preference or impose any disability on account of religious belief or religious status, or affect prejudicially the right of any child to attend a school receiving public money without attending a religious instruction at the school, or make any discrimination as respects State aid between schools under the management of different religious denominations, or divert from any religious denomination or any educational institution any of its property except for public utility purposes and on payment of compensation.

TRANSITIONAL

16. That by way of transitional arrangement for the Administration of Ireland during the interval which must elapse between the date hereof and the setting up of a Parliament and Government of Ireland in accordance herewith, the members elected for constituencies in Ireland since the passing of the British Government of Ireland Act in 1920 shall, at a meeting summoned for the purpose, elect a transitional Government to which the British Government and Dail Eireann shall transfer the authority, powers, and machinery requisite for the discharge of its duties, provided that every member of such transition Government shall have signified in writing his or her acceptance of this instrument. But this arrangement shall not continue in force beyond the expiration of twelve months from the date hereof.

RATIFICATION

17. That this instrument shall be submitted for ratification forthwith by His Britannic Majesty's Government to the Parliament at Westminster, and by the Cabinet of Dail Eireann to a meeting of the members elected for the constituencies in Ireland set forth in the British Government of Ireland Act, 1920, and when ratifications have been exchanged shall take immediate effect.

ANNEX

1. The following are the specific facilities referred to in Article 8 (*a*):

Dockyard Port at Berehaven

(*a*) British Admiralty property and rights to be retained as at the date hereof. Harbour defences to remain in charge of British care and maintenance parties.

Queenstown

(*b*) Harbour defences to remain in charge of British care and maintenance parties. Certain mooring buoys to be retained for use of His Britannic Majesty's ships.

Belfast Lough

(*c*) Harbour defences to remain in charge of British care and maintenance parties.

Lough Swilly

(*d*) Harbour defences to remain in charge of British care and maintenance parties.

Aviation

(*e*) Facilities in the neighbourhood of the above Ports for coastal defence by air.

Oil Fuel Storage

(*f*) Haulbowline and Rathmullen	To be offered for sale to commercial companies under guarantee that purchasers shall maintain a certain minimum stock for British Admiralty purposes.

2. A Convention covering a period of five years shall be made between the British and Irish Governments to give effect to the following conditions:

(*a*) That submarine cables shall not be landed or wireless stations for communications with places outside Ireland be established except by agreement with the British Government; that the existing cable landing rights and wireless concessions shall not be withdrawn except by agreement with the British Government; and that the British Government shall be entitled to land additional submarine cables or establish additional wireless stations for communication with places outside Ireland.

(*b*) That lighthouses, buoys, beacons, and any navigational marks or navigational aids shall be maintained by the Government of Ireland as at the date hereof and shall not be removed or added to except by agreement with the British Government.

(*c*) That war signal stations shall be closed down and left in charge of care and maintenance parties, the Government of Ireland being offered the option of taking them over and working them for commercial purposes subject to British Admiralty inspection and guaranteeing the upkeep of existing telegraphic communication therewith.

(The Addendum, given below, which concerns North-East Ulster, was to be proposed as a separate resolution by de Valera.)

ADDENDUM

North-East Ulster

Resolved:

That, whilst refusing to admit the right of any part of Ireland to be excluded from the supreme authority of the Parliament of Ireland, or that the relations between the Parliament of Ireland and any subordinate Legislature in Ireland can be a matter for treaty with a government outside Ireland, nevertheless, in sincere regard for internal peace, and in order to make manifest our desire not to bring force or coercion to bear upon any substantial part of the province of Ulster, whose inhabitants may now be unwilling to accept the national authority, we are prepared to grant to that portion of Ulster which is defined as Northern Ireland in the British Government of Ireland Act of 1920, privileges and safeguards not less substantial than those provided for in the Articles of Agreement for a Treaty between Great Britain and Ireland signed in London on December 6th, 1921.

Appendix H

CRAIG-COLLINS AGREEMENT[8]

Agreement signed by Collins, Kevin O'Higgins, Craig, Churchill and others on March 30th, 1922. Ireland.

Heads of agreement between the Provisional Government and Government of Northern Ireland:

(1) Peace is today declared.

(2) From today the two Governments undertake to co-operate in every way in their power with a view to the restoration of peaceful conditions in the unsettled areas.

(3) The Police in Belfast to be organised in general in accordance with the following conditions:

(1) Special police in mixed districts to be composed half of Catholics and half of Protestants, special agreements to be made where Catholics or Protestants are living in other districts. All specials not required for this force to be withdrawn to their homes and their arms handed in.

(2) An Advisory Committee, composed of Catholics, to be set up to assist in the selection of Catholic recruits for the special police.

(3) All police on duty, except the usual secret service, to be in uniform and officially numbered.

(4) All arms and ammunition issued to police to be deposited in barracks in charge of a military or other competent officer when the policeman is not on duty, and an official record to be kept of all arms issued, and of all ammunition issued and used.

(5) Any search for arms to be carried out by police forces composed half of Catholics and half of Protestants, the military rendering any necessary assistance.

(4) A Court to be constituted for the trial without jury of persons charged with serious crime, the Court to consist of the Lord Chief Justice and one of the Lord Justices of Appeal of Northern Ireland. Any person committed for trial for a serious crime to be tried by that court:

(*a*) If he so requests, or
(*b*) If the Attorney-General for Northern Ireland so directs.

Serious crime should be taken to mean any offence punishable with death, penal servitude, or imprisonment for a term exceeding six months. The Government of Northern Ireland will take steps for passing the legislation necessary to give effect to this Article.

(5) A Committee to be set up in Belfast of equal number Catholics and Protestants with an independent Chairman, preferably Catholic and Protestant alternately in successive weeks, to hear and investigate complaints as to intimidation, outrages, etc., such Committee to have direct access to the heads of the Government. The local Press to be approached with a view to inserting only such reports of disturbances, etc., as shall have been considered and communicated by this committee.

(6) I.R.A. activities to cease in the Six Counties, and thereupon the method of organising the special police in the Six Counties outside Belfast shall proceed as speedily as possible upon lines similar to those agreed for Belfast.

(7) During the month immediately following the passing into law of the Bill confirming the constitution of the Free State (being the month within which the Northern Parliament is to exercise its option) and before any address in accordance with Article 12 of the Treaty is presented, there shall be a further meeting between the signatories to this agreement with a view to ascertaining:

(*a*) Whether means can be devised to secure the unity of Ireland.
(*b*) Failing this, whether agreement can be arrived at on the boundary question otherwise than by recourse to the Boundary Commission outlined in Article 12 of the Treaty.

(8) The return to their homes of persons who have been expelled to be secured by the respective Governments, the advice of the Committee mentioned in Article 5 to be sought in cases of difficulty.

(9) In view of the special conditions consequent on the political situation in Belfast and neighbourhood, the British Government will submit to Parliament a vote not exceeding £500,000 for the Ministry of Labour of Northern Ireland to be expended exclusively on relief work, one-third for the benefit of Roman Catholics and two-thirds for the benefit of Protestants. The Northern signatories agree to use every effort to secure the restoration of the expelled workers, and wherever this proves impracticable at the moment, owing to trade depression, they will be afforded employment on the relief works referred to in this Article so far as the one-third limit will allow. Protestant ex-servicemen to be given first preference in respect to the two-thirds of the same fund.

(10) The two Governments shall in cases agreed upon between the signatories arrange for the release of political prisoners in prison for offences before the date hereof. No offences committed after March 31st, 1922, shall be open to consideration.

(11) The two Governments unite in appealing to all concerned to refrain from inflammatory speeches and to exercise restraint in the interests of peace.

Signed on behalf of the Provisional Government:

MICHAEL O COILEAIN E. S. O. DUGAIN
CAOIMHGIN O hUIGIN ART O GRIOBHTHA

Signed on behalf of the Government of Northern Ireland:

JAMES CRAIG LONDONDERRY E. M. ARCHDALE

Countersigned on behalf of the British Government:

WINSTON S. CHURCHILL L. WORTHINGTON-EVANS

Appendix I

CORRY'S ACCOUNT OF THE FATAL AMBUSH*

There were two drivers in charge of the car, M. Quinn and myself. Make of car was a Leyland Thomas racing type, straight eight cylinder; no armour of any sort being attached at any time to bodywork or engine; canvas top folded back to rear.

General Collins and Major-General Emmet Dalton were seated in the back, the two drivers in the front seat.

We were aware of I.R.A. Flying Column being about at various places during our journey down to Cork; but not a shot was fired at us. We arrived in Cork city at 10.30 p.m.—due to road obstructions, blown bridges, etc.

The day of the ambush.

Ahead of us two Crossley tenders with ten armed men in each. Also one Crossley tender containing ropes, saws, picks, food, etc., for emergency use. Leading our column a motor-cyclist guide. At the rear of our car, a Rolls Royce Whippet armoured car, name 'Slievenamon'.

Two men of the convoy observed the time of departure from Bandon town as being 8 p.m. (G.M.T.) After doing some five miles, we came around a sharp curve and were then on a straight stretch of road. A single shot rang out from across the hill on our extreme left, some 440 yards away (approximately).

General Collins' command 'Stop!' was obeyed at once. There was no obstruction on the road ahead of us at the time. On leaving our car, we were met by heavy fire; but no one was hit.

General Collins walked back some fifty yards, followed by Major-General Dalton, Quinn and myself. We took cover at a hedge or ditch about two feet high. The firing was heavy at this time from enemy position right in front. On our extreme right our men were replying. On our extreme left a clear road. At our backs a steep hillside. Firing came from directly in front only.

Major-General Dalton observed that the armoured car machine-gun was not firing. He called to the gunner, who replied, 'Gun is jammed, sir.'

Gen. Collins, who had been lying firing from a position six feet from me, now stood erect, and after firing several rounds, fell on the roadside, with a gaping wound near the left ear lobe extending to the upper section of the skull; there was also a tear in the front of the forehead, and a hole nipped in the front of his cap close to the badge.

Major-General Dalton said to me, 'The General is finished.'

We placed the body across the rear seat of the General's car; my hands holding the head, Major-General Dalton the feet of General Collins.

Firing had ceased as General Collins died on the roadside. Nightfall was coming on and there was some drizzle as we started on our eighteen miles' journey back to Cork.

Appendix J

Major-General Dalton's Account of the Fatal Ambush[10]

'About three miles from Clonakilty,' says General Dalton, 'we found the road blocked with felled trees. We spent about half an hour clearing the road. General Collins, always ready for emergencies, great or small, directed the work, and took a hand in carrying it out. Active and powerful in body as in mind, he handled axe and saw with the same vigour as he could exhibit in the direction of affairs of state, military or civil.

Having at last cleared a way, we went into the town of Clonakilty, which is the home town of General Collins. Here he interviewed the garrison officer, and had conversation with many of his friends. It was pleasant to see with what delight and affection they met him. We had lunch in a friend's house in the town before setting out for Roscarbery.'

It may be mentioned here that, on his arrival in Clonakilty, the whole town turned out to welcome him. . . .

'Just outside the town of Bandon,' says Dalton, 'General Collins pointed out to me several farmhouses, which he told me were used by the lads in the old days of "The Terror". He mentioned to me the home of one particular friend of his own, remarking, "It's too bad he's on the other side now, because he is a damn good soldier." Then he added pensively—"I don't suppose I will be ambushed in my own country."

It was now about a quarter past seven, and the light was failing. We were speeding along the open road on our way to Macroom. Our motor-cyclist scout was about fifty yards in front of the Crossley tender, which we followed at the same interval in the touring car. Close behind us came the armoured car.

We had just reached a part of the road which was commanded by hills on all sides. The road itself was flat and open. On the right we were flanked by steep hills; on the left there was a small two-foot bank of earth skirting the road. Beyond this there was a marshy field bounded by a small stream, with another steep hill beyond it.

About half way up this hill there was a road running parallel to the one that we were on, but screened from view by a wall and a mass of trees and bushes. We had just turned a wide corner on the road when a sudden and heavy fusillade of machine-gun and rifle fire swept the road in front of us and behind us, shattering the windscreen of our car.

I shouted to the driver—"Drive like hell!" But the Commander-in-Chief, placing his hand on the man's shoulder, said—"Stop! Jump out and we'll fight them."

We leaped from the car, and took what cover we could behind the little mud bank on the left hand side of the road. It seemed that the greatest volume of fire was coming from the concealed roadway on our left-hand side. The armoured car now backed up the road and opened a heavy machine-gun fire at the hidden ambushers.'

It may be mentioned here that the machine-gun in the armoured car 'jammed' after a short time. The machine-gunner, MacPeake, not long after this occurrence, deserted to the Irregulars, bringing an armoured car with him.

It was the Crossley tender, which was in charge of Commandant

O'Connell, which received the first shot. The road had been barricaded by an old cart, which the occupants of the tender promptly removed out of the way. After a few minutes the firing at these ceased, and the ambushers concentrated their fire on Collins and the other men who had occupied the touring car. Sean O'Connell then ran down the road and joined them.

'General Collins and I,' says Dalton, 'were lying within arm's length of each other. Captain Dolan, who had been on the back of the armoured car, together with our two drivers, was several yards further down the road to my right.

General Collins and I, with Captain Dolan who was near us, opened a rapid rifle fire on our seldom visible enemies. About fifty or sixty yards further down the road, and round the bend, we could hear that our machine-gunners and riflemen were also heavily engaged.

We continued this fire fight for about twenty minutes without suffering any casualties, when a lull in the enemy's attack became noticeable. General Collins now jumped up to his feet and walked over behind the armoured car obviously to obtain a better view of the enemy's position.

He remained there, firing occasional shots and using the car as cover. Suddenly I heard him shout—"Come on boys! There they are, running up the road." I immediately opened fire upon two figures that came in view on the opposite road.

When I next turned round the Commander-in-Chief had left the car position, and had run about fifteen yards back up the road. Here he dropped into the prone firing position, and opened up on our retreating enemies.'

Dalton, Dolan and O'Connell took up positions on the road further down. Presently the firing of Collins ceased, and Dalton heard, or fancied he heard, a faint cry of 'Emmet!' He describes how he and Sean O'Connell 'rushed to the spot with a dreadful fear clutching our hearts. We found our beloved Chief and friend lying motionless in a firing position, firmly gripping his rifle, across which his head was resting.

There was a fearful gaping wound at the base of the skull behind the right ear. We immediately saw that General Collins was almost beyond human aid. He could not speak to us.

The enemy must have seen that something had occurred to cause a sudden cessation of our fire, because they intensified their own.

O'Connell now knelt beside the dying but still conscious Chief, whose eyes were wide open and normal, and he whispered into the ear of the fast-sinking man the words of the Act of Contrition. For this he was rewarded by a slight pressure of the hand.

Meanwhile I knelt beside them both, and kept up bursts of rapid fire, which I continued whilst O'Connell dragged the Chief across the road and behind the armoured car. Then, with my heart torn with sorrow and despair, I ran to the Chief's side. Very gently I raised his head on my knee and tried to bandage his wound, but, owing to the awful size of it, this proved very difficult.

I had not completed my grievous task when the big eyes closed, and the cold pallor of death overspread the General's face. How can I describe the feelings that were mine at that bleak hour, kneeling in the mud of a country road not twelve miles from Clonakilty, with the still bleeding head of the Idol of Ireland resting on my arm.

My heart was broken, my mind was numbed. I was all unconscious of the bullets that still whistled and ripped the ground beside me. I think that the weight of the blow must have caused the loss of my reason had I not abruptly observed the tear-stained face of O'Connell, now distorted with anguish, and calling also for my sympathy and support.

We paused for a moment in silent prayer, and then, noting that the fire of our enemies had greatly abated, and that they had practically all retreated, we two, with the assistance of Lieutenant Smith, the motor-cyclist scout officer, who had come on the scene, endeavoured to lift the stalwart body of Michael Collins on to the back of the armoured car.

It was then that we suffered our second casualty—Lieutenant Smith was shot in the neck. He remained on his feet, however, and helped us to carry our precious burden around a turn in the road and under cover of the armoured car.

Having transferred the body of our Chief to the touring car, where I sat with his head resting on my shoulder, our awe-stricken little party set out for Cork.'

Appendix K

Notes on Sources and Sources Listed

Apart from the letters which Collins wrote, to Sean Deasey and Harry Boland for example, the chief sources for this assessment of Collins will be found in the following items:

(1) Collins' private notebooks.
(2) Collins' notes.
(3) Personal papers.
(4) Day-book.
(5) Collins' letters to John O'Kane.
(6) The Collins-Griffith Memorandum.

The present writer is indebted to four persons for the use of this material, though the name of only one of these persons can be divulged: the name is that of Miss Eithne O'Kane, to whose uncle Collins addressed a great deal of correspondence.

Regarding these sources, the present writer gave a promise not to divulge the present whereabouts of this material; but, at the same time, understands that the notebooks, at least, can be produced if they should be required as a further guarantee of the present writer's integrity. Further, the present writer is prepared to depose on oath that the documents have been in his possession, and that the material in this book in no way distorts the originals. A description of each of these items is appended.

(1) *Private notebooks.* Six in number, each loosely bound with string and tie-in clips. Dates of entries range from Friday, 30th December, 1921, to Sunday, 6th August, 1922. One entry only is written in pencil; otherwise the handwriting is in ink and the script is neat, clean and tidy—a characteristic of Collins' handwriting. These notebooks have been carefully preserved: there are no torn pages nor even any sign of yellowing in the paper. The entries are daily, except from Thursday, 5th January, 1922, to Tuesday, 10th January, 1922, when a brief note is inserted which states 'Dail meetings during this period'.

(2) *Notes.* Seventeen items all of which concern the Treaty discussions in London. These documents, loosely bound in a folder, show signs of deterioration, in particular the ones which concern Collins' assessments of the British delegation. It would appear that they have, at some time or other, been subjected to a damp atmosphere, and the writing is difficult to decipher. The opinions of two independent handwriting experts were secured in the task of deciphering these documents.

(3) *Personal papers.* The handwriting on these documents is a study in itself and it expresses three stages of penmanship: the handwriting of Collins as a youth, the style of penmanship evident in the photostats of the Stafford-Frongoch period, and the neat clear script of the later years. The early dated documents are now somewhat yellowed and torn, but for their age they are in good condition.

(4) *Day-book.* Concerns the month of June, 1922, only, although the total pages number two hundred and ten. Quarto size, writing on both sides of the pages, it contains only the brief details of appointments; of value, nevertheless, because it indicates the strain to which Collins was put in attempting to cope with a mass of persons, details, and government work.

(5) *Collins-O'Kane letters.* These letters, and others also not mentioned in this biography, are in matchless condition owing to the fact that they have been treated, pasted onto paper and carefully bound. Papers of various sizes, in colour white or blue, are used, and, as many of them were written when Collins was pressed for time, they are invariably headed 'Cad Gdns' [Cadogan Gardens], where Collins stayed during the time he was in London for the Treaty discussions. On three of the letters the heading 'Dail Eireann' is obliterated. For the purposes of fully indicating the state of Collins' mind at this critical period they are invaluable.

(6) *Collins-Griffith Memorandum.* Contained on three sheets of foolscap paper each headed 'Dail Eireann'. The contents are typewritten and several alterations are in Collins' handwriting. Each page is initialled by Collins and Griffith, but the documents are undated. In fair condition, though the edges of the papers are torn and bear the marks of constant creasing. The present writer endeavoured to rectify these damages, and, before they were returned to their present source, bound them in a folder.

SOURCES

Introductory Note

1 P. S. O'Hegarty: *A History of Ireland under the Union, 1801-1922*, p. 415.

Chapter 1

1 Mrs. Anna Kelly.
2 Private source.
3 Mrs. Anna Kelly.
4 Private source.

Chapter 2

1 Full references to the O Coileain will be found in the Rev. Patrick Woulfe's *Sloinnte Gaedheal is Gall*, pp. 470 and 694.
2 Tone, *Life Washington*, 1826, Vol. I, pp. 51-2.
3 Letter to Kevin O'Brien, dated 16th October, 1916.
4 Lyons' personal papers. (Private source.)
5 Lyons' personal papers. (Private source.)
6 Personal papers. (Private source.)
7 Personal papers. (Private source.)
8 Personal papers. (Private source.)
9 Letter from Sean Deasey to the present writer, dated 16th November, 1955.
10 Letter from Patrick Hodges to the present writer, dated 19th March, 1955.
11 Personal papers. (Private source.)
12 Second page of a letter in Collins' handwriting, found among his personal papers. (Private source.)
13 Undated letter to Sean Deasey. (In Deasey's possession.)
14 In Deasey's possession.
15 To Sean Deasey, dated February 12th, 1915. (In Deasey's possession.)
16 Letter from Kevin O'Brien to the present writer, dated January 12th, 1956.

Chapter 3

1 Communicated to the present writer by Mr. P. Moylett.
2 To Sean Deasey, dated April 5th, 1916. (In Deasey's possession.)

3 *See* Wells and Marlowe: *History of the Irish Rebellion of 1916*, p. 90.
4 W. B. Yeats: *Collected Poems*, pp. 204-5.
5 These figures (the result of much painstaking research) were given to the present writer by Florence O'Donoghue.
6 *Sinn Fein Rebellion Handbook*, Easter, 1916, p. 4b.
7 *Sinn Fein Rebellion Handbook*, Easter, 1916, p. 4b.
8 *Sinn Fein Rebellion Handbook*, Easter, 1916, p. 7.
9 Private source.
10 Frank O'Connor: *The Big Fellow*, p. 37.
11 Frank O'Connor: *The Big Fellow*, p. 37.
12 To Sean Deasey, dated May, 1916. (In Deasey's possession.)

Chapter 4
1 *Sinn Fein Rebellion Handbook*, Easter, 1916, p. 4.
2 *Sinn Fein Rebellion Handbook*, Easter, 1916, p. 4.
3 Mr. Frank Kelly was a witness to this incident.
4 Compiled from the *Sinn Fein Rebellion Handbook*, Easter, 1916, pp. 71, 72, 78, 79, 80, 81.
5 To Sean Deasey, dated May, 1916. (In Deasey's possession.)
6 To Sean Deasey, dated May, 1916. (In Deasey's possession.)
7 To Sean Deasey, dated May, 1916. (In Deasey's possession.)
8 To Mollie (Mrs. M. Delaney), dated June 24th, 1916.
9 To Sean Deasey, dated 12th September, 1916. (In Deasey's possession.)
10 Told to the present writer by a number of former Irish internees.
11 To Sean Deasey, dated 29th September, 1916. (In Deasey's possession.)
12 To Mollie (Mrs. M. Delaney).
13 To Sean Deasey, undated. (In Deasey's possession.)
14 *Sinn Fein Rebellion Handbook*, Easter, 1916, p. 62.
15 Sean O Luing: *Art O Griofa*, p. 268.
16 17th September, 1916.
17 To Sean Deasey, dated October 12th, 1916. (In Deasey's possession.)
18 To Sean Deasey, dated October 22nd, 1916. (In Deasey's possession.)
19 In Frongoch Collins was noted for the happy outlook which he preserved.
20 To Kevin O'Brien, dated November 9th, 1916.
21 To Sean Deasey. (In Deasey's possession.)
22 Anecdote—told to the present writer.

Chapter 5
1 To Sean Deasey, dated January 19th, 1917. (In Deasey's possession.)
2 To Sean Deasey, undated. (In Deasey's possession.)
3 Contemporary newspapers.

4 *See* Frank O'Connor: *The Big Fellow*, pp. 54-5.
5 Personal papers. (Private source.)
6 A draft note (one of several) written by Ashe, undated. (Private source.)
7 Contemporary newspapers.
8 To Sean Deasey, dated September 6th, 1917. (In Deasey's possession.)
9 *See* P. S. O'Hegarty: *A History of Ireland under the Union, 1801-1922*, p. 717.

Chapter 6
1 *See* Macardle: *The Irish Republic*, p. 273.
2 *See* Callwell: *Wilson: Life and Diaries.*
3 Told to the present writer by the person concerned.
4 In the possession of Gerard Costelloe of Killalee.
5 In the possession of Gerard Costelloe of Killalee.
6 In the National Library of Ireland.
7 In the National Library of Ireland.
8 In the possession of Gerard Costelloe of Killalee.
9 In the National Library of Ireland.
10 In the National Library of Ireland.
11 In the National Library of Ireland.
12 Mrs. Anna Kelly.
13 In the National Library of Ireland.
14 In the National Library of Ireland.
15 Told to the present writer by the person concerned.
16 In the possession of Gerard Costelloe of Killalee.
17 In the National Library of Ireland.
18 In the possession of Gerard Costelloe of Killalee.
19 Private source.

Chapter 7
1 Told to the present writer by Mrs. Anna Kelly.
2 *See* Macardle: *The Irish Republic*, p. 295.
3 Sean O Luing.
4 Frank Pakenham: *Peace by Ordeal*, p. 95.
5 'Sceilg' (J. J. O'Kelly): *Stepping Stones*, pp. 15-16.

Chapter 8
1 In the National Museum of Ireland.
2 Private source.
3 Private source.
4 Private source.
5 Private source.
6 Private source.
7 Private source.
8 Anecdote.
9 Told to the present writer by (the then) Private McCallum.
10 Private source.

11 Private source.
12 Private source.
13 Told to the present writer by the person concerned.
14 Private source.
15 Letter to the present writer.
16 *See* Frank O'Connor: *The Big Fellow*, pp. 174-5.
17 Callwell: *Wilson: Life and Diaries*, p. 269, Vol. II.
18 Callwell: *Wilson: Life and Diaries*, p. 269, Vol. II.
19 Callwell: *Wilson: Life and Diaries*, p. 270, Vol. II.
20 Told to the present writer by Mr. Moylett.
21 Private source.

Chapter 9
1 'Sceilg' (J. J. O'Kelly): *A Trinity of Martyrs*, p. 10.
2 Frank O'Connor: *The Big Fellow*, p. 157.
3 Denis Gwynn: *De Valera*, p. 129.
4 Private source.
5 One of many witnesses.
6 Frank O'Connor: *The Big Fellow*, p. 217.
7 Found among Collins' personal papers. Perhaps intended as a letter. Headed 'Harcourt Terrace, July 13th, 1921'.
8 Callwell: *Wilson: Life and Diaries*, p. 297, Vol. II.
9 Callwell: *Wilson: Life and Diaries*, p. 299, Vol. II.

Chapter 10
1 Private source.
2 Callwell: *Wilson: Life and Diaries*, p. 305, Vol. II.
3 Private source.
4 *See* Callwell: *Wilson: Life and Diaries*, p. 505, Vol. II.
5 P. S. O'Hegarty: *A History of Ireland under the Union, 1801-1922*, p. 752.
6 'Sceilg' (J. J. O'Kelly): *Stepping Stones*, p. 17.
7 P. S. O'Hegarty: *The Victory of Sinn Fein*, pp. 86-7.
8 The Earl of Birkenhead: *Frederick Edwin Earl of Birkenhead, The Last Phase*, p. 150.
9 The Earl of Birkenhead: *Frederick Edwin Earl of Birkenhead, The Last Phase*, p. 150.
10 Dail Debate on the Treaty, p. 333.
11 The quotes on this page are taken from *Frederick Edwin Earl of Birkenhead, The Last Phase*, p. 150.
12 Communicated to the present writer by Mr. Michael Collins, nephew of the subject of this biography.

Chapter 11
1 Private source.
2 Letter to John O'Kane, dated November 6th, 1921.
3 Collins' notes. (Private source.)
4 Collins' notes. (Private source.)
5 Collins' notes. (Private source.)

6 Collins' notes. (Private source.)
7 Collins' notes. (Private source.)
8 Collins' notes. (Private source.)
9 Collins' notes. (Private source.)
10 Letter to John O'Kane, dated October 19th, 1921.
11 Letter to John O'Kane, dated October 23rd, 1921.
12 Letter to John O'Kane, dated October 27th, 1921.

Chapter 12

1 Letter to John O'Kane, dated October 17th, 1921.
2 Letter dated November 2nd, 1921.
3 The Earl of Birkenhead: *Frederick Edwin Earl of Birkenhead, The Last Phase*, p. 157.
4 Collins' notes. (Private source.)
5 Sean O Luing: *Art O Griofa*, p. 367.
6 Collins' notes. (Private source.)
7 Collins' notes. (Private source.)

Chapter 13

1 Told to the present writer by Sean McBride, S.C.
2 Told to the present writer by Sean McBride, S.C.
3 To John O'Kane. (Undated.)
4 Collins' notes. (Private source.)
5 *See* article by David Hogan: 'Tom Jones and the Welsh Wizard', *Irish Press*, October 21st, 1955.
6 *Hansard*, Vol. 127, Col. 1114.
7 *Ireland's Right to Unity*, p. 9.
8 *Ireland's Right to Unity*, p. 9.
9 Collins' notes. (Private source.)
10 Collins' notes. (Private source.)
11 Collins' notes. (Private source.)
12 Collins' notes. (Private source.)
13 Collins' notes. (Private source.)
14 Private source.

Chapter 14

1 *See* Terence de Vere White's *Kevin O'Higgins*, p. 62, and Frank Pakenham's *Peace by Ordeal*, p. 255.
2 *See* Frank O'Connor: *The Big Fellow*, p. 232.
3 Sean O Luing: *Art O Griofa*, pp. 412, 413, 414.
4 Frank O'Connor: *The Big Fellow*, p. 232.
5 Private source.
6 *See* article by David Hogan: 'Tom Jones and the Welsh Wizard', *Irish Press*, October 21st, 1955.
7 Contributed to the world's Press; reproduced in *The Republic of Ireland*, February 14th, 1922.
8 Dail debate on the Treaty, p. 97.
9 Dail debate on the Treaty, p. 86.

10 Sean O Luing: *Art O Griofa*, facsimile opposite p. 384.
11 Private source.

Chapter 15
1 *See* Frank O'Connor: *The Big Fellow*, p. 236.
2 Macardle: *The Irish Republic*, p. 617.
3 *See* Frank O'Connor: *The Big Fellow*, p. 237.
4 P. S. O'Hegarty: *A History of Ireland under the Union, 1801-1922*, p. 769.
5 P. S. O'Hegarty: *A History of Ireland under the Union, 1801-1922*, pp. 769-770.
6 Batt O'Connor: *With Michael Collins*, p. 180.
7 Macardle: *The Irish Republic*, p. 618.
8 To Joseph McGarrity, who was prominent in Irish-American circles. (*See* O'Hegarty: *A History of Ireland under the Union, 1801-1922*, p. 768.)
9 P. S. O'Hegarty: *A History of Ireland under the Union, 1801-1922*, p. 754.

Chapter 16
1 *See* Macardle: *The Irish Republic*, p. 659.
2 'The Times': *History of The Times*, Vol. IV, p. 1116.
3 Padraig de Burca and John F. Boyle: *Free State or Republic?*, pp. 67-8.

Chapter 17
1 Padraig de Burca and John F. Boyle: *Free State or Republic?*, p. 88.
2 Private source.
3 Collins' private notebook.
4 O'Rourke's letter in the possession of Sean Deasey.
5 P. S. O'Hegarty: *A History of Ireland under the Union, 1801-1922*, pp. 786-7.
6 *See* Frank O'Connor: *The Big Fellow*, p. 260.
7 *See* Frank O'Connor: *The Big Fellow*, p. 260.
8 Letter from Frank O'Connor to the present writer.
9 Frank O'Connor: *The Big Fellow*, p. 260.
10 *Irish Independent*, 17th March, 1922.
11 *Irish Independent*, 18th March, 1922.
12 *Irish Independent*, 18th March, 1922.
13 *Irish Independent*, 20th March, 1922.
14 Condensed from (p. 741) *The Irish Republic*, by Dorothy Macardle.
15 Macardle: *The Irish Republic*, p. 1006.
16 Michael Collins: *The Path to Freedom*, pp. 15-17.
17 Sean O Luing: *Art O Griofa*, p. 396.
18 Terence de Vere White: *Kevin O'Higgins*.
19 In the National Museum of Ireland.

20 In the National Museum of Ireland.
21 Frank O'Connor: *The Big Fellow*, p. 276.

Chapter 18
1 *See* Frank O'Connor: *The Big Fellow*, p. 278.
2 Told to the present writer by Sean McGarry.
3 *See* Frank O'Connor: *The Big Fellow*, p. 281.
4 *Irish Independent*, 23rd June, 1922.
5 Macardle: *The Irish Republic*, p. 771.
6 *See* Frank O'Connor: *The Big Fellow*, p. 285.
7 *See* Frank O'Connor: *The Big Fellow*, p. 286.
8 Private source.
9 In the National Museum of Ireland.
10 Private notebook, dates from 27th June to 6th August, 1922.
11 Anecdote.
12 Private source.
13 Private source.
14 Anna Kelly: *Irish Press*, 1st August, 1938.
15 Told to the present writer by Mr. Moylett.
16 *See* Frank O'Connor: *The Big Fellow*, p. 291.
17 *See* Frank O'Connor: *The Big Fellow*, p. 291.
18 Frank O'Connor: *The Big Fellow*, p. 292.

Chapter 20
1 *Guerilla Days in Ireland*, p. 180.
2 Sir John Lavery: *The Life of a Painter*, p. 217.
3 Quoted in the *Irish Independent*, August 24th, 1922.
4 Quoted in the *Irish Independent*, August 24th, 1922.
5 Quoted in the *Irish Independent*, August 24th, 1922.
6 Quoted in the *Irish Independent*, August 24th, 1922.
7 Quoted in the *Irish Independent*, August 24th, 1922.
8 Quoted in the *Irish Independent*, August 24th, 1922.
9 Quoted in the *Irish Independent*, August 24th, 1922.
10 Quoted in the *Irish Independent*, August 24th, 1922.
11 Quoted in the *Irish Independent*, August 24th, 1922.
12 *Daily Sketch*, August 24th, 1922.
13 *Daily Sketch*, August 24th, 1922.
14 *Daily Sketch*, August 24th, 1922.
15 Sir John Lavery: *The Life of a Painter*, pp. 218-19.
16 Sir John Lavery: *The Life of a Painter*, p. 217.
17 *Forum*: Treaty Commemoration issue, December, 1946.

Chapter 21
1 Speech at Cork, March 12th, 1922. (Arguments for the Treaty, pp. 18-24.)
2 Speech at Skibbereen, March 17th, 1922. (Arguments for the Treaty, pp. 25-7.)
3 Michael Collins: *The Path to Freedom*, pp. 33-42.

4 Michael Collins: *The Path to Freedom*, pp. 43-54.
5 Michael Collins: *The Path to Freedom*, pp. 127-41.

Appendices

A Macardle: *The Irish Republic*, pp. 172-4.
B Macardle: *The Irish Republic*, pp. 955-6.
C Sean O Luing: *Art O Griofa*, pp. 410-11.
D Private source.
E Macardle: *The Irish Republic*, pp. 990-5.
F Official Report: *Debate on the Treaty between Great Britain and Ireland*, pp. 378-9.
G Macardle: *The Irish Republic*, pp. 996-1000.
H Macardle: *The Irish Republic*, pp. 1003-1005.
I Signed account in the present writer's possession.
J Published in the *Freeman's Journal*; reprinted by kind permission of the *Irish Independent*, Dublin.

Bibliography

BOOKS

BARRY, TOM, COMMANDANT-GENERAL. *Guerilla Days in Ireland.* Cork, 1949. (Mercier Press.)
BEASLAI, PIARAS, MAJOR-GENERAL. *Michael Collins and the Making of a New Ireland.* London. (Harrap, 2 vols.)
BIRKENHEAD, THE EARL OF. *Frederick Edwin Earl of Birkenhead, The Last Phase.* London. (Thornton Butterworth.)
DE BURCA, PADRAIG, AND BOYLE, JOHN F. *Free State or Republic?*, 1922. (Talbot Press—T. Fisher Unwin.)
CALLWELL, C. E., MAJOR-GENERAL, K.C.B. *Field-Marshal Sir Henry Wilson, Bart., G.C.B., D.S.O.: His Life and Diaries.* London, 1927. (Cassell, 2 vols.)
COLLINS, MICHAEL. *The Path to Freedom.* 1922. (Talbot Press—T. Fisher Unwin.)
CONNOLLY, JAMES. *Labour in Ireland.* Dublin, 1922. (Maunsel and Roberts.)
Dail Eireann Official Report, 16th August, 1921, to 8th June, 1922. (Talbot Press.)
Debate on the Treaty between Great Britain and Ireland. (Talbot Press.)
Dublin's Fighting Story. Tralee, 1949. (Kerryman.)
DUFFY, CHARLES GAVAN. *Four Years of Irish History.*
FIGGIS, DARRELL. *Recollections of the Irish War.* London, 1927. (Benn.)
GREGORY, LADY. *Journals, 1916-30*, Ed. Lennox Robinson. London, 1946. (Putnam.)
GWYNN, DENIS. *De Valera.* London, 1933. (Jarrolds.)
Hansard, Vol. 127.
HEADLAM, MAURICE, C.B., C.M.G. *Irish Reminiscences.* London. (Hale.)
LAVERY, SIR JOHN. *The Life of a Painter.* London, 1940. (Cassell.)
MACARDLE, DOROTHY. *The Irish Republic.* London, 1937. (Gollancz.)
MACDONAGH, MICHAEL. *William O'Brien.* London, 1928. (Benn.)
MACMANUS, M. J. *Eamon de Valera.* Dublin, 1944. (Talbot Press.)
O'CONNOR, BATT. *With Michael Collins in the Fight for Irish Independence.* London, 1929. (Peter Davies.)
O'CONNOR, FRANK. *The Big Fellow.* London, 1937. (Nelson.)
O'HEGARTY, P. S. *A History of Ireland under the Union, 1801-1922.* London, 1952. (Methuen.)
The Victory of Sinn Fein. Dublin, 1924. (Talbot Press.)

O LUING, SEAN. *Art O Griofa.* Dublin, 1953. (Sairseal Agus Dill.)
PAKENHAM, FRANK (now Lord). *Peace by Ordeal.* London, 1935. (Cape.)
'SCEILG' (J. J. O'Kelly). *A Trinity of Martyrs.* Dublin. (Irish Book Bureau.)
Sinn Fein Rebellion Handbook. Dublin, 1917. (*Irish Times.*)
TALBOT, HAYDEN. *Michael Collins' Own Story.* London, 1923. (Hutchinson.)
WELLS, W. E., AND MARLOWE, N. A. *History of the Irish Rebellion of 1916.* Dublin, 1917. (Maunsel.)
WHITE, TERENCE DE VERE. *Kevin O'Higgins.* London, 1948. (Methuen.)
WOULFE, REV. PATRICK. *Sloinnte Gaedheal is Gall.*
YEATS, W. B. *Collected Poems.* London, 1939. (Macmillan.)

PAMPHLETS

'A.E.' (George Russell). *Ireland and the Empire at the Court of Conscience.* Dublin, 1921. (Talbot Press.)
Thoughts for a Convention. Memorandum on the State of Ireland. Dublin, 1917. (Maunsel.)
The Inner and the Outer Ireland. Dublin, 1921. (Talbot Press.)
COLLINS, MICHAEL. *Arguments for the Treaty.* Dublin, 1922. (Martin Lester.)
Erskine Childers.
Ireland's Right to Unity.
MAIRE NI SUIBNE (Miss Mary MacSwiney). *The Republic of Ireland.*
RYAN, DESMOND. *Ireland, Whose Ireland?* London. (Fore Publications.)
'SCEILG' (J. J. O'Kelly). *Stepping Stones.* Dublin. (Irish Book Bureau.)
SKEFFINGTON, HANNA SHEEHY. *British Militarism as I Have Known It.* Tralee, 1946. (Kerryman.)
What the Treaty Means. (Republic of Ireland.)

PERIODICALS

Forum, Treaty Commemoration Issue. Dublin, 1946. (Fine Gael.)
Free State. The Michael Collins Memorial Number. (No. 28, Vol. I, 1922.)
Leader, The. October 28th, 1944, and September 6th, 1947.
Star, The. Treaty Commemoration Number, 1921-31. Dublin, 1931. (Star Publishing Co.)
Wolfe Tone Annual. Dublin. (O'Higgins.)

NEWSPAPERS

Belfast Telegraph.
Daily Chronicle.
Daily Express.
Daily Sketch.
Daily Telegraph.
Eire.
Evening Post.
Evening Press.
Irish Independent.
Irish Press.
Irish Times.
Midland Reporter.
New Ireland, July 6th, 1918.
Plain People, The, May 14th, 1922 and June 11th, 1922.
Republic of Ireland, February 14th, 1922 and November 11th, 1922.
Sunday Express.
Sunday Independent.
Sunday Press.
The Mail.
The Nationalist and Leinster Times.
The Times.
Wexford People.
Young Ireland, December 31st, 1921.